EUROJARGON

A dictionary of European Union acronyms, abbreviations and sobriquets

6th edition

Edited by
Anne Ramsay FLA

CPI Limited
United Kingdom

Fitzroy Dearborn Publishers
Chicago • London

Published in the United Kingdom by
CPI Limited
91 High Street, Bruton
Somerset BA10 0BH

ISBN 1-898869-67-7

British Library Cataloguing in Publication Data. A record
for this book is available from the British Library

Published in the United States of America by
Fitzroy Dearborn Publishers
919 North Michigan Avenue
Chicago, Illinois 60611

ISBN 1-57958-274-5

A-Cataloging-in-Publication record for this book is
available from the Library of Congress

Printed and bound in Great Britain
by Haynes Publishing
Sparkford, Yeovil
Somerset BA22 7JJ

CONTENTS

PREFACE

Many abbreviations, acronyms and sobriquets have crept into everyday use over recent years and have almost become a language in themselves. EUROJARGON is an attempt to bring together those used within the context of the European Union (EU). The principle for selection has been of a pragmatic nature.

Not every abbreviation in EU documents has been cited, as several may be found in general dictionaries of abbreviations. Some have been included which are from a wider context than that of the EU, such as European associations and organisations recognised by the EU. There will certainly be omissions and inaccuracies. I invite the zealous browser to draw my attention to these, so that they may be considered and corrected in a future edition.

EUROJARGON does not claim to offer multilingual access, although a few '*See*' references for abbreviations in a language other than English are cited, if the foreign abbreviation is in common use in this country. Addresses are given where appropriate and this edition contains a vastly increased number of Internet addresses. No attempt has been made to index the names of Rapporteurs of European Parliament documents. Uniquely, the references to official texts are cited in brackets after the description, wherever these have been traced. They are believed to be correct as at the end of December 1999. The reader is, however, always advised to check the currency of the information in published and/or electronic sources. The alphabetical listing follows the principle of 'letter by letter'. Any descriptive text in capital letters indicates that there is an entry under that heading in the alphabetical sequence. EUROJARGON contains a large number of additional acronyms, abbreviations and sobriquets as well as updated information on terms which have appeared in earlier editions.

EUROJARGON is aimed at a wide range of user, such as specialist consultants in EU information, academics, documentalists, librarians, journalists, local authority staff, civil servants, economists and politicians, in addition to those with a penchant for serendipity.

Whilst every care has been taken to ensure the accuracy of the information contained in this publication, the editor cannot accept any liability for loss or damage resulting from its use.

Anne Ramsay
Newcastle upon Tyne

ACKNOWLEDGMENTS

For this edition, special thanks are due to Lillian Stevenson and Jackie Woollam in the European Documentation Centre at the University of Wales Aberystwyth for their contribution to the updating of the text - especially with regard to Internet addresses and project acronyms. They in turn, thank the Director of Information Services at the University of Wales Aberystwyth, Dr Mike Hopkins, for his encouragement and support whilst they were engaged on the project. Professor Christopher Harding and Stephen Skinner in the Law Department of the University of Wales Aberystwyth are also thanked for their contributions, in particular with regard to some revised text following the provisions of the Amsterdam Treaty.

My thanks - as always - are due to a number of experts in the field of European Union information provision, without whose help this edition would have been even more incomplete. They include Tim Kelly at the Commission Representation in Dublin, Avis Furness at the European Parliament office in London and European Documentation Centre Librarians Grace Hudson (University of Bradford), Maimie Balfour (University of Northumbria at Newcastle) and Wendy Sage (Wye College). Also to Judith Barton at the Local Government International Bureau and Marianne Sheppard of the Newcastle City Council, European Team. I am grateful for their expertise, patience and kindness in helping me to track down elusive information and for words of encouragement from a wide range of EU information providers.

Finally, special thanks to my husband, without whose continued patience, support and tea making skills, this edition would not have been completed.

Anne Ramsay

SYMBOLS AND ABBREVIATIONS NOT EXPLAINED IN THE TEXT

*	No longer in use
ed	edition
HMSO	Her Majesty's Stationery Office (now The Stationery Office)
No	Number
p	page
R&D	Research and Development
RTD	Research and Technological Development
S.I.	Statutory Instrument
TSO	The Stationery Office (formerly Her Majesty's Stationery Office)
vol(s)	volume(s)

3 PILLARS	*See* PILLARS
3SNET	Short Sea Shipping Network. Project to improve the direct information and communication links between the different participants in the transport chain (TRANSPORT project)
3 WISE MEN	*See* THREE WISE MEN REPORT
5mail	An e-mail newsletter launched by the Employment and Social Affairs DG of the European Commission in 1999 to give a short overview of the latest news on employment, industrial relations and social affairs 5mail@dg5.cec.be
30th MAY MANDATE	Declaration following the Congress of Europe (organised by the EM) held in Paris in May 1980 to celebrate the 30th anniversary of the SCHUMAN DECLARATION. Published in *Bulletin of the EC Supplement 1/1981*
48 HOUR Directive	*See* WORKING TIME Directive
1992	*See* SEM (Single European Market)
XIII MAGAZINE	*See* I&T MAGAZINE
A (point)	A Council of the European Union agenda item for formal adoption without discussion
AA	Agricultural Acreage
AAD	Accompanying Administrative Document
AALBORG CHARTER	of European cities and towns towards sustainability. A European Conference held in Aalborg 24-27 May 1994
*AAMS	Associated African States and Madagascar
AAT	Advanced Authoring Tools (DELTA project)

ABC	Internet access to basic factual information on the EU. *See also* EUROPA http://europa.eu.int/abc-en.htm
ABC MALE	Accreditation Board of Clinical Movement Analysis Laboratories in Europe (a Telematics for Healthcare project within the TELEMATICS APPLICATIONS programme) http://www.ehto.org/vds/projects/abc-male.html
ABEAM	Across the Borders Effects of ATM (an Air Transport project within the TRANSPORT programme)
*ABEL	*See* EUDOR
ABSTRACT	External trade statistical domain on the NEW CRONOS databank Also available as a CD-ROM from EUROSTAT data shops
AC	Advisory Committee
ACACIA	A Concerted Action towards a Comprehensive climate Impacts and Adaptation assessment for the EU (ENVIRONMENT AND CLIMATE project)
ACAFS	Automatic Control of an Asic Fabrication Sequence as demonstrated in the plasma ETCH Area (ESPRIT project)
ACC	Article 113 of the ROME TREATY regarding the passage of a COM DOC for CCP legislation
ACCEE	Associated Countries of Central and Eastern Europe
ACCESS	Advanced Customer Connection: an Evolutionary Strategy (RACE project)
ACCESS	Development platform for unified access to enabling environments (TIDE project)

ACCESSION COUNTRIES	Countries preparing for accession to the EU. *See* APPLICANT COUNTRIES
ACCESSION CRITERIA	In June 1993 the Copenhagen European Council recognised the right of the CEEC to join the EU when they had fulfilled certain political and economic criteria and incorporated the ACQUIS COMMUNAUTAIRE. These criteria were confirmed at the Madrid European Council in December 1995
ACCESSION PARTNERSHIPS	Part of the new pre-accession process as set out in AGENDA 2000, between the Commission and each of the candidate countries. It is a framework covering in detail the priorities for adopting the ACQUIS COMMUNAUTAIRE
ACCESSION TREATY	signed by Belgium, France, Germany, Italy, Luxembourg, the Netherlands, Denmark, Ireland, Norway and the United Kingdom. Came into force 1st January 1973. Norway did not ratify the Treaty
ACCOR	Articulatory-acoustic Correlations in CoarticulatORy (ESPRIT project)
ACCORD	Computer-aided engineering software for advanced workstations in the CIM environment (ESPRIT project)
*ACE	Action by the Community relating to the Environment (1987-1991) (OJ L207/87). *Continued as* ACNAT
ACE	Action Centre for Europe c/o 2 Queen Anne's Gate, London SW1H 9AA, United Kingdom
ACE	Action for Cooperation in the field of Economics in favour of Poland, Hungary, Yugoslavia, Bulgaria, Romania and Czechoslovakia (within the PHARE and TACIS programmes) (1990-). *See also* PHARE ACE

ACE-2	Aerosol Characterisation Experiment (EI project)
ACEA	European Automobile Manufacturer's Association rue de Noyer 211, B–1000 Brussels, Belgium http://www.acea.be/
ACES	Courseware Engineering System (DELTA project)
ACI EUROPE	Airports Council International European Region sq de Meeûs 6, B-1000 Brussels, Belgium http://www.aci-europe.org
ACKNOWLEDGE	ACquisition of Knowledge (ESPRIT project)
ACMDP	Advisory Committees on the Management of Demonstration Projects
ACME	Adaptive Control of Marine Engines. One of the eight interrelated Community-funded projects in the field of design, production and operation for safer, more efficient, environmentally friendly and user-friendly ships, coordinated by NETS
*ACNAT	Action by the Community relating to Nature Conservation (1992-1993) (OJ L370/91). *Previously* ACE. *Continued as* LIFE
ACOR	Advisory Committee on Own Resources
ACORD	Construction and interrogation of KBs bases using natural language text and graphics (ESPRIT project)
ACP	African, Caribbean and Pacific States Secretariat: ave Georges-Henri 451, B-1200 Brussels, Belgium http://www.oneworld/acpsec
ACP-ALA-MED	A compendium of short- and long-term macroeconomic indicators of 117 countries. *See also* Ptiers Access via CD-ROM from CONTEXT and EUR-OP official agents

ACPC	Advisory Committee on Procurements and Contracts
ACPM	Advisory Committee on Programme Management
ACQUILEX	Acquisition of Lexical knowledge for natural language processing systems (ESPRIT project)
ACQUIRED RIGHTS Directive	Dir 77/187/EEC on the safeguarding of employees' rights in the event of transfers of undertakings, businesses or parts of businesses (OJ L61/77 with latest amendment in OJ L201/98). *See also* TUPE
ACQUIS COMMUNAUTAIRE	A short hand term denoting the whole body of law and policy which has been developed under the EC and the EU
ACRuDA	Assessment and Certification Rules for Digital Architecture (a Rail Transport Research project within the TRANSPORT programme)
ACSTT	Advisory Committee on Scientific and Technical Training
ACTA	The study of the use of metaphors as a means for assessment of currently unavailable technology (CSCW project) http://orgwis.gmd.de/projects/ACTA
ACTION	Assisting Carers using Telematics Interventions to meet Older persons Needs (a Telematics for Disabled and Elderly People project within the TELEMATICS APPLICATIONS programme)
ACTIP	Animal Cell Technology INDUSTRIAL PLATFORM http://europa.eu.int/comm/dg12/biotech/ip2.html#ACTIP
ACT IT	Application of Computer-based systems for Training in IT (TIDE project)

*ACTS	Council Decision 94/572/EEC for Advanced Communications Technologies and Services (1994-1998) (OJ L222/94). *Previously* RACE. *Continued as* IST. *See also* ICT
ACTS	High resolution speech recognition (ESPRIT project) http://www.cordis.lu/acts/home.html
*ACU	Administration of the Customs Union
ACUSE	Action Committee for the United States of Europe. Set up in 1956 by the architect of the European Community, Jean Monnet
ACVT	Advisory Committee on Vocational Training
ADAM	Advanced Architecture in Medicine (AIM project)
ADAM	A European Commission Budget DG database http://europa.eu.int/adam/start
*ADAPT	COMMUNITY INITIATIVE for the Adaptation of workers to industrial change (1994-1999) (OJ C180/94). *Continued as* EQUAL
ADAPT-BIS	Building the Information Society (1996-1999) (Guidelines in OJ C200/96)
ADCIS	Analog-Digital CMOS ICS (ESPRIT project)
ADDITIONALITY	The principle of receiving sums of money from Brussels for projects (primarily from the STRUCTURAL FUNDS) which are additional to national Member State contributions
ADECO	Dismantling workshop for Orgel fuels (JRC - safety of nuclear materials programme)
ADEPT	Advanced Distributed Environment for Production Technology (ESPRIT project)

ADEQUAT	Advanced Developments for 0.25 um CMos Techniques (JESSI/ESPRIT project)
ADEXP	Air traffic services Data EXchange Presentation. One of two EUROCONTROL standards adopted by Dir 97/15/EC (OJ L95/97). The Directive covers the definition and use of compatible technical specifications for the procurement of Air Traffic Management equipment and systems. *See also* OLDI
adf	Additional Duty on Flour
ADFORA	Advertising in electronic publishing and commerce (a Telematics Information Engineering project within the TELEMATICS APPLICATIONS programme)
ADKMS	Advanced Data and Knowledge Management Systems (ESPRIT project)
ADMIN	Personnel and Administration DG of the European Commission
ADONIS	Analysis and Development Of New Insights into Substitution of short car trips by cycling and walking (an Urban Transport project within the TRANSPORT programme)
ADONNINO REPORT	on a People's Europe. *See* PEOPLE'S EUROPE
ADORA	Analysis and Definition of Operational Requirements for ATM (an Air Transport project within the TRANSPORT programme)
ADOT	Advanced Display Optimisation Tools (ESPRIT project)
ads	Additional Duty on Sugar
ADVANCE	Network and customer administration systems (RACE project)

ADVICE	Automatic Design Validation of Integrated Circuits using E-beam (ESPRIT project)
ADVISER	ADded Value Information Service for European Research Results (TELEMATICS APPLICATIONS project)
AEBR	Association of European Border Regions Adenauerallee 139, D-5300 Bonn, Germany
*AEDCL	Association of EDC Librarians in the UK. *See* EIA (European Information Association)
AEGEE	Forum of European Students PO Box 72, Etterbeek 1, B-1040 Brussels, Belgium http://www.aegee.org
AEGIS	European air traffic management group for the improvement of scenarios (EURET project)
AEIC	European Agency of Information on Consumer Affairs rue Barthélémy Delespaul 47 bis, F-59000 Lille, France
AEIDL	European Association for Information on Local Development. The service of support to European Information networks was closed down in January 1999 ch St Pierre 260, B-1040 Brussels, Belgium http://www.rural-europe.aeidl.be/
AEIF	European Association for Railway Interoperability bd de l'Impératrice 15, B-1000 Brussels, Belgium
AEMI	Advanced Environment for Medical Image interpretation (AIM project)
AEOLUS II	Development and construction of two windpower stations (EUREKA project)
AEPPC	*See* EIPA (European Insolvency Practitioners Association)

AER	Assessment of Environmental Risk related to unsound use of technologies and mass tourism (ENVIRONMENT AND CLIMATE project)
AER	*See* ARE (Group of the European Radical Alliance)
AERONOX	Project on the impact of nitrogen oxide emissions from air traffic in the upper atmosphere (ENVIRONMENT AND CLIMATE project)
AESOPIAN	Awareness of European SOlutions and best Practices for telematics applications (a telematics Engineering project within the TELEMATICS APPLICATIONS programme)
AFC	Appropriations for Commitment (in the budget)
AFCO	Committee on Constitutional Affairs (of the EP)
AFET	Committee on Foreign Affairs, Human Rights, Common Security and Defence policy (of the EP)
AFFET	Association for European Training of Workers on the Impact of Technologies bd Emile Jacqmain 155, B-1210 Brussels, Belgium http://www.etuc.org/etuco/afett.cfm
AFG	Association of the Glucose Producers in the EEC ave de la Joyeuse Entrée 1-5, Boîte 10, B-1040 Brussels, Belgium
AFP	Appropriations for Payment (in the budget)
AGATA	Advanced Gas Turbine for Automobiles (EUREKA project)

AGEFT	Agricultural Electronic Fund Transfer. A project to communicate daily data from the disbursing agencies to the EAGGF (CADDIA project). *Merged with* AGREX
AGENCIES	*See* CEDEFOP; CPVO; EEA; EFILWC; EMCDDA; EMEA; ETF; EU-OSHA; FVA; OHIM; TCEU
AGENDA 2000	An initiative for the millennium covering enlargement to Eastern Europe and new provisions for the financing of EU activity. Completed in 1999. (COM(97) 2000 and also available as *Bulletin of the EU Supplement 5/1997*) http://europa.eu.int/comm/agenda2000/index_en.htm
AGGEFFECT	Effectiveness of international environmental agreements (ENVIRONMENT AND CLIMATE project)
AGINFO	An on-line database of the CAP and European trade in food and agricultural commodities Access via AGRA EUROPE
AGMASCO	Airborne Geoid Mapping System for Coastal Oceanography (MAST III project)
AGORA	A CEDEFOP forum for open, multilateral discussion
AGORA	Network of SME networks using telematics (an Education and Training Sector project under the TELEMATICS APPLICATIONS programmme)
AGRA EUROPE	*See* AGINFO
*AGREP	A database consisting of a permanent inventory of agricultural research projects in EU Member States
AGREX	Agricultural Guarantee Fund Expenditure. A system to monitor expenditure under the Guarantee Section of the EAGGF (CADDIA project). *Includes* AGEFT

AGRI	Agriculture DG of the European Commission
AGRI	Committee on Agriculture and Rural Development (of the EP)
*AGRIMED	Mediterranean Agriculture (1989-1993) (OJ L58/90)
AGRI-R	Regional Agricultural statistical domain on the REGIO database
AGRO-BIOTECH	Applications of Biotechnology in Agriculture and Agro-Food industries (COMETT project)
AGROMET	A meteorological database within the CADDIA programme
AHSEA	Advanced driver assistance systems in Europe (a Telematics for Integrated Applications for Digital Sites project within the TELEMATICS APPLICATIONS programme)
AIDA	Advanced Integrated circuit Design Aids (ESPRIT project)
AIDA	Alternatives for International Document Availability (project within Area 5 of the TELEMATIC SYSTEMS programme)
AIDMED	Assistant for Interacting with Multimedia Medical Databases (AIM project)
AIEC	*See* AEIC
AILE	Innovative Local Integration and Exchange Activities (HELIOS project)
*AIM	Advanced Informatics in Medicine in Europe (1988-1990) (OJ L314/88). *Previously* BICEPS. *Continued as* Area 3 of the TELEMATIC SYSTEMS programme and ESPRIT IV

AIM	AIP application to IBCN maintenance (RACE project)
AIMBURN	Advanced Intelligent Multi-sensor system for control of Boilers and fURNaces (ESPRIT project)
AIMS	Advanced Integrated Millimeter wave Sub-assemblies (ESPRIT project)
AIMS	Aerospace Intelligence Management and development tool for embedded Systems (EUREKA project)
*AIMS	Assistance to Industry Mainframe System. A database of information on funding. *Replaced by* INFOGRANT
AIN-ED	The exchange of state aid data (CADDIA project)
AIPCEE	EU Fish Processors Association ave de Roodebeek, B-1030 Brussels, Belgium
*AIR	Agriculture and Agro-Industrial (including fisheries research) programme (1990-1994) (OJ L265/91). Incorporates ECLAIR; FLAIR; FOREST; JOULE (Biomass area). *Continued as* FAIR. *See also* FAP; FAR
AIR	Innovative theme-based rehabilitation activities (HELIOS project)
AIRBASE	EEA Air Quality database http://www.etcaq.rivm.nl/airbase/index.html
AIRE Centre	Advice on Individual Rights in Europe 74 Eurolink Business Centre, 49 Effra Rd, London SW2 1BZ, United Kingdom
*AISE	Archive of Socio-Economic Information. A EUROSTAT system
AITRAS	An intelligent real-time coupled system for signal understanding (ESPRIT project)
ALA	Asian and Latin American countries

ALAMEDSA	Asia, Latin America, the MEDiterranean and South Africa
ALAMOS	Automatic Lidar for Air Monitoring Operating System (EUREKA project)
ALCOM	ALgorithms and COMplexity (ESPRIT project)
ALDICT	Access of persons with Learning Disabilities to Information and Communication Technologies (a Telematics for Disabled and Elderly People project within the TELEMATICS APPLICATIONS programme)
ALDUV	ALgan Detectros for low cost solar UV-band monitoring systems (THESEO project)
ALE	*See* EFA (European Free Alliance Group)
ALECT	Advanced ceramic materials for aluminium electrolysis technology (EUREKA project)
ALF	Advanced software engineering environment logistics framework (ESPRIT project)
ALFA	Amérique Latine-Formation Académique. Cooperation between higher education establishments in 18 Latin American countries and the EU (1994-1999) (Information in OJ C281/96)
ALIM	Future of the food system (FAST programme)
ALINVEST	Reg 443/92. An Industrial cooperation and Investment promotion programme for the countries of Latin America (1991-1995) (OJ L52/92 with extension to 2000 in OJ C154/96)

ALIPOR	Autonomous Lander Instrument Packages for Oceanographic Research. Project to develop a series of instrumentation packages for measurement, monitoring and sampling on the sea floor (MAST III project)
ALL-INN	Allergy Innovations (EUREKA project)
ALPES	Advanced Logical Programming Environments (ESPRIT project)
ALPSOLAR	Field testing and optimisation of photovoltaic solar power plant equipment in alpine regions (EUREKA project)
ALTEC	Algorithms for future Technologies (PHARE project)
ALTENER II	Council Decision 98/352/EC concerning a multiannual programme for the promotion of renewable energy sources in the Community (1998-2002) (OJ L159/98) http://europa.eu.int/en/comm/dg17/altener.htm
ALTER	Alternative Traffic in Towns project. Launched at the first Environment and Transport Ministers' European Council in April 1998. The project aims to create a demand for zero and low emission vehicles among European local and regional authorities
ALURE I and II	Council Regulation 443/92 for financial and technical assistance in the energy sector for developing countries in Asia and Latin America (1995-) (OJ L52/92) http://www.alure.net
AMADEUS	Development, marketing and operation of a European-based global computerised distribution system to meet the future needs of the travel industry (EUREKA project)
AMADEUS	Multi-method Approach for DEveloping Universal Specifications (ESPRIT project)

AMADIS	Development of advanced training activities and educational software in computational engineering (COMETT project)
AMBAR	Science Park networking (SPRINT project)
AMBER WASTES	*See* WASTES
AMBULANCE	Mobile unit for health care provision via telematics support (a Telematics for Healthcare project within the TELEMATICS APPLICATIONS programme)
AmCham-EU	EU Committee of the American Chamber of Commerce
AMES	Advanced Microelectronics Educational Service (COMETT project)
AMES	European network on reactor pressure vessel embrittlement and annealing. A network established by the JRC. The IAM acts as operating agent and reference laboratory
AMFEP	Association of Manufacturers of Fermentation Enzyme Products ave de Roodebeek, B-1030 Brussels, Belgium
AMICE	European Computer Integrated Manufacturing Architecture (ESPRIT project)
AMIS	Agricultural Market Intelligence System (a database within the CADDIA programme). *See also* FIS
AMODEUS	Assimilating Models Of Design, Users and Systems (ESPRIT project)
AMR	Advanced Mobile Robots for public safety applications (EUREKA project)
AMRIE	Alliance of Maritime Regional Interests in Europe ave Michel Ange 68, B-1000 Brussels, Belgium http://www.amrie.org

AMS	Advanced Manufacturing System (ESPRIT project)
AMSTERDAM TREATY	Signed by the 15 Member States at Amsterdam on 2 October 1997. Came into force 1 May 1999 http://europa.eu.int/abc/obj/amst/en/index.htm
AMUE	Association for the Monetary Union of Europe rue de la Pépinière 26, F-75008 Paris, France http://amue.lf.net
AMUFOC	Association of Fodder Seed Producer Houses in the EC rue de la Science 25, Boîte 10, B-1040 Brussels, Belgium
ANA	Agricultural Numerical Annexes (CADDIA project)
ANCAT	Abatement of Nuisance Caused by Air Transport. It comprises a group of experts from within the ECAC
ANEC	European Association for the Coordination of Consumer Representation in Standardisation ave de Tervuren 36, Boîte 4, B-1040 Brussels, Belgium http://www.anec.org
ANIMA	An office established by the Commission to help with its Community action programme on equal opportunities for women and men. Council Decision 95/593/EEC on Equal opportunities for men and women (1996-2000) (OJ L335/95)
ANIMATE	Added support to strategy, cohesion and dissemination for Transport and Environment projects (a Telematics for Environment project within the TELEMATICS APPLICATIONS programme) http://www.trentel.org/environment/research/projects/animate.html

ANIMO	ANImal MOves management system. An information network on the transportation of live animals. Set up under the IDA programme (OJ L221/91)
ANNIE	Application of Neutral Networks for Industry in Europe (ESPRIT project)
ANTARES	A New Traffic Approach Regarding Energy Saving (THERMIE project) http://europa.eu.int/en/comm/dg17/thermie/antares.htm
ANTICI GROUP	An informal group composed of the personal assistants to the Permanent Representatives (COREPER)
ANTI-RAIDER Directive	Dir 88/627/EEC on rules to inform the public of significant changes in the ownership of shares of companies listed on the Stock Exchange (OJ L348/88)
AOCTS	Associated Overseas Countries and Territories
AOIS	Alps Observation and Information System. An Environmental Monitoring Unit at the EI in the JRC at ISPRA
AORS	Abnormal Occurrences Reporting System (a database which forms part of ERDS)
AORTICS	Advanced Open Resources Telematics In Critical Care Situations (a Telematics for Healthcare project within the TELEMATICS APPLICATIONS programme)
APACHIP	Advanced Packaging for High Performance (ESPRIT project)
APACO	Recurrent agricultural acts and management committees (a word processing system within the CADDIA programme)
APAS	Preparatory, Accompanying and Support Actions (in the FP5 Framework programme)

APBB	Advanced PROM Building Blocks (ESPRIT project)
*APC	A European Commission database which monitored Commission Proposals and Communications which were forwarded to the Council of the European Union. *Replaced by* PreLex
APECE	Advanced Production Engineering Continued (sic) Education (COMETT project)
APECS	Amphibious Plant for Environmental Control and Safeguard (EUREKA project)
APE-THESEO	Airborne Platform for Earth observation - THird European Experiment on Stratospheric Ozone (THESEO project)
APEX	Advanced Project for European information EXchange: application to the aerospace industry (EUREKA project)
APHRODITE	A PCTE host-target distributed testing environment (ESPRIT project)
API	Association of Producers of Isoglucose of the EU ave de la Joyeuse Entrée 1-5, Boîte 10, B-1040 Brussels, Belgium
*APOLLO	Article Procurement with On-Line Local Ordering. A joint project of the ESA and the Commission for satellite document delivery (1984-1988)
APPE	Association of Petrochemical Producers in Europe ave Van Nieuwenhuyse 4, B-1160 Brussels, Belgium

APPLICANT COUNTRIES	The following countries have applied to join the EU. Turkey in April 1987; Cyprus and Malta in July 1990; Hungary in March 1994; Poland in April 1994; Romania and Slovakia in June 1995; Latvia in October 1995; Estonia in November 1995; Lithuania and Bulgaria in December 1995; Czech Republic in January 1996; Slovenia in June 1996
APPSN	Application Pilot for People with Special Needs (RACE project)
APR	Action Programme for Research
APs	*See* ACCESSION PARTNERSHIPS
APSIS	Application Software Prototype Implementation Scheme (ESPRIT project)
AQUA	Advanced QUAntum-well lasers for multi-gigabit transmission (RACE project)
AQUACON	A water quality project carried out by the EI
AQUA EUROPA	European Water Conditioning Association rue de Louvranges 58, B-1325 Dion-Valmont, Belgium
AQUARELLE	Sharing cultural heritage through multimedia telematics (a Telematics Information Engineering project within the TELEMATICS APPLICATIONS programme)
AQUARIUS	AQUAtic Research Institutions for the development of USer friendly applications in telematics (a Telematics for Education and Training project within the TELEMATICS APPLICATIONS programme)
AQUARIUS	A project to encourage the safeguarding of the sea (1987). Launched under the EYE programme

19

ARAL	Rehabilitation of the Lebanese Administration project European Commission External Relations DG, rue de la Loi 200, B-1049 Brussels, Belgium
ARAMIS	Advanced Runway Arrivals Management to Improve airport Safety and efficiency (an Air Transport project within the TRANSPORT programme)
ARBRE	ARable Biomass Renewable Energy (THERMIE project)
*ARC	Rainbow group (of the EP)
ARCADIA REPORT	House of Lords Select Committee on the European Communities *report on policies for rural areas in the EC*. Published by HMSO as House of Lords paper 1979-80 (129)
ARC ATLANTIQUE	See ATLANTIC ARC
ARCDEV	ARctic Demonstration and Exploratory Voyage (TRANSPORT project) http://www.cordis.lu/transport/src/arcdev.htm
ARCHISPLUS	A database of historical archives of the Commission http://europa.eu.int/comm/secretariat_general/archisplus/htdocs/en/htm/home.htm
ARCHITECTS' Directive	Dir 85/384/EEC on the mutual recognition of diplomas, certificates and other evidence of formal qualifications in architecture (OJ L223/85)
*ARCHITECTURAL HERITAGE	An annual pilot project to conserve and promote the EU's architectural heritage. (incorporated within the RAPHAEL programme)
ARCHITECTURE OF EUROPE	Refers to the various organisations, Institutions, Treaties and traditional relations making up the European area within which members work together on problems of shared interest. An essential part of this are the PILLARS

ARCHON	ARchitecture for Cooperative Heterogenous ON-line Systems (ESPRIT project)
*ARCOME	ECHO database of organisations, researchers and publications in the communications field
ARE	Assembly of the Regions of Europe pl des Halles 20, F-67054 Strasbourg, France
*ARE	Group of the European Radical Alliance (of the EP)
ARGOSI	Applications Related Graphics and OSI standards integration (ESPRIT project)
ARI	Appraisal of the Regional Impact
ARIADNE	Access, information and navigation support in the labyrinth of large buildings (a Telematics for Disabled and Elderly People project within the TELEMATICS APPLICATIONS programme)
ARIADNE	Development of an intelligent driver and navigation support system (DRIVE project)
ARIADNE II	Alliance of Remote Instructional Authoring and Distribution Networks for Europe (a Telematics for Education and Training project within the TELEMATICS APPLICATIONS programme)
*ARIANE	Council Decision 2085/97/EC establishing a programme of support, including translation, in the field of books and reading (1997-1998) (OJ L291/97 with an extension to 1999 in OJ L57/99). *Replaced by* CULTURE 2000 http://europa.eu.int/comm/dg10/culture/ariane/index_en.html
ARIES	Applied Research and Information-transfer Enhanced Services rue Jean Calvin 6, F-75005 Paris, France

ARIN	Advancing Rural Information Networks (a Telematics for Integrated Applications for Digital Sites project within the TELEMATICS APPLICATIONS programme)
*ARION	Actieprogramma: Reizen met een Instructief Karakter voor Onderwijsspecialisten (1978/79-1994). *Previously* Study visits for education specialists. *Continued as* part of Action 3 within the SOCRATES programme
ARIS Network	Action for Research and Information Support in civilian demining (an SAI project for the detection and positioning of mines)
ARISE	Anaesthesia Risks Intelligent Supporting Environment (EUREKA project)
ARISE	A Reusability Infrastructure for Software Engineering - off line (RACE project)
ARMS	Advanced Robotics Manipulation System (ESPRIT project)
ARP	*See* AIR (Agriculture and Agro-Industrial programme)
ARPS	Agricultural Report Production System (CADDIA project)
ARS	Adverse environment Recognition of Speech (ESPRIT project)
Art	Article
ARTEMIS	Application Research and Testing for Emergency Management Intelligent Systems (a Telematics for Environment project within the TELEMATICS APPLICATIONS programme) http://www.trentel.org/environment/research/projects/artemis.html

ARTERI	ARctic Terrestrial Ecosystems Research Initiative: coordination of research in European Arctic and Alpine areas (TERI project)
ARTICLE 6 COMMITTEE	Commission committee to implement Financial Protocols in Mediterranean countries
ARTICLE 55	of the PARIS TREATY for technical coal and steel research (1994-1999) (OJ C67/94)
ARTICLE 56	of the PARIS TREATY for READAPTATION GRANTS
ARTICLE K.4 Committee	A coordinating committee set up to do the preparatory work for Council of the European Union deliberations on justice and home affairs
ARTIFACTS	Advanced RoboTIcs in Flexible Automation: Components, Tools and Strategies (ESPRIT project)
ARTISAN	Intelligent framework for the industrial environment (DELTA project)
ARTM	Agency for Trans-Mediterranean Networks set up in 1993 for the coordination of MED-Campus; MED-Media and MED-Urbs
ARTMA	Advanced Real-Time Motion Analysis (EUREKA project)
ARTS-IP	Arts-IP satellite data (ESPRIT project)
ASAC	Application Specific Architecture Compilation (ESPRIT project)
ASAP	Amsterdam Special Action Programme. Launched by the EIB in June 1997 in response to the European Council meeting in Amsterdam, to step up action in support of job-creating investments (1997-2000) (OJ C10/98) http://eib.eu.int/pub/press/asap.htm

ASCIS	Behavioural synthesis, partitioning and architectural optimisation for complex systems on silicon (ESPRIT project)
ASCOT	Assessment of Systems and Components for Optical Telecommunications (RACE project)
ASEAN	Association of South-East Asian Nations 70-A Jalan Sisingamangaraja, PO Box 2072, Jakarta 12110, Indonesia http://www.aseansec.org/
*ASFALEC	*See* EDA
ASHORED	Adaptable Smarter HOmes for Residents who are Elderly or Disabled (TIDE project)
ASIA INVEST	A programme to facilitate business cooperation between the EU and Asian countries with whom Agreements have been concluded (1996-2000) (Information in OJ C344/95) http://www.asia-invest.com
ASIA URBS	A programme to develop cooperation between local authorities in Asia and EU Member States (1996-1998-2000) (Information in OJ C2/96). *See also* URB-LA http://www.asia-urbs.com
ASIC	*Agricultural Situation in the European Union*: the annual agricultural report published by EUR-OP
ASOR	Council Decision 82/505/EEC regarding the Agreement on the international carriage of passengers by road by means of occasional coach and bus services (OJ L230/82)
ASP	Advanced Sandwich Panel (EUREKA project)
ASPEC	Association of Sorbitol Producers within the EC ave de Gaulois 9, B-1040 Brussels, Belgium

ASPIS	Application Software Prototype Implementation System (ESPRIT project)
ASSENT	ASSEssmeNt of Telematics programme (a project within the TELEMATICS APPLICATIONS programme)
ASSENT PROCEDURE	Introduced by the SEA so that the Council of the European Union must obtain the approval of the EP for Association Agreements, Accession Agreements and some legislation
ASSET	Automated Support for Software Engineering Technology (ESPRIT project)
ASSIFONTE	Association of the Processed Cheese Industry in the EU Godesberger Allee 157, D-53175 Bonn 1, Germany
*ASSILEC	*See* EDA
ASSIST	ASSessment of Information Systems and Technologies in medicine (AIM project)
ASSOCIATION AGREEMENTS	are those drawn up with non-EU countries and organisations to allow specific rights and obligations, but which fall short of full EU membership
ASTEP	Advanced Software for Teaching and Evaluation of Processes (EMTF project)
ASTERISK	System and scenario simulation for testing RTI systems (DRIVE project)
ASTRA	Advanced and integrated office systems prototypes for European public administration (ESPRIT project)
ASTRID	Amorphous Silicon Technology for Radiological Imaging Diagnostics (EUREKA project)

ASTRID	A Socio-Technical Response to the needs of Individuals with Dementia and their carers (a Telematics for Disabled and Elderly People project within the TELEMATICS APPLICATIONS programme)
ATA	Fast prototypeable Analogue Transistor Array development of an analogue ASIC (EUREKA project)
ATES	Advanced Techniques integration into Efficient Scientific application software (ESPRIT project)
ATEX Directive	Dir 94/9/EC concerning equipment and protective systems intended for use in potentially explosive atmospheres (OJ L100/94). This replaces the EXPLOSIVE ATMOSPHERES' Directives
ATIS	AIT Touring Information System (IMPACT project)
ATLANTIC	The deployment of coherent systems for digital television (ACTS project)
ATLANTICA	Developing training methodologies for the European Atlantic regions (COMETT project)
ATLANTIC ARC	The 26 regions of the EU which border the Atlantic together with the islands of the Atlantic and other regions with close economic, ethnic and cultural ties with the Atlantic seaboard regions (EP DOC A3-304/92). Map and list in *Innovation and Technology Transfer 4/1995*
ATLANTIC AXIS	*See* ATLANTIC ARC
ATLAS	A Commission study to integrate communications, navigation and surveillance technologies to support a single air traffic management system for Europe

ATLAS	Study to provide independent information to help determine and prioritise the next steps in terms of RTD, demonstration and market stimulation in the energy field (THERMIE project)
ATM	Air Traffic Management
ATMOSPHERE	Advanced Techniques and MOdels of System Production in a Heterogeneous Extensible and Rigorous Environment (ESPRIT project)
ATOMOS	Optimisation of manpower in marine transport (EURET project)
ATOMS	High densities mass storage memories for knowledge and information storage (ESPRIT project)
ATRE	ATM and Telecollaboration for Research and Education (a Telematics for Research project within the TELEMATICS APPLICATIONS programme)
ATT	Advanced Transport Telematics
ATTACH	Advanced Trans-European Telematics Applications for Community Help (a Telematics for Urban and Rural Areas project within the TELEMATICS APPLICATIONS programme)
ATTAIN	Applicability in Transport and Traffic of Artificial Intelligence (DRIVE project)
ATTRACT	Applications in Telemedicine Taking Rapid Advantage of Cable Television network evolution (a Telematics for Healthcare project within the TELEMATICS APPLICATIONS programme) http://www.ehto.org/vds/projects/attract.html
AUDETEL	AUdio DEscription of TELevision for the visually disabled and the elderly (TIDE project)

AUDIT	Financial control DG of the European Commission
AULIS	Biomarkers of genotoxicity of urban air pollution, a dose response study (an Environmental Health and Chemical Safety Research project within the ENVIRONMENT AND CLIMATE programme)
AUSA	Agricultural Usable Surface Area
AUTOCODE	Intelligent system for automatic processing of design codes of practice (ESPRIT project)
AUTO-OIL programme	set up in 1993 and resulting in Dir 96/44/EC on the measures to be taken against air pollution by emissions from motor vehicles (OJ L210/96) and Dir 98/70/EC on fuel quality (OJ L350/98). *See also* AUTO-OIL II programme
AUTO-OIL II programme	Further research is currently being undertaken on fuel quality and proposals are due later in 2000. *See also* AUTO-OIL programme
AUTOPOLIS	AUTOmatic POLicing Information System (DRIVE project)
AUVIS	Audiovisual Information System statistical domain on the NEW CRONOS databank
AVC	d'Avis Conforme (regarding the passage of a COM DOC)
AVEC	Association of Poultry Processors and Poultry Import and Export Trade in the EU Trommesalen 5, DK-1614 Copenhagen V, Denmark
AV EUREKA	European programme for audiovisual networks. A French initiative (1989-) Secretariat: ave des Arts 44, B-1040 Brussels, Belgium
AVIATION	Air transport statistical domain on the NEW CRONOS databank

AVICA	Advanced Video endoscopy Image Communication and Analysis (AIM project)
AVICENNE INITIATIVE	Scientific and technical cooperation with MAGHREB and Mediterranean Basin countries (1991-) (Information in OJ C173/92 and OJ C106/94)
AWG	Permanent Working Group 'Information on Agriculture'
AWU	Annual Work Unit
B	Belgium
B (point)	A Council of the European Union agenda item which is likely to be discussed at great length
BABEL	Broadcasting Across the Barriers of European Language c/o European Broadcasting Union, Ancienne Route 17A, Case Postale 67, Grand-Saconnex, CH-1218 Geneva, Switzerland
BABEL	Integrating cultural differences in telematics engineering (a Telematics Engineering project within the TELEMATICS APPLICATIONS programme)
BACH	Base for the Accounts of Companies Harmonised. A database of statistical data on company accounts http://europa.eu.int/comm/economy_finance/databases/bach_en.htm
BACIP	BACillus subtilis genome INDUSTRIAL PLATFORM http://europa.eu.int/comm/dg12/biotech/ip2.html#BACIP
BALAI Directive	Dir 92/65/EEC on the international transport of live animals (OJ L268/92 with latest amendment in OJ L117/95)

BANGEMANN CHALLENGE	A competition initiated by Stockholm in 1994 calling on all European cities with more than 400,000 inhabitants to present their most interesting information technology applications
BANGEMANN REPORT	*Europe and the global information society: recommendations to the European Council* 1994. Published by the Council of the European Union
*BAP	Biotechnology Action programme (1985-1989) (OJ L206/88). *Previously* BEP. *Continued as* BRIDGE
BARCELONA CONVENTION	Council Decision 77/585/EEC for the protection of the Mediterranean Sea against pollution (OJ L240/77) with Protocols as follows:

Prevention of pollution of the Mediterranean by dumping from ships and aircraft (OJ L240/77 with latest amendment in OJ L322/99)
Council Decision 81/420/EEC Cooperation in combatting pollution of the Mediterranean by oil and other harmful substances in cases of emergency (OJ L162/81)
Council Decision 83/101/EEC Protection of the Mediterranean against pollution from land-based sources (OJ L67/83 with latest amendment in OJ L322/99)
Council Decision 84/132/EEC on Mediterranean specially protected areas (OJ L68/84 with latest amendment in OJ L322/99)
Protection of the Mediterranean against pollution resulting from the exploration and exploitation of the continental shelf, the seabed and its subsoil (COM(92) 169 and COM(94) 397)
Protection of the Mediterranean against pollution from land-based sources and...pollution resulting from transboundary movements of hazardous wastes and their disposal (COM(96) 63)

| BARRE PLANS | for monetary union. Published in *Bulletin of the EC Supplements 3/69; 2/70* |

BARRIER	Development of a multimedia database providing information on the accessibility in public buildings for people with handicaps to their mobility (a Telematics for Disabled and Elderly People project within the TELEMATICS APPLICATIONS programme)
BARTOC	Bus Advanced Real Time Operational Control (DRIVE project)
Bas	*See* Business Angels
BASEL CONVENTION	Council Decision 93/98/EEC on the control of transboundary movements of hazardous wastes and their disposal (OJ L39/93 with latest amendment in OJ L272/97)
BASELINE	Baseline data for user validation in information engineering (a Telematics Information Engineering project within the TELEMATICS APPLICATIONS programme)
BASIS	The Barents Sea Impact Study (ELOISE project)
BASLE CONVENTION	*See* BASEL CONVENTION
BASYS	The Baltic Sea System Study (a project within the MAST III programme). *See also* CANIGO; MATER; OMEX
BAT	Best Available Techniques
BBP	Biotechnology for Biodiversity INDUSTRIAL PLATFORM http://europa.eu.int/comm/dg12/biotech/ip2.html#BBP
BC	Budget Committee
BCC	Biotechnology Coordination Committee
BCC	Business Cooperation Centre rue d'Arlon 80, B-1040 Brussels, Belgium

BC-NET	Business Cooperation Network. Set up by the BCC to encourage SMEs to develop links with SMEs in other Member States http://europa.eu.int/comm/dg23/bos_cooperation/cooper_net/bc-net.html
*BCR	Community Bureau of Reference
*BCR	R&D programme in the field of applied metrology and chemical analysis (1988-1992) (OJ L206/88)
BCS	BC-NET Central System
BDII	Development of a database for distributed expert systems on low-level computers (EUREKA project)
*BEACON EUROPE 1992	A European initiative to light beacons throughout the EC to herald the SEM on 1 January 1993
BEAM II	Biomedical Equipment Assessment and Management (a Telematics for Healthcare project within the TELEMATICS APPLICATIONS programme)
BEC	Broad Economic Categories
BECOS	A natural language front-end to databases with speech facilities (EUREKA project)
BEDA	Bureau of European Designers' Associations Postbus 91526, NL-2509 EC Den Haag, Netherlands
BEI	*See* EIB
BEMA	Biogenic Emissions in the Mediterranean Area (EI project)
BENELUX	Benelux Economic Union comprising Belgium, the Netherlands and Luxembourg
*BEP	Biomolecular Engineering programme (1982-1986) (OJ L305/83). *Continued as* BAP

BEQUEST	Building Environmental QUality Evaluation for Sustainability through Time (ENVIRONMENT AND CLIMATE programme)
BERD	*See* EBRD
BERI	Bog Ecostystem Research Initiative (TERI project)
BERNE CONVENTION	Council Decision 82/72/EEC concerning the conclusion of the Convention on the conservation of European wildlife and natural habitats (OJ L38/82)
BERTIE	Changes in the drive behaviour due to the introduction of RTI systems (DRIVE project)
BEST	*Bulletin of European Studies on Time.* Produced by a European network of experts (Business Environment Simplification Task Force) set up by the EFILWC
BEST	Methodological approach to IBC system requirements and specifications (RACE project)
Betel	Interconnection of broadband sites in France and Switzerland: a fibre interconnection initiative to prepare for TEN-TELECOMMUNICATIONS
BEUC	European Consumers' Organisation ave de Tervuren 36, Boîte 4, B-1040 Brussels, Belgium http://www.beuc.org/index_t.htm
BEVABS	European office for wine, alcohol and spirit drinks. A special unit at the EI in the JRC at ISPRA
BIA	Business Impact Assessment

BIBDEL	Libraries without walls: the delivery of library services to distant users (project within Area 5 of the TELEMATIC SYSTEMS programme)
BiblioTECA	Bibliographic TExts Compositional Analysis (project within Area 5 of the TELEMATIC SYSTEMS programme)
BIC	Blueprint for Interactive Classrooms (a Telematics for Education and Training project within the TELEMATICS APPLICATIONS programme)
BIC	Business and Innovation Centres. There are now around 150 such centres providing integrated support services for the creation of enterprises EBN, rue Froissart 89, Boîte 5, B-1040 Brussels, Belgium
*BICEPS	*See* AIM (Advanced Informatics in Medicine in Europe)
BICMOS	A high performance cmos-bipolar process for VLSI circuits (ESPRIT project)
BINOCULARS	A project to perfect a general system for managing the impact of fertilisers at river basin level (ENVIRONMENT AND CLIMATE programme)
BINTERMS	Basic INteroperability for TERMinals for telematic Services (ISIS Teleworking project) http://www.ispo.cec.be/isis/96binter.htm
BIO	Internal briefings of the European Commission Restricted access via RAPID
BIO COMAC	Biology Concerted Action Committee
BIODEPTH	BIODiversity and Ecological Processes in Terrestrial Herbaceous ecosystems: experimental manipulations of plant communities (TERI project)

BIOKIT	Clinical diagnosis of gonorrhoea (EUREKA project)
BIOLAB	Integrated Biomedical Laboratory (AIM project)
*BIOMED II	Council Decision 94/913/EC for a research and technological development programme in the field of biomedicine and health (1994-1998) (OJ L361/94). *See also* BIOTECH; ELSA; LST http://europa.eu.int/comm/dg12/biomed1.html
BIOMERIT	Increased innovation and industrial development in the European agro-food sector through biotechnology exploitation (COMETT project)
BIOREP	Permanent Inventory of Biotechnical Research Projects in the EU Access via DIMDI and CAB INTERNATIONAL
BIOSTANDARDS	Establishment of bioinformatic databases and access tools (ISIS Bioinformatics project) http://www.ispo.cec.be/isis/95biost.htm
*BIOTECH II	Council Decision 94/912/EC for a Biotechnology action programme (1994-1998) (OJ L361/94). *Previously* BRIDGE. *See also* BIOMED; LST http://europa.eu.int/comm/dg12/biotech/biot2.html
BIPED	Basic Business IBC Demonstrator (RACE project)
BIPMS	Building Industry Project Management System (ESPRIT project)
BIRDS Directive	Dir 79/409/EEC on the conservation of wild birds (OJ L103/79 with latest amendment in OJ L223/97)
BIS	Budget Information System
BIT	Biotechnology in Training (COMETT project)

BLACK LIST	of dangerous substances discharged into the aquatic environment. Dir 76/464 (OJ L129/76 - List 1. *See also* GREY LIST
BLEU	Belgium - Luxembourg Economic Union
BLIC	Liaison Office of the Rubber Industries of the EU ave des Arts 2, Boîte 12, B-1210 Brussels, Belgium
BLNT	Broadband Local Network Technology (RACE project)
BLOCK EXEMPTIONS	These are made to exempt certain categories of agreement from Article 85 of the ROME TREATY, which prohibits agreements affecting trade between Member States, or which restrict or distort competition eg KNOW-HOW LICENSING
BLUE FLAG CAMPAIGN	An annual award for EU bathing beaches which fulfil certain criteria. An initiative from FEEE
BME COMAC	Bio-Medical Engineering COncerted Action Committee
BOI	Binding Origin Information (with respect to customs matters)
BookTownNet	European Book Town Network. A telematics application based on a model for sustainable rural development within the cultural heritage (a Telematics for Urban and Rural Areas project within the TELEMATICS APPLICATIONS programme)
BOP	Balance of Payments statistical domain on the NEW CRONOS databank
BOPCom	Baltic Open Port Communication (a marine transport project within the TRANSPORT programme) http://cordis.lu/transport/src/bopcom.htm

BOPS	Back Office Performance Support (EMTF project)
BOSMAN CASE	Case C-415/93 in the ECJ on the freedom of movement for footballers (Case reported in ECR I - 1995/12)
*BRAIN	Basic Research in Adaptive Intelligence and Neurocomputing (part of the SCIENCE STIMULATION programme)
BRE	Bureau de Rapprochement des Entreprises. *See* BCC (Business Cooperation Centre)
BREVIE	Bridging REality and Virtuality with a graspable user IntErface (EMTF project)
BRIC	Biotechnology Regulations Inter-Service Committee
*BRIDGE	Biotechnology Research for Innovation, Development and Growth in Europe (1990-1994) (OJ L360/89). *Previously* BAP. *Continued as* BIOTECH
*BRITE	Basic Research in Industrial Technologies for Europe. *See* BRITE/EURAM III
*BRITE/EURAM III	Council Decision 94/571/EC on industrial and materials technologies (1994-1998) (OJ L222/94). *Replaced by* GROWTH. *See also* BRITE; CRAFT; IT http://www.cordis.lu/brite-euram/home.html
*BROKERSGUIDE	On-line directory of current information brokers in the EC. Merged with DIANEGUIDE to form I*M GUIDE
BRUSSELS CONVENTION	on jurisdiction and the enforcement of judgments in civil and commercial matters 1968. *See* LUXEMBOURG CONVENTION
BRUSSELS TREATY	Treaty amending certain financial provisions of the Treaties establishing the EC and of the Treaty establishing a Single Council of the EC. Signed in July 1975 and came into force in 1978

BSC	Biotechnolgy Steering Committee
BSCW	Basic Support for Cooperation Work (CSCW project partially funded by the EU under the TELEMATICS APPLICATIONS programme) http://bscw.gmd.de/
BSEC	Black Sea Economic Cooperation
BSPF	Baltic Small Projects Facility set up in 1995 with PHARE funding to establish INTERREG-type collaboration in Baltic Sea regions
BTI	Binding Tariff Information (with respect to customs matters) Available as a CD-ROM from TSO and EUR-OP official agents
*BTN	Brussels Tariff Nomenclature. *Replaced by* CCCN
BTR	Basic Technological Research
BTWC	Biological and Toxin Weapons Convention. A common position (99/346/CFSP) has been adopted (OJ L133/99)
BUDG	Budget DG of the European Commission
BUDG	Committee on Budgets (of the EP)
*BUILDING 2000	Solar energy pilot project (within the 1985-1988 non-nuclear energy R&D programme)
BUILDING EUROPE TOGETHER	A campaign within PRINCE
BURDEN OF PROOF	Dir 97/80/EC on the burden of proof in cases of discrimination based on sex (OJ L14/98 with latest amendment in OJ L205/98)

Business Angels	Entrepreneurs willing to invest time and money to support the creation and development of start-up companies. In 1999, the Enterprise DG of the European Commission launched a programme to promote networks of Business Angels. *See also* EBAN
CA	Commitment Appropriation (in the budget)
CA	Compensatory Amounts
CA	Concerted Action
CABOTAGE	A procedure whereby non-resident transport carriers may operate national transport services within another Member State: *Passenger transport:* Reg 2454/92 (OJ L251/92 with proposal for amendment in OJ C60/96); *Maritime transport:* Reg 3577/92 (OJ L364/92); *Road haulage:* Reg 3118/93 (OJ L279/93 with latest amendment in OJ L350/94 and detailed rules in OJ L92/94)
CACOHIS	Computer Aided Community Oral Health Information System (AIM project)
CACTI	Common Agricultural Customs Transmission of Information (CADDIA project)
CAD	CAD interfaces (ESPRIT project)
CAD	*See* CAPITAL ADEQUACY Directive
CADAM	Cancer and Aids Diagnosis and Monitoring (EUREKA project)
CADDIA	Cooperation in Automation of Data and Documentation for Imports-Exports and Agriculture (1985-1992) (OJ L96/85 and OJ L145/87)
CADEX	CAD Geometry Data Exchange (ESPRIT project)

CADP	Community Area Development Plan
CAFA	Committee for Administrative and Financial Affairs. Set up in 1998 by the Bureau of CoR
CAFAO	Customs and Fiscal Assistance Office. Established in 1996, this Taxation and Customs Union DG programme of the European Commission in Bosnia-Herzegovina aims to facilitate the implementation of the customs-related provisions of the Dayton/Paris Peace Agreements
CAFE	Conditional Access for Europe (ESPRIT project)
CAFÉ MONDIAL	Communication Applications for Education, Multi-user Open Network Design, Infrastructure and Logistics (a Telematics for Urban and Rural Areas project within the TELEMATICS APPLICATIONS programme)
CAGII	Second Competitiveness Advisory Group
CAJAL, Ramón y SCHOLARSHIPS	*See* RAMÓN y CAJAL SCHOLARSHIPS
CAKE	Advanced knowledge-based environments for large database systems (ESPRIT project)
CALIES	Computer-aided Locomotion by Implanted Electro-Stimulation (EUREKA project)
CALYPSO	Computational fluid dynamic in the ship-design process. One of the eight interrelated Community-funded projects in the field of design, production and operation for safer, more efficient, environmentally friendly and user-friendly ships, coordinated by NETS. *See also* CAMELLIA

CALYPSO	Contact and contact Less environments Yielding a citizen Pass integrating urban Services and financial Operations (a Telematics for Integrated Applications for Digital Sites project within the TELEMATICS APPLICATIONS programme)
CAM-A	Customs Assistance Mission to Albania (part of the 1997 PHARE programme in Albania)
CAMAC	Care-based Hospital Management and Clinical Evaluation in Europe (AIM project)
*CAMAR	Competitiveness of Agriculture and Management of Agricultural Resources (1989-1993) (OJ L58/90)
CAMARC	Computer-Aided Movement Analyses in a Rehabilitation Context (AIM project)
CAMBI	A research network for market based instruments for environmentally sustainable development (ENVIRONMENT AND CLIMATE project)
CAMCE	Computer-Aided Multimedia Courseware Engineering (DELTA project)
CAMELLIA	Environmentally compatible anti-fouling coatings. One of the eight interrelated Community-funded projects in the field of design, production and operation for safer, more efficient, environmentally friendly and user-friendly ships, coordinated by NETS. *See also* CALYPSO
CAM-ES	Customs Assistance Mission to Eastern Slavonia (part of the PHARE programme in the Balkans)
CAMILE	Concerted Action on Management Information for Libraries in Europe (TELEMATICS APPLICATIONS project)

*CAN	Committee of an Advisory Nature. A committee to assist in the management of DOSES
CANDI	Combined Analogue Digital Integration (ESPRIT project)
CANIGO	CANary Islands Azores Gibraltar Observatories (MAST III project). *See also* BASYS; MATER; OMEX
CANS	Citizens Access Networks and Services (a Telematics for Urban and Rural Areas project within the TELEMATICS APPLICATIONS programme)
CANTOR	Converging Agreement by Networking Telematics for Object Recognition (a Telematics for Healthcare project within the TELEMATICS APPLICATIONS programme) http:www.ehto.org/vds/projects/cantor.html
CAOBISCO	Association of the Chocolate, Biscuit and Confectionery Industries of the EEC rue Defacqz 1, Boîte 7, B-1000 Brussels, Belgium
CAP	Common Agricultural Policy
CAP	Computer Assisted Production (EUREKA project)
CAP	Concerted Action Programme
CAP2000	Studies carried out by the Agriculture DG of the European Commission examining the common agricultural policy http://europa.eu.int/comm/dg06/publi/cap2000/index_en.htm
CAPE 2000	Computer Aided Post in Europe in the year 2000 (a Telematics for Administrations project within the TELEMATICS APPLICATIONS programme)

CAPIEL	Coordinating Committee for Common Market Associations of Manufacturers of Industrial Electrical Switchgear and Controlgear Stresemannallee 19, D-60591 Frankfurt am Main, Germany
CAPITAL ADEQUACY Directive	Dir 93/6/EEC to ensure that banks and securities firms have reserves to cover normal trading risks (OJ L141/93 with latest amendment in OJ L204/98)
CAPITAL Directive	Dir 88/361/EEC which abolishes controls on the free movement of capital between Member States (OJ L178/88). Incorporated by Agreement 94/0103(62) (OJ L1/94)
CAPRI	Concerted Action for transport Pricing Research Integration (TRANSPORT project)
CAPS	Communication and Access to information for Persons with Special needs (TIDE project)
CAPT	Committee on Associations with Third Countries
CAPTION LIFE	Using Telematics to help those suffering with a hearing impairment (a Telematics for Disabled and Elderly People project within the TELEMATICS APPLICATIONS programme)
CAPTIVE	Collaborative Authoring, Production and Transmission of Interactive Videos for Education (DELTA project)
CAR	CAD/CAM for the automotive industry in Europe (RACE project)

CARA programme	Community Association and Reconstruction Assistance to the Western Balkans. Future programme for assistance to Albania, Bosnia and Herzegovina, Croatia, the Former Yugoslav Republic of Macedonia and the Federal Republic of Yugoslavia (2000-2006) (Guidelines in COM(99) 661)
CARDI-ASSIST	Improving cardiac telediagnosis and surgery enabling technologies and 3D ultrasound imaging (a Telematics for Healthcare project within the TELEMATICS APPLICATIONS programme)
Cardiff I	Commission report on economic and structural reforms: *Economic Reform: Report on the functioning of Community product and capital markets* (COM(99) 10). *See also* Cardiff II
Cardiff II	Commission report on economic and structural reforms: *Economic and structural reform in the EU* (COM(99) 61). *See also* Cardiff I
CARDIO EUG7	Feasibility study on the European component of the G7 global health care cardiovascular sub project (a Telematics for Healthcare project within the TELEMATICS APPLICATIONS programme)
CARDLINK 2	A patient held portable record for particular application in cases of medical emergency (a Telematics for Healthcare project within the TELEMATICS APPLICATIONS programme)
CARE	Council Decision 93/704/EC on the creation of a Community databank on road accident statistics (OJ L329/93)
CARE	Health information network involving HSSCD and HIEMS (IDA project)

CARGOES	Integration of Dynamic Route Guidance and Traffic Central System (DRIVE project)
CARISMA	Coordinated Architecture for the Interconnection of networks for Suitable Mobility with telematics applications (TRANSPORT project)
CARLOS	Communications Architecture for Layered Open Systems (ESPRIT project)
CARMAT 2000	Car structures using new Materials (EUREKA project)
CARMINAT	System for the acquisition, transmission, processing and presentation of information to improve the safety of the driver and to make trips easier and more efficient (EUREKA project)
CARNOT	Council Decision 1999/24/EC for a multiannual programme of technological actions promoting the clean and efficient use of solid fuels (1998-2002) (OJ L7/99) http://europa.eu.int/en/comm/dg17/carnot.htm
CARREFOUR	Rural Information Centre set up for the rural community. *See also* RELAYS
CART	Community Action to promote Rural Tourism (COM(90) 438)
CARTOON	An animation project under the MEDIA programme Contact: bd Lambermont 418, B-1030 Brussels, Belgium
CASA	A Cooperative Archive of Serials and Articles (project within the Telematics for Libraries programme). *See also* NFP
CASCADE	Contribution for ASsessment of Common ATM Development in Europe (an Air Transport project within the TRANSPORT programme)

CASEIN	Settling of a casein and by-products industrial pilot plant (EUREKA project)
CASSIOPE	Computer-Aided System for Scheduling, Information and Operation of Public Transport in Europe (DRIVE project)
CASSIS DE DIJON	Case 120/78 in the ECJ which established that any product lawfully produced and marketed in one Member State must (in principle) be admitted to the market of any other Member State (Case reported in ECR 1979/1)
CA.SS.TM	Administrative Commission on Social Security for Migrant Workers
Catalogue of Data Sources	*See* CDS
CATCH II	Citizens Advisory system based on Telematics for Communication and Health (a Telematics for Healthcare project within the TELEMATICS APPLICATIONS programme)
CATDIFF	Working title for the new web catalogue with access profiles for sales networks, internal Commission staff and public use, which replaces CATEL. This will be developed further in 2000. *See also* EUROCAT Test site: http://online.eur-op.eu.int
*CATEL	An electronic catalogue containing publicly available documents from EUR-OP. *Replaced by* CATDIFF
CAVA	Concerted Action on Voluntary Approaches (Coordinated by CERNA)
CAVIS	Intelligent automated optical inspection of printed circuit boards (EUREKA project)
CBC	Cross-Border Cooperation between the NIS and the EU and between the NIS and CCE (TACIS programme)

CBMC	Confederation of Common Market Breweries ch de la Hulpe 181, Boîte 20, B-1170 Brussels, Belgium http://www.cbmc.org/
CBNM	Central Bureau for Nuclear Measurements. Part of the JRC at GEEL
CBP	Dir 97/5/EC on cross-border credit transfers (OJ L43/97)
CBSS	Council of Baltic Sea States Baltic Sea States Support, c/o Ministry of Foreign Affairs, Box 16121, S-10323 Stockholm, Sweden http://www.baltinfo.org/CBSS.htm
CC	Information notes from the ECA Access via RAPID
CCACE	Coordinating Committee of EC Cooperative Associations c/o CECOP, rue Guillaume Tell 59, B-1060 Brussels, Belgium
CCAMLR	Reg 66/98 setting up the Commission for the Conservation of Antarctic Marine Living Resources (OJ L6/98)
CCBE	Council of the Bars of the European Community rue Washington 40, B-1050 Brussels, Belgium http://www.ccbe.org/
CCC	Reg 2913/92 establishing the Community Customs Code. The basic instrument underlying Community customs provision (OJ L302/92 with latest amendment in OJ L119/99)
CCCC	Community-COST Concertation Committee
*CCCN	Customs Cooperation Council Nomenclature. *Previously* BTN. *Replaced by* HS
CCD	Committee on Commerce and Distribution
CCE	Countries of Central Europe

CCFI	Advisory Committee on Training in Nursing
CCFP	Consultative Committee for the Fusion Programme. Set up in 1980
CCFR	Coordinating Committee on Fast Reactors
CCG	Policy Coordination Group for Credit Insurance, Credit Guarantees and Financial Credits
CCL	Common Command Language
CCN/CSI	Common Communications Network/Commons System Interface. The development of common facilities for the transfer of large files and interactive data exchange (IDA project)
CCP	Common Commercial Policy
CCP	Consultative Committee on Publications
CCPC	Consultative Committee on Purchases and Contracts
CCPF	Central Committee of Forest Ownership in the EEC quai Churchill 9, B-4020 Liège, Belgium
CCPI	Advisory Committee for the Management and Coordination of Data Processing programmes
CCPM	Consultative Committee for Programme Management
CCRP	*See* ACOR
*CCT	Common Customs Tariff. *Replaced by* CN
CCT	Compulsory Competitive Tendering
CD	Coordinated Development of Computerised Administrative Procedures (CADDIA project) (OJ L33/86)

CDBC	Commission Database Committee
CDI	Centre for the Development of Industry. Set up under LOME I to facilitate SME participation in EDF projects ave Herrmann Debroux 52, B-1160 Brussels, Belgium http://www.cdi.be
CDIC	Commission Informatics Steering Committee
CDIS	Steering Committee for Statistical Information
CDR	An application editors and software developers workbench for publishing multi-media information using optical read-only storage devices (ESPRIT project)
CdR	*See* CoR
CDS	Catalogue of Data Sources. A database containing descriptions of authoritative EEA and EIONET information resources developed by the ETC/CDS http://www.mu.niedersachsen.de/system/cds
CdT	Community's Translation Centre Nouvelle Hemicycle, niveau 4, rue de Fort Thungen 1, L-1499 Kirchberg, Luxembourg
CE	Compulsory Expenditure
CE	Council of Europe Palais de l'Europe, F-67075 Strasbourg Cedex, France http://www.coe.fr
CE (mark)	Dir 93/68/EEC on Conformity marking (OJ L220/93)
CEA	European Confederation of Agriculture rue de la Science 23-25, Boîte 23, B-1040 Brussels, Belgium
CEAS	Citizen's Europe Advisory Service UK Contact: AIRE Centre
CEBI	*See* EIC

CEC	Central European Countries statistical domain on the NEW CRONOS databank
CEC	Commission of the European Communities rue de la Loi 200, B-1049 Brussels, Belgium http://europa.eu.int/en/comm.html UK Representation Offices: Jean Monnet House, 8 Storey's Gate, London SW1P 3AT 7 Alva Street, Edinburgh EH2 4PH 4 Cathedral Road, Cardiff CF1 9SG Windsor House, 9-15 Bedford Street, Belfast BT2 7EG http://www.cec.org.uk
CEC	Confédération Européenne des Cadres (European Managers' Confederation) ave Carton de Wiart 148, B-1090 Brussels, Belgium
CECC	Cenelec Electronic Components Committee rue de Stassart 35, B-1050 Brussels, Belgium
CECCs	Central European Candidate Countries
CECCHINI REPORT	published in 1988 (English version by Wildwood House) entitled *The European challenge 1992: the benefits of a Single Market* (plus 16 research volumes published by OOPEC)
CECG	*See* CEG
CECODE	European Centre of Retail Trade c/o HDE, Gothaer Allee 2, D-50969 Köln, Germany
CECOP	European Committee of Workers Cooperatives, Social Cooperatives and Participative Enterprises rue Guillaume Tell 59, B-1060 Brussels, Belgium
CEDB	Component Event Data Bank which forms part of ERDS
CEDEFOP	A database of bibliographical references in the field of vocational training http://www.cedefop.gr/

CEDEFOP	European Centre for the Development of Vocational Training. Set up by Reg 337/75 (OJ L39/75 with amendments in OJ L127/94 and L30/95) PO Box 22427, Finikas, GR-55102 Thessaloniki, Greece http://www.cedefop.gr/
CEDI	European Self-employed Confederation Oberbexbacherstrasse 7, D-66450 Bexbach, Germany
CEDISYS	Models, languages and logics for concurrent distributed systems (ESPRIT project)
CEE	Central and Eastern Europe
CEE	*See* UK CEE
CEEC	Central and Eastern European Countries
CEEC	European Committee for Catholic Education ave Marnix 19A Boîte 6, B-1000 Brussels, Belgium
CEEP	European Centre of Enterprises with Public Participation rue de la Charité 15, Boîte 12, B-1210 Brussels, Belgium
CEEPUS	Central European Exchange Programme for University Studies http://www.adis.at/ceepus/
CEES	Central and Eastern European States
CEFES	Creating a European Forum in European Studies. A virtual seminar in European studies (SOCRATES programme) http://www.diff.uni-tuebingen.de/cefes
CEFIC	European Chemical Industry Council ave E van Nieuwenhuyse 4, B-1160 Brussels, Belgium http://www.cefic.be
CEFIR	European high temperature fibres (EUREKA project)
CEFS	European Committee of Sugar Manufacturers ave de Tervuren 182, B-1150 Brussels, Belgium http://www.ib.be/cefs/content.htm

CEFTA	Central European Free Trade Association. Established in 1992 to set up a free trade area and now consists of Poland, Hungary, Czech Republic, Romania, Bulgaria, Slovakia and Slovenia
CEG	Consumers in Europe Group 20 Grosvenor Gdns, London SW1W 0DH, United Kingdom http://www.ceg.co.uk
CEI	Central European Initiative. A regional cooperation instrument agreed in 1992 covering the political, cultural and economic fields in CEEC, Austria, Italy and Bavaria (as an observer) (COM(96) 601) *See also* CEInet
CEI-Bois	European Confederation of Woodworking Industries rue Royale 109-111, B-1000 Brussels, Belgium
CEIES	European Advisory Committee on Statistical Information in the Economic and Social Spheres (OJ L59/91)
CEInet	Internet information pages on CEI activities, contacts and projects http://www.ceinet.org/home1.htm
CEJA	European Council of Young Farmers rue de la Science 23-25, Boîte 3, B-1040 Brussels, Belgium
CEL	European Language Council Freie Universität Berlin ZE, Sprachlabor, Habelschwerdter Allee 45, D-14195 Berlin, Germany
CELEX	Communitatis Europae LEX : an inter-institutional computerised database for EU law covering legislation, proposals, opinions, case law and parliamentary questions http://europa.eu.int/celex (password required) Available on-line via CONTEXT; DATASTAR; EUR-OP; LEXIS-NEXIS. CD-ROM available from CONTEXT; ELLIS; EUR-OP; ILI

CEMR	Council of European Municipalities and Regions rue de Castiglione 14, F-75001 Paris, France UK contact: 35 Great Smith St, London SW1P 3BJ (where it is known as the Local Government International Bureau) http://www.ccre.org/
CEMR-EP	Council of European Municipalities and Regions Employers' Platform
CEN	European Committee for Standardisation (Comité Européen de Normalisation). *See also* CEN-STAR rue de Stassart 36, B-1050 Brussels, Belgium http://www.cenorm.be
CENELEC	European Committee for Electrotechnical Standardisation rue de Stassart 36, B-1050 Brussels, Belgium http://www.cenelec.be
CEN-STAR	European Standards Committee working group on Standards and Research. *See also* CEN
CENSUS	1990/1991 population census statistical domain on the NEW CRONOS databank
CENTAUR	Clean and Efficient New Transport Approach for Urban Rationalisation (Integrated Quality Targeted Project within the THERMIE programme) http://europa.eu.int/en/comm/dg17/thermie/centaur.htm
CENYC	Council of European National Youth Committees de Wavre 517-519, B-1040 Brussels, Belgium
CEO	Centre for Earth Observation. Part of the SAI at the JRC in ISPRA
CEOS	Conditions of Employment of Other Servants of the EU
CEPF	Central Environmental Protection Fund. Launched within PHARE's 1997 programme in Hungary to finance a wide range of environmental capital investments

CEPFAR	European Training and Development Centre for Farming and Rural Life rue de la Science 23-25, Boîte 10, B-1040 Brussels, Belgium
CEPLACA	Assessment of environmental contamination risk by platinum, rhodium and palladium from automobile catalysts (an Environmental Health and Chemical Safety Research project within the ENVIRONMENT AND CLIMATE programme)
CEPS	Centre for European Policy Studies pl du Congrès 1, B-1000 Brussels, Belgium http://www.ceps.be
CEPT	European Conference of Postal and Telecommunications Administrations Telecommunications Administration Centre, PO Box 53, FIN-00211 Helsinki, Finland
CER	Centre for European Reform. Think-tank devoted to improving the quality of the debate on the future of the EU 29 Tufton Street London SW1P 3QL, United Kingdom http://www.cer.org.uk
CER	Community of European Railways bd de l'Impératrice 15, Boîte 11, B-1000 Brussels, Belgium
CERACS	Comparative Evaluation of the Different Radiating Cables and Systems Technologies (DRIVE project)
CERAME-UNIE	Liaison Office of the European Ceramic Industries rue des Colonies 18-24, Boîte 17, B-1000 Brussels, Belgium
CERD	European R&D Committee
CEREC	European Committee for Business, Arts and Culture Handelskaai 14, B-1000 Brussels, Belgium

*CERES	Cascade Environment for the Realisation of Electronic Systems. A project in the microelectronics technology programme (1982-1986)
CERIF	Recommendation 91/337/EEC for a Common European Research Information Format to provide a standard format for European research databases (OJ L189/91)
CERISE	European centre for image synthesis: to improve and market computer imaging technology (EUREKA project)
CERNA	Centre d'Economie Industrielle bd Saint-Michel 60, F-75272 Paris Cedex 06, France
CERTIFIED	Conception and Evaluation of Roadside Testing Instruments to Formalise Impairment Evidence in Drivers (TRANSPORT project)
CES	Press releases of the ESC Access via RAPID
CESAR	Collaboration Environments and Service Architectures for Researchers (a CSCW Telematics for Research project, partially funded under the TELEMATICS APPLICATIONS programme) http://orgwis.gmd.de/projects/CESAR/
CESAR	European Centre for the Support of Rural Activities. A pilot project funded by the European Commission
CES DOC(UMENT)	Opinions and reports of the ESC
CET	Common External Tariff. See also CCT and CN
CETIL	Committee of Experts for the Transfer of Information between European Languages
*CETIS	European Scientific Data Processing Centre

CFCU	Central Financing and Coordination Unit (within the PHARE programme)
CFI	*See* ECFI
CFP	Common Fisheries Policy
CFSP	Common Foreign and Security Policy. Statements within the CFSP framework are issued as Press Releases Access via RAPID
CFSP	A database containing the text of CFSP Acts adopted by the Council of the European Union http://ue.eu.int/pesc/default.asp?lang=en
*CG	Left Unity Group (of the EP)
CGC	Council Decision 84/338/EURATOM, ECSC, EEC for a Management and Coordination Consultative Committee for a Research Action programme (OJ L177/84)
CGD	Waste Management Committee
CHABADA	CHAnges in BActerial Diversity and Activity in Mediterranean coastal waters as affected by eutrophication (ELOISE project)
CHAINE	Comprehensive Hospital and Ambulatory care Information Networking for Episode linkage (a Telematics for Healthcare project within the TELEMATICS APPLICATIONS programme) http://www.hiscom.nl/chaine/
CHAMELEON	Dynamic software migration between cooperating environments (ESPRIT project)
CHARME	Correct hardware design towards formal design and verification for provably correct VLSI hardware (ESPRIT project)
CHEDYN	Advanced dynamic simulator for chemical plants (EUREKA project)

CHEF	A kitchen management system for people with mental handicap (TIDE project)
CHEMICON	Chemistry and microphysics of Contrail formation (THESEO project)
CHEOPS	High order logic supported design for complex data processing (ESPRIT project)
CHESS	An EI project to study the influence of land-use and climate changes on pollutant loads to water bodies in a number of inland and coastal watersheds across Europe
CHEYSSON FACILITY	*See* ECIP (Investment Partners to promote joint ventures ...)
CHIC	Community Health Information Classification and Coding (AIM project)
CHIEF	Customs Handling of Import and Export Freight
CHILIAS	Children in Libraries: improving multimedia virtual library access and information skills (project within the Telematics for Libraries programme)
ChimEre	Statistical database for chemical products. *See* RISC Access via Internet (password required)
ChimStat	Statistical database for chemical products. *See* RISC Access via Internet (password required)
CHIN	Co-operative Health Information Networks for the community (a Telematics for Healthcare project within the TELEMATICS APPLICATIONS programme)

CHIP	Chemicals (Hazard Information and Packaging) Regulations S.I. 1993 No 1746; S.I. 1994 No 3247 and S.I. 1996 No 1092 (in the UK). *See* DANGEROUS PREPARATIONS Directive and DANGEROUS SUBSTANCES Directive
CHRISTINE	Characteristics and Requirements of Information Systems based on Traffic Data in an Integrated Network Environment (DRIVE project)
CI	Community Initiative. *See also* NPCI
CIAA	Confederation of the Food and Drink Industries of the EU ave des Arts 43, B-1040 Brussels, Belgium http://www.ciaa.org/
CICERO	Cultural Information Computer Exchange (a Telematics for Urban and Rural Areas project within the TELEMATICS APPLICATIONS programme)
CID	Centre for Information and Documentation (EURATOM)
CIDAM	CIM system based on a distributed database with individually configurable modules (ESPRIT project)
CIDIE	Committee of International Development Institutions on the Environment
CIDREE	Consortium of Institutions for Development and Research in Education in Europe Scottish CCC, Gardyne Rd, Broughty Ferry, Dundee DD5 1NY, United Kingdom http://claudius.sccc.ac.uk/cidhom.htm
CIDST	Committee for Scientific and Technical Information and Documentation
CIM	Computer Integrated Manufacturing (ESPRIT project)

CIMALIVE	Implementation Addressing Levels of Integration in Various Environments (ESPRIT project)
CIMCEE	Committee of the Mustard Industries of the EEC ave de Roodebeek 30, B-1030 Brussels, Belgium
CIM-PLATO	CIM system planning toolbox (ESPRIT project)
CIMSCEE	Committee of the Mayonnaise and Condiment Sauce Industries of the EEC ave de Roodebeek 30, B-1030 Brussels, Belgium
CIMSTEEL	Computer aided manufacturing for constructional steelwork (EUREKA project)
CIRCA	Collaborative software used by EUROSTAT and a number of DGs
CIRCCE	International Confederation of Commercial Representation in the EC rue d'Hauteville 2, F-75010 Paris, France
CIRCE	Application and enhancement of an experimental center for system integration in CIM (ESPRIT project)
*CIRCE	European Communities Information and Documentary Research Centre. *Replaced by* SII
CIRCLE	Centre of Information Resources for Collaboration on Environment. A customised version of the CIRCA software used on EIONET http://eea.eionet.eu.int:8980/eionet-circle/
CIRD	Interservice Committee for R&D
CIS	Commonwealth of Independent States
CIS	Community Innovation Survey. Carried out by Member States and coordinated by EUROSTAT on behalf of the INNOVATION programme

CIS	Customs Information System
CIT	Advisory Committee for Innovation and Technology Transfer
*CITE	Centre for Information Technologies and Electronics at the JRC. Merged in 1990 to form ISEI
CITES	Reg 338/97 on the Convention on International Trade in Endangered Species of Wild Fauna and Flora which commits Member States to the application of the rules prescribed by the Convention ((OJ L61/97 with latest amendment in OJ L279/98) http://europa.eu.int/comm/dg11/cites/home_en.htm
CITIES	Cities Telecommunications and Integrated Services (a Telematics for Administrations project within the TELEMATICS APPLICATIONS programme)
CITIZEN'S EUROPE	*See* PEOPLE'S EUROPE
CITIZEN'S FIRST	A campaign launched in November 1996 (within the PRINCE programme) to enable citizens to obtain information on their EU rights and how to benefit from them http://citizens.eu.int
CITIZEN'S NETWORK	A European Commission Communication on public passenger transport in Europe (COM(98) 431)
CITRA	System for the Control of Dangerous Goods Transport in International Alpine Corridors (DRIVE project)
CIVI	Committee on Civil liberties and internal affairs (of the EP)
CJE	Bulletin of the ECJ Access via RAPID
CJEC	*See* ECJ

CL4K	Cyberspace Learning for Kids (a Telematics for Education and Training project within the TELEMATICS APPLICATIONS programme)
CLAB Europa	European Database on Case Law About unfair contract terms http://europa.eu.int/clab/index.htm
CLAIR	Clean Air: Fluor hydrocarbon replacement in cleaning process during Mechadeck production for video recorders (EUREKA project)
CLAUDE	Coordinating LAnd Use and cover Date and analyses in Europe (ENVIRONMENT AND CLIMATE project)
CLC	CORINE Land Cover database for the analysis of land use in Europe http://natlan.eea.eu.int/datasets/viewmap3.htm#landcover#5
CLECAT	European Liaison Committee of Common Market Forwarders rue de l'Entrepôt 11, Boîte 4, B-1020 Brussels, Belgium
CLICOFI	Effects of climate induced temperature change on marine coastal fishes (ELOISE project)
CLICS	Categorical Logic in Computer Science (ESPRIT project)
CLIMFRESH	Impact of CLIMate change on carbon flux in FRESHwater ecosystems (a Water, Wetland and Acquatic Ecosystem Research project within the ENVIRONMENT AND CLIMATE programme)
CLIMOOR	Climate driven changes in the functioning of heath and moorland ecosystems (TERI project)
CLITRAVI	Liaison Centre for the Meat Processing Industry in the EEC bd Baudouin 21, 7e étage, B-1000 Brussels, Belgium

the 'CLUB'	Institutions of the EC specialising in long-term credit
CLUE	Changing Land Usage: Enhancement of biodiversity and ecosystem development (TERI project)
CLUSTER	Cooperative Link between Universities in Science and Technology for Education and Research Stichting Cluster, Den Dolech 2, NL-5612 AZ Eindhoven, Netherlands
CME	Compact Measure. TEMPUS and PHARE projects with a one or two year duration
CME	Complementary Measures. Technical assistance under the TEMPUS programme
CMGM	Committee on the Monitoring of the seriously ill
*CMO	Common Market Organisation
CMR	Substances which are Carcinogenic, Mutagenic and toxic to Reproduction
CMSO	CIM for Multi-Supplier Operations (ESPRIT project)
CN	Combined Nomenclature: an 8-digit goods nomenclature which is based on the HS and which replaces the CCT and NIMEXE nomenclatures. It is updated annually, the latest being in OJ L278/99
CNMA	Communication Network for Manufacturing Applications (ESPRIT project)
CNMB	*See* CBNM
CNS	*See* CONSULTATION PROCEDURE
COAST	Coordinated Action for Seaside Towns (Network of coastal tourist areas under RECITE)

COAST	*See* COASTER
COASTER	COurseware Authoring for Scientific Training: Extended Renewal of the original COAST project (a Telematics for Education and Training project within the TELEMATICS APPLICATIONS programme)
COAT	Coatings for advanced technology development of coatings and fabrication processes for smart windows (EUREKA project)
COBIP	Teleworking coordination services for CO-operative Business Processes (a Telematics for Urban and Rural Areas project within the TELEMATICS APPLICATIONS programme)
Co BRA+	Computerised Bibliographic Records Actions (TELEMATICS APPLICATIONS project)
COBROW	Collaborative Browsing in Information resources (a Telematics for Research project within the TELEMATICS APPLICATIONS programme)
COBUCO	COrdless BUsiness COmmunication system (ACTS project)
COCERAL	Committee of Cereals, Oilseeds, Animal Feed, Olive Oils, Oils and Fats and Agrosupply Trade in the EU sq de Meeûs 18, Boîte 1, B-1050 Brussels, Belgium
COCKFIELD WHITE PAPER	on plans to complete the SEM (COM(85) 310 and Commission. Document Series. *Completing the internal market.* 1985. Published by OOPEC)
Co-Co	Coordination Committee for European Integration

COCO	COordination and COntinuity in primary care: the regional healthcare information network (a Telematics for Healthcare project within the TELEMATICS APPLICATIONS programme)
COCOR	Iron and Steel Nomenclature Coordination Committee
COCOS	Components for Future Computing Systems (ESPRIT project)
COD	*See* CO-DECISION PROCEDURE
CO-DECISION PROCEDURE	Introduced in the TREATY ON EUROPEAN UNION. Where agreement cannot be reached between the Council of Ministers and the EP, the EP may finally veto the adoption of the measure by an absolute majority of its total membership. The AMSTERDAM TREATY has made this the normal method of legislation involving the EP and the Council of Ministers (Article 251 *Consolidated version of the Treaty establishing the EC* and OJ C340/97). *See also* CONCILIATION COMMITTEE
CODEPASS	COmmunity complexity and the DEcomposition Process in Acquatic SystemS: an ecosystem approach to manage biodiversity (TERI project)
CODEST	Committee for the European Development of Science and Technology. Set up in 1982 by Council Decision 82/835/EEC (OJ L350/82)
CODING	Colour desktop publishing (ESPRIT project)
CODP	2-D Coherent Optical Dynamic Processor (ESPRIT project)
CODRO	Council Working Group on Drugs. Part of the CFSP

COFACE	Confederation of Family Organisations in the EC rue de Londres 17, B-1050 Brussels, Belgium
COFIDEC	Compact CCITT G722 codec for digital telephone set development of a codec compliant... (EUREKA project)
COGECA	General Committee of Agricultural Cooperation in the EEC rue de la Science 23-25 Boîte 3, B-1040 Brussels, Belgium
COGEN Europe	European Association for the Promotion of Cogeneration rue Gulledelle 98, B-1200 Brussels, Belgium http://www.cogen.org/home.html
COHESION	Introduced in the SEA (additional Title V Articles 130A-130E) to provide economic and social cohesion and to reduce disparities between the various regions and the backwardness of the LFR. *See also* COHESION FUND; COHESION REPORT
COHESION FUND	Reg 1164/94 set up under the TREATY ON EUROPEAN UNION to establish a financial instrument in the fields of the environment and trans-European transport infrastructure networks in Member States with a per capita GNP of less than 90% of the EU average. (OJ L130/94 and amended by Reg 1264/99 and Reg 1265/99 in OJ L161/99).This is currently only applicable in Spain, Greece, Portugal and Ireland. *See also* COHESION
COHESION REPORT	A triennial report which analyses the contribution of national and EU policies in the reduction of social and economic development gaps (COM(96) 542). *Previously* PERIODIC REPORT. *See also* COHESION; SYNTHETIC INDEX

Coins	Collaborative Information Acquisition (CSCW project partially funded by the EC under the TELEMATICS APPLICATIONS programme) http://orgwis.gmd.de/projects/Coins/
COINS	Communication and Information Services statistical domain on the NEW CRONOS databank
COINS	Corporate Organisations Interactive Network Systems (a Telematics for Education and Training project within the TELEMATICS APPLICATIONS programme)
COLIPA	European Cosmetic, Toiletry and Perfumery Association rue du Congrès 5-7, B-1000 Brussels, Belgium
COM	Common Organisation of the Market
COMAC	Concerted Action Committee
COMAH Directive	Dir 96/82/EC on the Control of Major Accident Hazards involving dangerous substances (OJ L10/97). Implemented by Decision 98/433/EC (OJ L192/98). *See also* SEVESO I and II
COMANDOS	Construction and Management of Distributed Office Systems (ESPRIT project)
COMBAT	Cooperative Marketing to overcome the Barriers facing disabled Teleworkers (TIDE project)
COM DOC(UMENT)	Working Document of the European Commission
COMECE	Commission of the Bishop's Conferences of the EC rue Stévin 42, B-1000 Brussels, Belgium

COMEDI	Commercial Electronic Data Interchange for the collection, validation, grouping and dissemination of trade statistics (1993-1997) (OJ C87/93)
COMENIUS	School education initiative (within the SOCRATES programme) UK contact: Central Bureau for Educational Visits and Exchanges, 10 Spring Gdns, London SW1A 2BN
COMET	Computerised Molecular Evaluation of Toxicity (an Environmental Health and Chemical Safety Research project within the ENVIRONMENT AND CLIMATE programme)
*COMETT II	Community programme in Education and Training for Technology (1990-1994) (OJ L13/89). *Continued as* part of the LEONARDO DA VINCI programme
COMEXT	EUROSTAT databank of intra- and extra-EU trade statistics For on-line access contact EUR-OP Information Desk or EUROSTAT Data Shops. CD-ROM from EUR-OP official gateways and TSO. Data also available on request via e-mail and diskette from EUROSTAT Data Shops
COMIC	To investigate the integration of organisational context and notifications of interaction into CSCW systems (ESPRIT project) http://orgwis.gmd.de/projects/COMIC/
COMIS	Communication System for cooperative driving (DRIVE project)
COMIS	Standard for Coding of Moving Images on Digital Storage Media (ESPRIT project)
COMITOLOGY	Procedures laid down in Council Decision 1999/468/EC which give implementing powers for Council Decisions to be given to European Commission committees (OJ L184/99)

ComLégi	RISC legislative database. *See* RISC <small>Access via Internet (password required)</small>
COMMAL	Aluminium matrix composites (EUREKA project)
COMMON MARKET	*See* EEC (European Economic Community)
COMMON POSITION	The first stage of the Council of the European Union adoption of SEM legislation prior to the EP's second reading
COMMUNICATION TECHNOLOGIES	*See* ACTS (Advanced Communications Technologies and Services)
COMMUNITISATION	The transfer of a matter which is dealt with using the Intergovernmental Second and Third Pillars (of the three PILLARS) to the Community method of the First Pillar
COMMUNITY INITIATIVES	Programmes under the STRUCTURAL FUNDS to give financial support for EU-wide initiatives. For those in the 2000-2006 programme *See* EQUAL; INTERREG; LEADER+; URBAN
COMMUTE	COmmon Methodology for MUltimodal Transport Environmental impact assessment (A Strategic Transport project within the TRANSPORT programme)
COMNET	Community Network for European Education and Training <small>UETP-Toscana, via Cavur 82, I-50129 Firenze, Italy</small>
COMP	Competition DG of the European Commission
COMPASS-A	Comprehensive algebraic approach to system specification and development (ESPRIT project)
COMPESTELA FORET	Improved emergency services in forested regions (RECITE project)
COMPET	Indicators of Competitiveness statistical domain on the NEW CRONOS databank

COMPEX	System of Compensation to offset drops in export earnings for agricultural produce offered by the EU to LDCs
COMPRESIT	Compact reinforced composite development of ultra-high strength compact reinforced composite for civil and structural engineering applications (EUREKA project)
COMPRO	Committee for the Simplification of International Trade Procedures in the EC
COM PROGRAMME	New strategic industrial system of communication (FAST programme)
COMPULOG	Computational Logic (ESPRIT project)
COMQUEST	Oil pipelines statistical domain on the NEW CRONOS databank
COMSINE	COMmunication infrastructure for Inland Navigation in Europe (INCO project)
COMWEB	Comparative analysis of food webs based on flow networks (MAST III/ELOISE project)
CONACCOUNT	Coordination of regional and national material flow accounting for environmental sustainability (ENVIRONMENT AND CLIMATE project)
CONCILIATION COMMITTEE	Made up of members of the Council of the European Union and the EP in equal numbers to attempt to reach agreement on a joint text during the CO-DECISION PROCEDURE
CONCIM	Construction Computer-Integrated Manufacturing (EUREKA project)
CONCISE	COSINE Network's Central Information Service for Europe (within the COSINE programme)

CONCORD I	CONcertation CoorRDination (a programme Support Actions project within the TELEMATICS APPLICATIONS programme)
Concorde	Centre for Organisations and Networks Cooperating in R&D in Education rue de la Concorde 60, B-1050 Brussels, Belgium
CONCORDIA	Consensus and CoOrdination in TA Results (a Telematics Engineering project within the TELEMATICS APPLICATIONS programme)
CONCUR	Theories of Concurrency: unification and extension (ESPRIT project)
CONFIDENCE PACT	*See* EUROPEAN CONFIDENCE PACT
CONFORMITY MARK	*See* CE (mark)
CONGAS	Biospheric CONtrols on trace GAS fluxes in northern wetlands (TERI project)
CONNECT	Innovation and Connection of Community programme to promote synergy between such programmes as SOCRATES and LEONARDO DA VINCI and FP5. An Education and Culture DG initiative of the European Commission. There are two strands: CONNECT - Education, training and youth and CONNECT - Culture, education and training
CONPRI II	A training project in industrial relations and social dialogue in Europe (Employment and Social Affairs DG of the European Commission)
CONQUEST	Clinical Oncology Network for Quality in European Standards of Treatment (a Telematics for Healthcare project within the TELEMATICS APPLICATIONS programme)
Consleg	Consolidated Legislation of the EU

CONSULTATION PROCEDURE	This was the original method of legislation laid down in the ROME TREATY requiring only consultation of the EP and/or the ESC. The most important areas in which it is now used are in relation to CFSP and EMU
Consumerland	A 'Virtual World' produced by the Health and Consumer Affairs DG of the European Commission to explain the European aspect of consumer protection Access via the ISPO website
CONT	Committee on budgetary control (of the EP)
CONTRACTUAL NETTING	Dir 96/10/EC regarding the recognition of contractual netting by the competent authorities (OJ L85/96)
CONTROL-C	Concept for Transportation and Loading of Containers. Project coordinated by NETS
CONVENFL	Development of a new concept of uninterrupted power supply (EUREKA project)
CONVER	*See* KONVER
CONVERGENCE CRITERIA	for EMU as laid down in the TREATY ON EUROPEAN UNION. *See also* CONVERGENCE REPORT http://europa.eu.int/comm/enlargement/index.html
CONVERGENCE REPORT	*Euro 1999: report on progress towards convergence and recommendation...to the transition to the third stage of EMU* (COM(98) 1999)
CONVERSION LOANS	Job creation loans under Article 56 of the PARIS TREATY
COOPERATION PROCEDURE	Procedure introduced under the SEA which extended dialogue between the Council of Ministers and the EP but unlike the CO-DECISION PROCEDURE does not enable the EP to veto the Council's proposal (Article 252 *Consolidated version of the Treaty establishing the EC* and OJ C340/97)

CoopWWW	Interoperable tools for Cooperation support using the World Wide Web (CSCW Telematics Engineering project partly funded by the TELEMATICS APPLICATIONS programme) http://orgwis.gmd.de/projects/COOPWWW/
COPA	Committee of Agricultural Organisations in the EU rue de la Science 23-25, Boîte 3, B-1040 Brussels, Belgium
COPAS	Joint Welfare Committee...Section
COPEC	Commission Joint Committee for Equal Opportunities. Founded in 1984
Coped	Cooperative Programme on Energy and Development. A network of Third World and European research centres in the area of energy economics and planning. Supported by the Energy DG of the European Commission
COPENHAGEN CRITERIA	*See* ACCESSION CRITERIA
COPENHAGEN REPORT	on political cooperation between the Nine Member States 1973. Published in *Bulletin of the EC 9/1973*
Copenur	A Standing Committee of the Council of the European Union on Uranium Enrichment
*COPERNICUS	CO-operation in science and technology with Central and Eastern European countries (1992-94). Since 1995, the activities have become part of the INCO-COPERNICUS programme
*COPERNICUS-PECO	Community of Pan-European Research Networks of Eastern European countries. *Replaced by* INCO
COPERT	Computer Programme to Calculate Emissions from Road Traffic (CORINAIR project)

COPOL	Comparison of national and Community Policies
CoR	Committee of the Regions of the EU. An advisory body set up under the TREATY ON EUROPEAN UNION for consultation on COHESION; trans-European transport networks; health and culture. Previously known as the Consultative Council of Regional and Local Authorities rue Belliard 79, B-1040 Brussels, Belgium http://www.cor.eu.int/
*CORDI	Advisory Committee on Industrial R&D. *Replaced by* IRDAC
CORDIS	Community R&D Information Service. *See also* RTD-ACRONYMS; RTD-COMDOCUMENTS; RTD-CONTACTS; RTD-NEWS; RTD-PARTNERS; RTD-PROGRAMMES; RTD-PROJECTS; RTD-PUBLICATIONS; RTD-RESULTS http://www.cordis.lu
CORE	COnsenus creation and awareness for R&D activities in technology for disabled and Elderly people (TIDE project)
CORECOM	Ad hoc Advisory Committee on the Reprocessing of irradiated nuclear fuels
COREPER	Committee of Permanent Representatives of the Council of the European Union. *See also* UKREP
COREU	Correspondant Européen. An EU network for communication between the Member States to facilitate cooperation in the fields of foreign policy
CORINAIR	Commission Working Group on emission factors for calculating emissions from road transport

*CORINE	Council Decision 85/338/EEC on the Coordination of Information on the Environment in Europe (1985-1990) (OJ L176/85 and OJ L81/90). Work continued under the EEA
COSA	Economic accounts for the agriculture and forestry statistical domain on the NEW CRONOS databank
COSAC	Conference of European Community Affairs Committees of the Parliaments of the European Union. Set up in 1989 to bring together the various committees in the national parliaments of the Member States specialising in European affairs http://www1.europarl.eu.int/natparl/cosac/en/default.htm
COSACC	Coordination of Security Activities between Chambers of Commerce (a Telematics for Administrations project within the TELEMATICS APPLICATIONS programme)
COSEMCO	Seed Committee of the Common Market c/o NVZP, BP909, NL-3708 JA Zeist, Netherlands
COSIGA	A COncurrent engineering SImulation GAme using advanced multimedia and telecommunication for the education of European engineering students (EMTF project)
COSIMA	Control systems for integrated manufacturing: the CAM solution (ESPRIT project)
COSIMA	Integrated COntaminated SItes MAnagement (a Telematics for Environment project within the TELEMATICS APPLICATIONS programme) http://www.trentel.org/environment/research/projects/cosima.html

COSINE	Cooperation for Open Systems Interconnection Networking in Europe (EUREKA project)
COSMOS	Cost Management with Metrics of Specification (ESPRIT project)
COST	European Cooperation in the field of Scientific and Technical research involving 25 countries (1971-) Secretariat: Council of the European Union, Justus Lipsius Building, rue de la Loi 175, B-1048 Brussels, Belgium http://www.netmaniacs.com/cost/
COSTEL	Course System for Telecommunications training and innovation management (COMETT project)
COSYMA	Code System for MARIA (MARIA project)
COTANCE	Confederation of National Associations of Tanners and Dressers of the EU rue Belliard 3, B-1040 Brussels, Belgium
COUSTO	Integrated optic technologies for real time wide band optical signal processing (ESPRIT project)
COVIRA	Computer Vision in Radiology (AIM project)
CP	Community Programme
CP	Compact project. TEMPUS and TACIS projects which address precisely defined, short-term needs
CP	Cooperative Profile (in the BC-NET network)
*CPA	Classification of Products by Activity (OJ L342/93). The basis for the CPV
CPC	Central Product Classification. A United Nations Central Product Classification published by the United Nations

CPC	Council Agreement 89/695/EEC on the Community Patent Convention 1975 (OJ L401/89)
CPD	Dir 89/106/EEC on Construction Products (OJ L40/89 with latest amendment in OJ L267/96)
CPHS	Technological Development in Hydrocarbons
CPIV	Permanent International Vinegar Committee - Common Market Reuterstrasse 151, D-53113 Bonn, Germany
CPIV	Standing Committee of Glass Industries of the EEC ave Louise 89, B-1050 Brussels, Belgium
CPMP	Committee for Proprietary Medicinal Products. A scientific committee of the EMEA
CPMR	Conference of Peripheral Maritime Regions of Europe bd de la Liberté 35, F-35000 Rennes, France
CPR	Regional Policy Committee
CPS	Consumer Policy Service (Health and Consumer Affairs DG of the European Commission)
CPSA	Standing Committee on Agricultural Structures
CPV	Community Procurement Vocabulary. A classification of goods and services to be used in public procurement (OJ S169/96). *Previously* CPA
CPVO	Community Plant Variety Office. Set up under Reg 2100/94 (OJ L227/94 with latest amendment in OJ L258/95) PO Box 2141, F-49021 Angers Cedex 02, France http://www.cpvo.fr
CPVRO	*See* CPVO

CRAFT	European Cooperative Research Action for Technology set up in 1989 by IRDAC to help SMEs to carry out research. The concept is incorporated into FP5
CRE	Association of European Universities rue du Conseil Général 10, CH-1211 Geneva 4, Switzerland http://www.unige.ch/cre/
*CREA	Risk Capital for business start-ups. A Commission initiative (1998-2000)
CREDIT	Capabilities Registration, Evaluation, Diagnosis and advice through Internet Technologies (EMTF project)
CREDO	Cross-border cooperation between CEC and CEC countries and CEC and NIS border regions (PHARE multi-country programme) http://www.credoprogramme.org
CREDSTAT	Credit Institutions statistical domain on the NEW CRONOS databank
CREST	Clinical Rehabilitation using Electrical Stimulation via Telematics (a Telematics for Disabled and Elderly People project within the TELEMATICS APPLICATIONS programme)
CREST	Scientific and Technical Research Committee. Set up in 1974. *Previously* PREST
CREW	Centre for Research on European Women rue Capouillet 25, B-1060 Brussels, Belgium
CRIS	Current Research Information Systems in Europe. An umbrella organisation for the advancement of international cooperation among research information systems
CRIT	Cooperative Research in Information Technology (PHARE programme)

*CRL	Co-Responsibility Levy. Reg 1079/77 to expand the market in milk and milk products (OJ L131/77). Abolished on 1 April 1993
CRM	Committee on Medical and Public Health Research. Set up by PREST to advise CREST on the coordination of national policies
CROCINA	Feasibility study for automated indoor horticulture production and its development (EUREKA project)
*CROCODILE GROUP	Group of MEPs (formed in 1980) to draw up proposals to reform the Institutions of the EC
*CRONOS	*See* NEW CRONOS
CROSS BORDER PAYMENTS	*See* CBP
CROSS BORDER WORKERS	Workers who live in one EU country but work in another and go home at least once per week
CROW	Conditions of Roads and Weather (DRIVE project)
CRPM	*See* CPMR
CRS	Reg 2299/89 on Computerised Reservation Systems (OJ L220/89 with latest amendment in OJ L40/99)
CRTDE	Committee on Research, Technological Development and Energy
CSA	Communication Systems Architecture (ESPRIT project)
CSAs	Competitive Support Activities (part of the INNOVATION programme)
*CSC	CADDIA Steering Committee

CSCE	Conference on Security and Cooperation in Europe
CSCW	Computer Supported Cooperative Work. A research group of the Institute for Applied Information Technology (FIT). Much of its work has been partially funded by the EU under the TELEMATICS APPLICATIONS programme. *See also* BSCW; CESAR; Coins; CSCW-MIKMOD; KESO; NESSIE; POLITeam http://orgwis.gmd.de/
CSCW-MIKMOD	Microsimulation Models for legislative planning (a CSCW project partly funded by the TELEMATICS APPLICATIONS programme) http://orgwis.gmd.de/projects/mikmod
CSD	Committee for Spatial Development
C-SET	Interoperable Chip-Secured Electronic Transactions (ISIS electronic commerce project) http://www.ispo.cec.be/isis/96cset.htm
CSF	Community Support Framework under the STRUCTURAL FUNDS
CSO	COST Committee of Senior Officials
CSP	European Commission NGO Cofinancing Support Programme launched in 1997
CST	*See* STC
C-STAR	Coastal Sediment Transport Assessment using SAR (synthetic aperture radar) (MAST III project) http://www.soc.soton.ac.uk/SUDO/CSTAR/cstarweb.html
CSTEE	Commission Scientific Committee on Toxicity, Ecotoxicity and the Environment. *See also* SSC http://europa.eu.int/comm/dg24/health/sc/sct/index_en.html
CSTID	*See* CIDST

CT	Community Transit System
CTA	Technical Centre for Agricultural and Rural Cooperation. Established in 1983 under the LOME CONVENTION Postbus 380, NL-6700 AJ Wageningen, Netherlands http://www.cta.nl
CTE	European Theatre Convention (Convention Théâtrale Européenne) (KALEIDOSCOPE project) pl du Théâtre 9, L-2613 Luxembourg
CTIC	Trans-border information and consulting centres for consumers. Coordinated by the Consumer Affairs DG of the European Commission
CTMO	Community Trade Marks Office ave Aguilera 20, E-03080 Alicante, Spain
CTP	Common Transport Policy
CTS	Conformance Testing Services
CTS	European Continuous Tracking Survey. Results are released in EUROPINION
CU	Customs Union. Achieved in the EC on 1 July 1968
*CUBE	Concertation Unit for Biotechnology in Europe
CULT	Committee on Culture, youth, education, the media and sport (of the EP)
Culture 2000	Proposal for an EP and Council Decision establishing a single financing and programming instrument for cultural cooperation (2000-2004) (OJ C211/98). *Replaces* ARIANE; KALEIDOSCOPE; RAPHAEL http://europa.eu.int/comm/dg10/culture/program-2000_en.html

CUS	Customs Union Service (Taxation and Customs Union DG of the European Commission)
CUSTODIAN	Conceptualisation for User involvement in Specification and Tools Offering the efficient Delivery of system Integration Around home Networks (a Telematics for Disabled and Elderly People project within the TELEMATICS APPLICATIONS programme)
CUSTOMS 2000	EP and Council Decision 210/97/EC adopting an action programme for customs in the Community (OJ L33/97)
CVMP	Committee for Veterinary Medicinal Products. A scientific committee of the EMEA
CVS	CAD for VLSI Systems (ESPRIT project)
CVTS	Continuing Vocational Training Survey
CWASAR	Cooperative Wide Area Service Architecture (a Telematics for Urban and Rural Areas project within the TELEMATICS APPLICATIONS programme)
CYNAMUS	Mass multiplication of virus-free artichoke plants by in-vitro micropropagation (EUREKA project)
D	Germany
DA	Danish
DA	Differentiated Appropriations
DAB	Digital Audio Broadcasting System (EUREKA project)
DACAR	Data Acquisition and Communication techniques and their Assessment for Road transport (DRIVE project)

DAIDA	Advanced Interactive Development of Data-intensive Applications (ESPRIT project)
DAILY	Make Daily Life Easier (a Telematics for Disabled and Elderly People project within the TELEMATICS APPLICATIONS programme)
DALI	Delivery and Access to Local Information and Services (a Telematics for Urban and Rural Areas project within the TELEMATICS APPLICATIONS programme)
DAMS	Dynamically Adaptable Multi-service System (ESPRIT project)
DANGEROUS PREPARATIONS Directive	Dir 88/379/EEC relating to the classification, packaging and labelling of dangerous preparations (OJ L187/88 with latest amendment in OJ L265/96). *See also* CHIP
DANGEROUS SUBSTANCES Directive	Dir 67/548/EEC relating to the classification, packaging and labelling of dangerous substances (OJ L196/67 with latest amendment in OJ L355/98). *See also* CHIP
DANGEROUS SUBSTANCES AND PREPARATIONS Directive	Dir 76/769/EEC relating to restrictions on the marketing and use of certain dangerous substances and preparations (OJ L262/76 with latest amendment in OJ L315/97)
DAPHNE	Document Application Processing in a Heterogeneous Network Environment (applied in the COSINE project)
DAPHNE	Proposal for an EP and Council Decision adopting a programme of Community action on measures aimed to prevent violence against children, young persons and women (2000-2004) (Amended proposal in OJ C162/99) http://europa.eu.int/comm/sg/tfjai/project/daphne/en/index.htm

DAPRO	Data Protection in the EU (a Telematics Engineering project within the TELEMATICS APPLICATIONS programme)
DART	Dynamic Awareness Raising process regarding Telematics in the framework of NATURA (a Telematics for Education and Training project within the TELEMATICS APPLICATIONS programme)
DART	Dynamic Response of the forest-Tundra ecotone to environmental change (TERI project)
DARTS	Demonstration of Advanced Reliability Techniques (ESPRIT project)
DAS	Court of Auditors statement of assurances under Article 188c of the TREATY ON EUROPEAN UNION concerning the reliability of accounts
DASIQ	Distributed Automated System for Inspection and Quality control (ESPRIT project)
Data Warehouse	Used to maintain the data collected for the EEA's regular *State of the Environment* reports (EEA project) http://www.eea.eu.int/locate/Warehouse/default.htm
DAVIGNON PLAN	Guidelines for steel policy issued in 1977 and never published
DCLAA	Developing Countries in Latin America and Asia
DCP	Press releases from the CoR Access via RAPID
DE	German
*DECOM 3	Decommissioning of nuclear installations programme (1989-1993) (OJ L98/89)

DECT	Recommendation 91/288/EEC on Digital European Cordless Telecommunications (OJ L144/91). *See also* ERMES
DEDICA	Directory based EDI Certificate Access and management (a Telematics Engineering project within the TELEMATICS APPLICATIONS programme)
DEDICS	Distributed Environment Disaster Information and Control System (a Telematics for Environment project within the TELEMATICS APPLICATIONS programme) http://www.trentel.org/environment/research/projects/dedics.html
Deepening	Term used to describe the strengthening of certain policies which may be coupled with institutional reforms designed to develop European integration
DEFIED	Disabled and Elderly people Flexible Integrate (sic) Environment (TIDE project)
DEGREE	Diversity Effects in Grassland Ecosystems of Europe (TERI project)
DEI	Declaration of European Interest
DELILAH	Designing and Evaluating Learning Innovations and Learning Applications (TSER project)
DELORS PACKAGE	*See* DELORS PLAN
DELORS PLAN	Proposal *Making a success of the Single Act* (COM(87) 100)
DELORS REPORT	*on economic and monetary union in the EC.* Published in 1990 by the Committee for the Study of Economic and Monetary Union
DELORS WHITE PAPER	on growth, competitiveness, employment: the challenges and ways forward into the 21st Century (COM(93) 700 and *Bulletin of the EC Supplement 6/93* in 2 parts)

DELOS	DEveloping Learning Organisation models in SME clusters (TSER project)
DELOS Working Group	Digital Library Working Group. To promote research into the further development of digital library technologies http://www.iei.pi.cnr.it/DELOS//
*DELTA	Developing European Learning through Technological Advance (1988-1990) (OJ L206/88). *Continued in* the TELEMATIC SYSTEMS and TELEMATICS APPLICATIONS programmes
DELTA-4	A dependable open distributed systems architecture (ESPRIT project)
DEMETER	Digital Electronic Mapping of European Territory (EUREKA project)
DEMETER	Distance Education, Multimedia Teleservices and Telework for farmers (a Telematics for Urban and Rural Areas project within the TELEMATICS APPLICATIONS programme)
DEMILITARISED	Regions affected by a reduced military presence (RECITE project)
DEMO	Demography statistical domain on the NEW CRONOS databank
DEMO	Prototype Fusion Reactor to follow ITER
DEMON	Design Methods Based on Nets (ESPRIT project)
DEMO-R	Demography statistical domain on the REGIO database
DEMOS	Distance Education and tutoring in heterogeneous telematics environments (a Telematics for Education and Training project within the TELEMATICS APPLICATIONS programme)

DENEMA	Development of a New Market for telematics products in central Asia (a Telematics for Education and Training project within the TELEMATICS APPLICATIONS programme)
DEP	European Depository Library in major national libraries worldwide. *See also* RELAYS
DEPB	Duty Entitlement PassBook scheme. An export subsidy scheme under which any eligible exporter can apply for credits which are calculated as a percentage of the value of exported finished products. *Previously* PBS. *See also* EOU; EPCGS; EPZ; ITES
DESCARTES	Debugging and Specification of ADA Real-time Embedded Systems (ESPRIT project)
DESIMA	Decision Support for Integrated coastal zone Management (an SAI marine environment activity)
DESIRE	Development of a European Service for Information on Research and Education (a Telematics for Research project within the TELEMATICS APPLICATIONS programme) http://www.desire.org
DESIRE	Development of an all dry single-layer photolithography technology for sub-micron devices (EUREKA project)
DESON	Disorder and Electrical properties in Silicon OxyNitrides (ESPRIT project)
DETER	Detection, Enforcement and Tutoring for driver Error Reduction (DRIVE project)
DETERMINE	Dissemination of Environment and Transport telematics Results and needs analysis in Central and Eastern Europe (a Telematics for Environment project within the TELEMATICS APPLICATIONS Programme) http://www.trentel.org/environment/research/projects/determine.html

DEUCE	Electronic University for Citizens of Europe (DELTA project)
DEV	Development DG of the European Commission
DEVE	Committee on Development and cooperation (of the EP)
DFCC	Development Finance Cooperative Committee. Set up under Article 325 of the 4th LOME CONVENTION to examine whether the objectives of financial cooperation have been attained
DG	Directorate-General of the European Commission http://europa.eu.int/comm/dgs_en.htm
DIABCARD 3	Improved communication in DIABetes care based on chipCARD technology (a Telematics for Healthcare project within the TELEMATICS APPLICATIONS programme)
DIABCARE Q-NET	Diabcare Quality Network in Europe (a Telematics for Healthcare project within the TELEMATICS APPLICATIONS programme)
Dialogue Youth	improvement of information services to young people by developing cooperation between European Youth networks (YOUTH FOR EUROPE project) http://europa.eu.int/en/comm/dg22/eurodesk/dyhome.html
DIAMOND	Development and Integration of Accurate Operations in Numerical Data Processing (ESPRIT project)
DIANE	Automatic Integrated system for NEutronography (EUREKA project)
*DIANEGUIDE	An on-line description of databases now merged with BROKERSGUIDE to form I*M GUIDE

DIAS	Distributed Intelligent Actuators and Sensors (ESPRIT project)
DICTUM	Development of an Interactive Communication Training system Using teleworkers (TIDE project)
DIDAMES	Distributed Industrial Design and Manufacturing of Electronic Subassemblies (RACE project)
DIECAST	Medium pressure Die Casting (EUREKA project)
DIGICULT	Digital heritage and Cultural content. KEY ACTION 3 of the IST http://www.cordis.lu/ist/ka3/digicult
DIGISAT	Advanced Digital Satellite Broadcasting and Interactivity Services (ACTS project)
*DIME	Development of Integrated Monetary Electronics. This programme never became operational
DIMPE	Distributed Integrated Multi-Media Publishing Environment (RACE project)
DIMUN	DIstributed Manufacturing Using existing and developing public Networks (RACE project)
DIPECHO	ECHO initiative involving natural and manmade disaster preparedness and prevention (excluding conflicts) (1996-1998). To be extended to cover the period 2000-2001 http://www.disaster.info.desastres.net/dipecho
DIPLOMAS Directives	*1st Dir* 89/48/EEC on the recognition of higher education diplomas awarded on completion of professional education (OJ L19/89). *2nd Dir* 92/51/EEC…for the recognition of professional education and training (OJ L209/92 with latest amendment in OJ L184/97)

Dir	A Directive, which Member States must implement in national laws
DIRAC	Database for Reliability Calculations (RACE project)
DIRECTORIA	Convention for local and regional authorities. A Regional Policy DG initiative of the European Commission
DIRTYSUPRA	Study of the influence of impurities on the properties of High TC superconductors (ESPRIT project)
DIS	Decentralised Implementation System (part of the PHARE programme)
DIS	Drug Information Systems (PHARE project)
DiSCiPl	Debugging Systems for Constraint Programming (partly funded by the ESPRIT programme) http://discipl.inria.fr
DISCUS	Distance Information, Support and Communication for European carers (a Telematics for Disabled and Elderly People project within the TELEMATICS APPLICATIONS programme)
DISNET	Domain-Independent Information and Services Network (IMPACT project)
DISTANCE SELLING Directive	Dir 97/7/EC on the protection of consumers in respect of distance contracts (OJ L144/97)
DISTINCT	Deployment and Integration of Smartcard Technology and Information Networks for Cross-sector Telematics (a Telematics for Integrated Applications for Digital Sites project within the TELEMATICS APPLICATIONS programme)
DIVIDEND	Dealer Interactive Video (RACE project)
DK	Denmark

DMA	Depth and Motion Analysis (ESPRIT project)
DOBRÍS ASSESSMENT	A report published by the EEA in 1995 on *Europe's environment*. Dobrís Castle is near Prague http://www.eea.eu.int/frdocu.htm
doc	document
DOC	Key, public documents issued by the European Commission and the Council of the European Union Access via RAPID
DOCED	A programme covering a number of infrastructure activities in the agricultural databases (CADDIA project)
DOEOIS	Design and Operational Evaluation of Distributed Office Information Servers (ESPRIT project)
DOM	*See* FOD
DOMINC	Advanced control strategies and methods for motorway RTI - system of the future (DRIVE project)
*DOMIS	ECHO directory of Materials Data Information Sources
DOMITEL	Domestic Interactive Telematic Education and Learning (a Telematics for Education and Training project within the TELEMATICS APPLICATIONS programme)
DOMUS	DOMestic consumption and Utility Sectors (ENVIRONMENT AND CLIMATE project)
DOOGE report	on Institutional affairs presented to the European Council in March 1985. Published in the *Bulletin of the European Communities 3/1985* p102

DOORSTEP SELLING Directive	Dir 85/577/EEC on contracts negotiated away from business premises which protects consumers from high-pressure door-to-door salesmen (OJ L372/85)
DORIS	Digital and Organisational Regeneration Initiative for urban and rural Sites which are declining (a Telematics for Integrated Applications for Digital Sites project within the TELEMATICS APPLICATIONS programme)
*DOSE	EP internal database for the management of EP Working Documents. *Replaced by* PARDOC
*DOSES	Development of Statistical Expert Systems (1989-1993) (OJ L200/89). *Continued as* DOSIS
DOSIS	Development of Statistical Information Systems. A EUROSTAT project within the 4th RTD Framework programme (1994-1998). *Previously* DOSES
DOUCEUR	Documents Utiles et Communs pour EUROSTAT
DPSIR	Driving forces, Pressures, States, Impacts, Responses: a model for environmental management adopted by the EEA
*DR	Technical group of the European Right (of the EP)
DRACO	Driver and Accident Coordinated Observer (DRIVE project)
DRAGON	Distribution and Re-usability of ADA R/T Applications through Graceful and On-line Operations (ESPRIT project)
DRAMA	Developments for Rehabilitation of the Arm – a Multimedia Approach (a Telematics for Disabled and Elderly People project within the TELEMATICS APPLICATIONS programme)

DREAM	Feasibility study for monitoring driver status (DRIVE project)
DRINS REPORT	Proposed legislation on aldrin, dieldrin and endrin discharges (OJ C146/79; OJ C341/80; OJ C309/86)
DRIVAGE	Factors in elderly people's driving abilities (DRIVE project)
*DRIVE	Dedicated Road Infrastructure for Vehicle Safety in Europe (1988-1991) (OJ L206/88). *Continued as* Area 2 of the TELEMATIC SYSTEMS programme
DRUMS	Defeasible Reasoning and Uncertainty Management Systems (ESPRIT project)
DRYDEL	Dry Develop optical lithography for VLSI (ESPRIT project)
DSDIC	Design Support for Distributed Industrial Control (ESPRIT project)
DSIS	Distributed Statistical Information Services. A framework which aims to support the Community statistical system (a EUROSTAT initiative sponsored by the IDA programme)
DTCS	Policy analysis and spatial conflicts in transport policy (ENVIRONMENT AND CLIMATE project)
DUAL-PRICING Directive	Dir 98/6/EC on consumer protection in the indication of the prices of products offered to consumers (OJ L80/98)
DUAL-USE GOODS	Council Decision 94/942/CFSP on joint action concerning the control of exports of dual-use goods (OJ L367/94 with latest amendment in OJ L73/99)
DUBLIN FOUNDATION	*See* EFILWC

DUFIMESHT	Dust Filtration with Metal Screens at High Temperature (EUREKA project)
DUMIP	Ultrasonic Mechanised Devices for Internal Pipeline Inspection (EUREKA project)
DUNDALK CASE	Case 45/87 in the ECJ on public works contracts (Case reported in ECR 1988/8)
*DUNDIS	ECHO Directory of United Nations Databases and Information Systems
DURATION Directive	Dir 93/98/EEC harmonising the term of protection of copyright and certain related rights (OJ L290/93)
DVBIRD	Digital Video Broadcasting Integrated Receiver Decoder (ACTS project)
DYANA	Dynamic interpretation of natural language (ESPRIT project)
DYNAMO	DYNAmic MOdels to predict and scale-up the impact of environmental change on biogeochemical cycling (TERI project)
DYONISOS	Wine growing regions (RECITE project)
E	Spain
E111	An EU form which entitles the holder to free or reduced-cost emergency medical treatment when visiting another Member State. The form is available from post offices in the UK
E (numbers)	Code numbers for antioxidants, colouring matters and preservatives in foodstuffs as specified in various Directives
E2RC	European Environmental Reference Centre http://www.eea.eu.int/locate/default.htm
EA	European Association. Proposal for a Statute to enable associations to take advantage of the SEM (OJ C236/93)

EAA	Economic Accounts for Agriculture
EAAA	European Association of Advertising Agencies rue St Quentin 5, B-1000 Brussels, Belgium
EAAF	European Association of Animated Film. *See* CARTOON
*EAB	ESPRIT Advisory Board
*EABS	Database of references to the published results of scientific and technical research programmes, wholly or partly sponsored by the EU. Now on CORDIS as RTD-PUBLICATIONS
EAC	Education and Culture DG of the European Commission
EAC	European Accident Code (JRC - reactor safety programme)
EAC	European Association for Cooperation rue Archimède 17, B-1000 Brussels, Belgium
EAC	*See* EUROPE AGAINST CANCER
EACF	Extension and Acceleration of Financial Confidence. A BUSINESS ANGELS project to look into the possibility of setting up a 'virtual community' on the Internet where people with new ideas can meet investors and entrepreneurs
EACN	European Association of Community Networking http://www.eacn.org/
EACRO	European Association of Contract Research Organisations ave des Arts 53, B-1000 Brussels, Belgium
EAEC	*See* EURATOM
EAF	Economic Accounts for Forestry

EAFR	Reg 2454/99 amending the OBNOVA Reg, in particular by the setting up of a European Agency for Reconstruction (OJ L299/99)
EAG	External Advisory Group
EAGGF	European Agricultural Guidance and Guarantee Fund (1962-) (Latest Reg 1257/99 in OJ L160/99 with detailed rules in OJ L214/99)
EAGLE	European Association for Grey Literature Exploitation. *See also* SIGLE

Secretariat: Postbus 90407, NL-2509 LK The Hague, Netherlands
UK contact: Mr A Smith, Sigle Officer, British Library Document Supply Centre, Boston Spa, Wetherby, Yorkshire LS23 7BQ
http://www.konbib.np/sigle/

EAHIL	European Association for Health Information and Libraries

c/o ICP-NTI, POBox 23213, NL-1100 DS Amsterdam, Netherlands

EAP	(5th) Environmental Action Programme (1993-2000) (OJ C138/93)
EAPN	European Anti-Poverty Network

rue Belliard 205, Boîte 13, B-1040 Brussels, Belgium
http://www.epitelio.org/eapn/maineapn.htm

EARN	Euro Area Reference Notes. Established by the EIB in March 1999 as part of the EURO borrowing strategy
EARN	*See* TERENA
EARNING	Harmonised Earnings statistical domain on the NEW CRONOS databank
EARSEC	European Airborne Remote Sensing Capabilities (ISPRA project)

EASE	Project to investigate cross-border sulphur pollution in the Black Triangle area, which is found at the border of the former East Germany, the Czech Republic and Poland (within the INCO programme)
EASHW	European Agency for Safety and Health at Work. *See* EU-OSHA
EASI	European Applications in Surgical Interventions (a Telematics for Healthcare project within the TELEMATICS APPLICATIONS programme)
EASI-ISAE	Educating Authors for Simulated Interaction: Intercommunication Software for Appreciating Educators (EMTF project)
EASOE	European Arctic Stratospheric Ozone Experiment
EAST	EUREKA Advanced Software Technology: development of software factories incorporating software engineering (EUREKA project)
EAST	European Assistance for Science and Technology. An EP own-initiative proposal (EP Doc A3 174/90)
EASYTEX	Aesthetical, adjustable, serviceable and mainstay textiles for disabled and elderly (a Telematics for Disabled and Elderly People project within the TELEMATICS APPLICATIONS programme)
EAT	European Advertising Tripartite ave de Tervuren 267, B-1150 Brussels, Belgium
EATA	European Association for Telematic Applications 8-10 Methonis Street, GR-10680 Athens, Greece

EATCHIP	European Air Traffic Control Harmonisation and Integration Programme. Managed by EUROCONTROL to implement the ECAC strategy to harmonise and integrate European Air Traffic Management Services
EATI	European Addiction Training Institute. Part of the five-year Community programme for the prevention of drug dependence (1996-2000) (OJ L19/97) Stadhouderskade 125, NL-1974 AV Amsterdam, Netherlands http://www.eati.org
EATMS	European Air Traffic Management System
EATS	Efficiency of Assistive Technology and Services (a Telematics for Disabled and Elderly People project within the TELEMATICS APPLICATIONS programme)
EAVE	European Audiovisual Entrepreneurs (set up under the MEDIA programme) rue de la Presse 14, B-1000 Brussels, Belgium
EBA	ECU Banking Association rue de Galliéra, F-75116 Paris, France
EBAN	European BUSINESS ANGELS Network c/o Eurada, ave des Arts 12, Boîte7, B-1210 Brussels, Belgium http://www.eban.org
EBES	European Board for EDI Standardisation
EBIC	European Business Information Centre. See EIC
EBIP	Environmental Biotechnology INDUSTRIAL PLATFORM http://europa.eu.int/comm/dg12/biotech/ip2.html#EBIP http://www.ebip.org/
EBLIDA	European Bureau of Library, Information and Documentation Associations PO Box 43300, NL-2504 The Hague, Netherlands UK contact: Library Association, 7 Ridgmount Street, London WC1E 7AE http://www.eblida.org/

EBLUL	European Bureau for Lesser Used Languages Brussels Information Centre, rue Saint-Josse 49, B-1210 Brussels, Belgium
EBN	European Business and Innovation Centre Network ave de Tervuren 188A, B-1150 Brussels, Belgium http://www.ebn.be/
EBNIC	The European Biotechnology Node for Interaction with China, to facilitate direct contact between European academic and industrial biotechnologists and their Chinese counterparts (an INCO activity) http://www.ebnic.org/
EBO	European Community Baroque Orchestra
EBP	European Books in Print (project within Area 5 of the TELEMATIC SYSTEMS programme)
*EBP	European Business Programme to train management specialists at Business Institutes in the EC
EBR II	European Business Register - phase II. Designed to connect national registers which contain data on 15 million European companies (a Telematics for Administrations project within the TELEMATICS APPLICATIONS programme)
EBRD	European Bank for Reconstruction and Development. Established in 1991 by Council Decision 90/674/EEC (OJ L372/90) to foster the transition towards open market economies and to promote private and entrepreneurial initiatives in the CEEC and CIS 1 Exchange Sq, London EC2A 2EH, United Kingdom http://www.ebrd.com

EbS	Europe by Satellite. A television programme transmitted on the EUTELSAT II satellite Monday-Friday to inform citizens of current events and procedures in the European Commission and the EP. A Press and Communication DG initiative of the European Commission http://europa.eu.int/comm/dg10/ebs/index_en.html
EBT	European Business Trends statistical domain on the NEW CRONOS databank
EBTI	European Binding Tariff Information. Classification decisions in the customs nomenclature. *Now within* the IDA programme
EC	European Communities
*EC	European Council (of Ministers). Now known as the Council of the European Union Justus Lipsius Building, rue de la Loi 170, B-1048 Brussels, Belgium
ECA	European Catering Association c/o Catering and Allied Services, Central House, Balfour Road, Hounslow TW3 1HA, United Kingdom
ECA	European Court of Auditors which audits EU revenue and expenditure rue Alcide de Gasperi 12, L-1615 Luxembourg rue de la Loi 83-85, B-1040 Brussels, Belgium http://www.eca.eu.int
ECAC	European Civil Aviation Conference 3bis, Villa Emile Bergerat, F-92522 Neuilly-sur-Seine, France http://www.ecac-ceac.org
ECAP	EC/ASEAN Patents and Trademarks Programme. Managed by the EPO
ECARDA	European Common Approach for R&D in ATM (a Telematics for transport project within the TELEMATICS APPLICATIONS programme)

ECAS	Euro-citizen Action Service. An independent non-profit making organisation to help European citizens rue de la Concorde 53, B-1050 Brussels, Belgium http://www.ecas.org/
ECAT	Environmental Centres for Administration and Technology. A network of centres involved in environment-related EU policies
ECATA	European Consortium in Advanced Training for Aeronautics (COMETT project)
ECB	European Central Bank. Established on 1st June 1998 to replace the EMI Kaiserstrasse 29, D-60066 Frankfurt am Main, Postfach 160319, Germany http://www.ecb.int
ECB	European Chemicals Bureau (within the JRC)
ECBA	European Communities Biologists' Association Association des Professeurs de Biologie et Géologie, BP 8337, F-69356 Lyon, France
ECBS	European Committee for Banking Standards ave de Tervuren 12, B-1040 Brussels, Belgium
ECC	*See* CEC (Commission of the European Communities)
ECCAIRS	European Coordination Cente for Aircraft Incident Reporting Systems (part of ISIS)
ECCN	European Child Care Network Contact: European Commission Employment and Social Affairs DG UK Contact: Ms B Cohen, Princes House, 5 Shandwyck Pl, Edinburgh EH2 4 RG
ECCOFEX	European Commission Coordinating Committee of Options and Future Exchanges

ECDIN	Environmental Chemicals Data and Information Network. The database also contains EINECS Available as a CD-ROM from Springer Verlag or via the Internet at: http://ecdin.etomep.net
ECDL	European Computer Driving Licence http://pcie.nice.iway.fr/
ECDPM	European Centre for Development Policy Management which aims to improve cooperation between Europe and countries in Africa, the Caribbean, and the Pacific http://www.oneworld.org/ecdpm/
ECDVT	*See* CEDEFOP
ECE	Economic Commission for Europe (United Nations) Palais des Nations, CH-1211 Geneva 10, Switzerland http://www.unece.org/
ECETOC	European Centre for Exotoxicology and Toxicology of Chemicals Michelangelo Building, ave E Van Nieuwenhuyse 4, Boîte 6, B-1160 Brussels, Belgium
ECF	European Cyclist Federation ave de Broqueville, B-1200 Brussels, Belgium http://www.dcf.dk/ecf/
ECFI	European Court of First Instance at the ECJ bd Konrad Adenauer, L-2925 Luxembourg
ECFIN	Economic and Financial Affairs DG of the European Commission
*ECFTU	European Confederation of Free Trade Unions in the Community. *See* ETUC
*ECG	*See* EEIG
ECHO	Electronic Case-Handling in Offices (RACE project)
*ECHO	European Commission Host Organisation. The ECHO database was closed in Oct 1998

ECHO	European Community Humanitarian Aid Office rue de la Loi 200, B-1049 Brussels, Belgium http://europa.eu.int/en/comm/echo/echo.html
ECHOES	Educational Hypermedia Online System (EMTF project)
ECHP	European Community Household Panel
ECI	Dir 96/335/EC on the European Cosmetics Inventory (OJ L132/96) Access via EINECS-Plus
ECI	EURATOM Classified Information
ECIA	European Council for Information Associations http://www.aslib.co.uk/ecia/index.html
ECICS	European Customs Inventory of Chemical Substances: a database of chemical names and synonyms to disseminate information on tariff classifications Access via EINECS-Plus
ECIP	European CAD Integration Project (ESPRIT project)
ECIP	Reg 319/92 on the European Communities Investment Partners to promote joint ventures between firms in the Member States and those in Latin America, Asia and the Mediterranean (1992-1994) (OJ L35/92 and extended to 1999 with Reg 213/96 in OJ L28/96)
ECIR	European Centre for Industrial Relations via San Domenico 70, I-50133 Firenze, Italy
ECISS	European Committee for Iron and Steel Standardisation c/o CEN, rue de Stassart 36, B-1050 Brussels, Belgium
ECJ	Court of Justice of the European Communities Palais de la Cour de Justice, bd Konrad Adenauer, BP 1406, L-2925 Luxembourg http://www.curia.eu.int

ECLA	European Company Lawyers' Association Bezuidenhoutseweg 12, PO Box 93002, NL-2509 AA The Hague, Netherlands
*ECLAIR	European Collaborative Linkage of Agriculture and Industry through Research (1988-1993) (OJ L60/89). *See also* FLAIR. *Continued as* AIR
ECLAS	European Commission Library Automated System: the database of the Commission Library in Brussels created in 1982 http://europa.eu.int/eclas
*ECM	European Common Market
ECMAST	European Conference on Multimedia Applications, Services and Techniques (coordinated by COST and the ACTS programme)
ECMM	European Community Monitoring Mission. A non-United Nations body formed to monitor ceasefires
ECOBULB	ECOlogical flower BULB farming and its automated mechanisation (EUREKA project)
*ECO-COUNSELLORS	Counsellors appointed in 12 EC towns during EYE to advise on environmental issues
ECO/FIN	Economic and Financial Council of the EU
ECOFLAT	The ECO-metabolism of an estuarine tidal FLAT (ELOISE project)
ECOIN	European Core Inventory of existing chemical substances. *See* EINECS
ECO-LABEL	Reg 880/92 for a seal of approval for least polluting products (OJ L99/92 with a Proposal for revision in COM(96) 603 and an amended Proposal in COM(99) 21). Commission Decision 93/517/EEC on standard contracts covering terms of use (OJ L243/93)

ECOLE/GRIP	European Collaboration in Oncology Literature Evaluation/to Practice (a Telematics for Healthcare project within the TELEMATICS APPLICATIONS programme)
ECOLES	Development of representation in machine learning (ESPRIT project)
ECOMAC	ECO-MAanagement accounting as a tool of environmental management (ENVIRONMENT AND CLIMATE project)
ECOMANAGEMENT	To help SMEs in the development of their environmental management (a Telematics for Environment project within the TELEMATICS APPLICATIONS programme) http://www.trentel.org/environment/research/projects/ecomanagement.html
ECOMONT	ECOlogical effects of land use changes on European terrestrial MOuNTain ecosystems (TERI project)
ECON	Committee on Economic and Monetary Affairs (of the EP)
ECON DEV	Network of Science Centres (RECITE project)
ECONET	Environmental Enforcement Officers. A network set up at Community level to develop common approaches to implementation and to exchange information Contact: c/o IGC, Presidio Building 1012, 1st Floor, Torney ave, PO Box 29904, San Francisco CA 94129-0904, United States of America
ECON-R	Economic accounts statistical domain on the REGIO database
ECOPAC	Econometrics of Impacts projects (TRANSPORT project) http://www.cordis.lu/transport/src/ecopac.htm

ECOPAVE	Development of a multi-purpose composite pavement system (BRITE project)
ECOPOINTS	Reg 3298/94 laying down detailed measures concerning the system of Rights of Transit for heavy goods vehicles transiting through Austria (OJ L341/94 with latest amendment in OJ L190/96)
ECO-R	Regional Economic accounts statistical domain on the REGIO database
*ECOS	European City Cooperation Scheme. *Now within* INTERREG
ECOSA	European Consumer Safety Association c/o Dutch Consumer Safety Institute, Rijswijkstraat 2, PO Box 75169, NL-1070 AD Amsterdam, Netherlands
ECOSIM	ECOlogical and environmental monitoring and SIMulation system for management decision support in urban areas (a Telematics for Environment project within the TELEMATICS APPLICATIONS programme) http://www.trentel.org/environment/research/projects/ecosim.html
ECOSOC	ESC opinions and bulletins in full-text http://www.ces.eu.int/en/docs/fr_docs_default.htm
ECOSOC	Economic and Social Committee. *See* ESC
ECOTTRIS	European Collaboration On Transition Training for Improved Safety (TRANSPORT project)
ECOWAT	Energy Efficiency and Water Supply (RECITE project)
ECP	European Cooperation Programmes for language - teacher training (Action A within LINGUA)
ECPC	European Civil Peace Corps

ECPI	European Consumer Price Index produced by EUROSTAT and based on the HCPIs of the Member States (OJ C84/95)
ECPRD	European Centre for Parliamentary Research and Documentation to promote the exchange of information between parliaments Contact: European Parliament, L-2929 Luxembourg
ECR	European Commercial Register of companies, which is maintained by the ECJ
ECR	European Court Reports: Reports of Cases before the ECJ. Published by EUR-OP
ECR-SC	European Court Reports - Staff Cases
ECS	European Company Statute (OJ C138/91)
ECSA-Europe	European Community Studies Association Secretariat: rue de Trèves 67, B-1040 Brussels, Belgium http://www.ecsanet.org/
ECSC	European Coal and Steel Community Bâtiment Jean Monnet, rue Alcide de Gasperi, Plateau du Kirchberg, L-3424 Luxembourg
ECSC TREATY	*See* PARIS TREATY
ECSI	European Customer Satisfaction Index http://europa.eu.int/comm/dg03/directs/dg3a/a3/quality/cust/index_en.htm#c3
ECT	The use of terrestrial model ecosystems to assess environmental risks in ecosystems (an Environmental Health and Chemical Safety Research project within the ENVIRONMENT AND CLIMATE programme)
ECTA	European Communities Trade Mark Association Bisschoppenhoflaan 286, Box 5, B-2100 Deurne-Antwerpen, Belgium http://www.ecta.org

ECTARC	European Centre for Traditional and Regional Cultures Parade Street, Llangollen, Clwyd, Wales LL20 8RB, United Kingdom
ECTN	European Children's Television. A network supported by the KALEIDOSCOPE programme
EC TREATY	*See* ROME TREATY
ECTS	European Community Course Credit Transfer System (established under the ERASMUS programme)
*ECU	European Currency Unit. *See also* EMS. *Replaced by* EURO
EC-UNRWA	Community contribution to the United Nations Relief and Works Agency for Palestine Refugees
Ecup+	European Copyright User Platform (TELEMATICS APPLICATIONS project)
ECURIE	Council Decision 87/600/Euratom on a European Community Urgent Radiological Information Exchange (OJ L371/87)
ECVAM	European Centre for the Validation of Alternative Methods (part of the JRC at ISPRA)
ECVP	European Community's Visitors' Programme. Established by the Commission and the EP to enable young leaders from the USA, Canada, Latin American countries, Australia, New Zealand and Japan to visit Europe
*ED	European Democratic group (Conservatives in the EP). *See* EPP/ED
ED	*See* EUROPEAN DOCUMENTATION

EDA	European Dairy Association (formed from ASSILEC and ASFALEC) rue Montoyer 14, B-1000 Brussels, Belgium
EDA	*See* RDE
E-Day	1 January 2002, the date of the final changeover to the EURO
EDC	European Documentation Centre set up in Universities and Higher Education institutions. *See also* RELAYS
EDCOMER	European Documentation Centre and Observatory on Migration and Ethnic Relations. Launched in June 1995 with financial support from the Employment and Social Affairs DG of the European Commission EDCOMER, Utrecht University, P.O.Box 80.140 - 3508 TC Utrecht, Netherlands http://www.ruu.nl/ercomer/edcomer/index.html
EDD	Europe of Democracies and Diversities Group (of the EP)
EDDRA	Exchange on Drug Demand Reduction activities. An information system set up by EMCDDA http://www.emcdda.org/html/demand_reduction.html
EDF	European Development Fund (1958-) which operates under the LOME CONVENTION
EDF	European Disability Forum. A representative consultative body on disability issues in the EU sq Ambiorix 32, B-1000 Brussels, Belgium http://www.edf.unicall.be
EDI	Electronic Data Interchange project. A European system of electronic links for transborder trade between businesses
EDIC	EC translation service query language on the EURODICAUTOM database

Edicom	Council Decision 96/715/EC for Electronic Data Interchange on Commerce (OJ L327/96)
EDIE	European Direct Investment in Europe
EDIFLOW	Inventory of dataflows exchanged between EUROSTAT and Member States (EUROSTAT project)
EDIL	Electronic Document Interchange between Libraries (project within Area 5 of the TELEMATIC SYSTEMS programme)
EDILIBE	Electronic Data Interchange for Libraries and Booksellers in Europe (project within Area 5 of the TELEMATIC SYSTEMS programme)
EDINBURGH FACILITY	A temporary lending facility agreed at the December 1992 Edinburgh Council to fund infrastructure projects from EIB resources, especially for trans-European transport, telecommunications and energy networks, environmental protection and conservation. Proposal to extend the facility to SMEs (OJ C210/93). *See also* EDINBURGH GROWTH INITIATIVE
EDINBURGH GROWTH INITIATIVE	Set up at the December 1992 Edinburgh Council to promote economic recovery in Europe. (COM(93) 54 and COM(93) 164). *See also* EDINBURGH FACILITY; EIF
EDI-ROAD	EDI project under the TEDIS programme
EDIT	EU Databases Information and Training consultancy Donnington House, Trinity Street, Coventry CV1 1FJ, United Kingdom
EDITRANS	EDI project under the TEDIS programme
EDITYRE	EDI project under the TEDIS programme
EDIUS	European Direct Investment in the USA

EDMC	*See* EMCDDA
*EDN	Europe of Nations Group (Coordination Group) (of the EP). *See* UEN
EDP	European Development Pole. A transfrontier reconversion zone around Longwy-Aubange-Petange which receives some STRUCTURAL FUNDS aid
EDPEC	Energy Demonstration Project of the European Communities
EDPS	European Data Protection Supervisor. An independent supervisory body to be established to protect individuals with regard to the processing of personal data by the Institutions and bodies of the Community and the free movement of such data (COM(99) 337)
EDPW	European Drug Prevention Weeks held in November 1992, October 1994 and November 1998
EDS	European Declarative System (ESPRIT project)
E-DSRR	Enhanced Digital Short Range System Applications (a Telematics for Education and Training project within the TELEMATICS APPLICATIONS programme)
*EDU	European Democratic Union
EDU	EUROPOL Drugs Unit
EDUCATE	End-user courses in information access through communication technology (project within Area 5 of the TELEMATIC SYSTEMS programme)

EEA	European Economic Area which strengthens trade and economic relations between the Member States and EFTA countries. It came into effect on 1 January 1994 (OJ L1/94). Liechtenstein joined on 1 May 1995 (OJ L86/95). Switzerland has not yet joined
EEA	European Environment Agency. Set up under Reg 1210/90 (OJ L120/90 with latest amendment in OJ L117/99). *See also* EIONET Kongens Nytorv 6, DK-1050 Copenhagen, Denmark http://www.eea.eu.int/
EEA-CC	European Economic Area Consultative Committee
EEA/EIONET Regulation	*See* EEA (European Environment Agency); EIONET
EEB	European Environmental Bureau bd de Waterloo 34, B-1000 Brussels, Belgium
*EEB	European Export Bank
EEC	European Economic Community
EEC TREATY	*See* ROME TREATY
EEG6	EBES Expert Group 6 - statistics (sponsored by the IDA programme)
EEIG	Reg 2137/85 on European Economic Interest Grouping (OJ L199/85). *Previously* ECG
EEIS	European Environmental Information Services (a Telematics for Environment project within the TELEMATICS APPLICATIONS programme) http://www.trentel.org/environment/research/projects/eeis.html http://eeis.ceo.sai.jrc.it/
EEMIN	European Environment Monitoring and Information Network (OJ L120/90)

EEMR	Exchange of Experience, Monitoring and Reporting activities (part of the PHARE programme)
EEP	European Educational Project (within Action 1 of COMENIUS)
EEP	European Exchange Programme (RAPHAEL programme)
EERO	European Environment Research Organisation Dr J V Lake, PO Box 191, General Foulkesweg 70, NL-6700 AD, Wageningen, Netherlands
EES	European Employment Strategy
EES	European Economic Space. *See* EEA (European Economic Area)
EESD	Council Decision 1999/170/EC adopting a specific programme for research, technological development and demonstration on energy, environment and sustainable development (1998-2000) (OJ L64/99). One of the THEMATIC PROGRAMMES which form part of FP5. *Previously* ENVIRONMENT AND CLIMATE programme; JOULE-THERMIE; MAST III. *See also* ENERGIE
EETP	European Educational Teleports (a Telematics for Education and Training project within the TELEMATICS APPLICATIONS programme)
e-EUROPE	An information society for all. A Commission initiative launched in December 1999 to bring the benefits of the IS to all Europeans (COM(99) 687) http://europa.eu.int/comm/information_society/eeurope/index_en.htm
*EF	European File. A series of pamphlets published by OOPEC which ceased publication with 7/92

EF	European Foundation. *See* EFILWC
EFA	European Federation of Agricultural Workers' Unions rue Fossé-aux-Loups 38, Boîte 8, B-1000 Brussels, Belgium
EFA	European Film Academy (set up under the MEDIA programme)
EFA	European Free Alliance Group (of the EP). *See* GREENS/EFA
EFA	Federation of European Accountants rue de la Loi 83, B-1040 Brussels, Belgium http://www.euro.fee.be
EFAH	European Forum for the Arts and Heritage rue de la Concorde 53, B-1050 Brussels, Belgium http://www.eurplace.org/orga/efah/index.html
EFER	European Foundation for Entrepreneurship Research bd Saint Michel 15, B-1040 Brussels, Belgium
EFEX	European Financial Expertise network to mobilise European public and private sector financial sector expertise for technical assistance programmes in Asian countries (OJ C57/99) EFEX Clearing House, C107, 3/36, rue de la Loi 200, B-1049 Brussels, Belgium http://europa.eu.int/comm/dg15/efex/
EFFAS	European Federation of Financial Analysts Societies Palais de la Bourse, pl de la Bourse, F-75002 Paris, France http://www.effas.org
EFFECT	Environmental Forecasting for the Effective Control of Traffic (a Telematics for Environment project within the TELEMATICS APPLICATIONS programme) http://www.trentel.org/environment/research/projects/effect.html

EFICS	Reg 1615/89 on a European Forestry Information and Communications System (1989-1992) (OJ L165/89). Modified and extended until 2002 by Reg 1100/98 (OJ L157/98)
EFIEA	European Forum on Integrated Environmental Assessment (ENVIRONMENT AND CLIMATE project)
EFIFC	European Federation of Investment Funds and Companies sq de Meeûs 20, B-1050 Brussels, Belgium
EFILWC	European Foundation for the Improvement of Living and Working Conditions. Set up by Reg 1365/75 (OJ L139/75) Wyattville Road, Loughlinstown, IRL-Co. Dublin, Ireland http://www.eurofound.ie http://www.eurofound.eu.int
EFMD	European Foundation for Management Development rue Gachard 88, B-1050 Brussels, Belgium
EFPA	European Food Service and Packaging Association bd Saint Michel 15, B-1040 Brussels, Belgium
EFPIA	European Federation of Pharmaceutical Industries Associations ave Louise 250, Boîte 91, B-1050 Brussels, Belgium http://www.efpia.org
EFQM	European Foundation for Quality Management ave des Pléiades 19, B-1200 Brussels, Belgium
EFTA	European Free Trade Association consisting of Iceland, Liechtenstein, Norway and Switzerland rue de Varembé 9-11, CH-1202 Geneva 20, Switzerland
EGE	European Group on Ethics in Science and New Technologies. *Previously* GAEIB http://europa.eu.int/comm/sg/sgc/ethics/en/index/htm

EGLEI	European Group for Local Employment Initiatives sq Ambiorix 45, B-1000 Brussels, Belgium
EHCR	Electronic Health Care Records support action (a Telematics for Healthcare project within the TELEMATICS APPLICATIONS programme)
EHLASS	Council Decision 3092/94/EC on a European Home and Leisure Accident monitoring Surveillance System (1994-1997) (OJ L331/94). From 1999 it has been integrated into INJURY-PREV C. *Previously* HASS http://www.santel.lu/EHLASS/uk_home.html
EHT	Employment in high-tech statistical domain on the NEW CRONOS databank
EHTO	European Health Telematics Observatory (a Telematics for Healthcare project within the TELEMATICS APPLICATIONS programme) http://www.ehto.org/
EI	Environment Institute (part of the JRC at ISPRA)
EIA	Environmental Impact Assessment. *See* IMPACT Directive
EIA	European Information Association. *Previously* AEDCL Manager: Ms C Webb, Manchester Central Library, St Peter's Sq, Manchester M2 5PD, United Kingdom http://www.eia.org.uk/
EIARD	European Initiative for Agricultural Research for Development (COM(97) 126). *See also* Infosys http://www.dainet.de/eiard/homepage/
EIB	European Investment Bank bd Konrad Adenauer 100, L-2950 Luxembourg http://www.eib.org UK Information Office: 68 Pall Mall, London SW1Y 5ES

EIC	EuroInfoCentre (for SMEs). *See also* RELAYS
EICC	Euro Info Correspondence Centre. Set up, with financial support from the PHARE programme, to facilitate collaboration between OCTs and EU firms
EICP	European Index of Consumer Prices
EIESP	European Institute of Education and Social Policy J-P Jallade, c/o Univerity of Paris, IX-Dauphiné, pl du Maréchal de Lattre de Tassigny, F-75116 Paris, France
EIF	Council Decision 94/375/EC to establish a European Investment Fund. Set up under the EDINBURGH GROWTH INITIATIVE to provide financial guarantees to aid economic growth (OJ L173/94). *See also* ETF; I-TEC 2 ave J.F.Kennedy 43, L-2968 Luxembourg http://www.eif.org
EIF	European Internet Forum. An initiative launched by the Information Society DG to raise awareness across Europe on Internet related questions http://www.ispo.cec.be/eif/
EIIA	European Information Industry Association BP 262, L-2012 Luxembourg
*EIL	European Innovation Loan. A proposed initiative which was never agreed
*EIMI	European Innovation Monitoring Initiative. Set up under SPRINT. *Continued by* EIMS
EIMS	European Innovation Monitoring System (part of the INNOVATION programme). *Previously* EIMI http://www.cordis.lu/eims/home.html
EINECS	European Inventory of Existing Chemical Substances. *See also* ECDIN; EINECS-Plus; ELINCS Access via EINECS-Plus

EINECS-Plus	Electronic access to ECI; ECICS; EINECS; ELINCS Available via the Internet or on CD-ROM from EUR-OP and SILVERPLATTER
E-INTERFACE	Standardisation of integrated LAN services and service access protocols (ESPRIT project)
EIOAPP	EIONET telematics APPlication development group (a Telematics for Environment project within the TELEMATICS APPLICATIONS programme) http://www.trentel.org/environment/research/projects/eioapp.html
EIOL	European Infrastructure for Open Learning (DELTA project)
EIONET	European Environment Information and Observation Network. Set up within the IDA programme under Reg 1210/90 (OJ L120/90 with latest amendment in OJ L117/99). *See also* EEA; MCE http://www.eionet.eu.int/
EIOP	European Integration On-line Papers. A web journal http://eiop.or.at/eiop/
EIP	Euro Info Point. Information offices set up by the European Commission in the Member States, where the public may obtain free literature about the EU. *See also* RELAYS Brussels Contact: Rond-Point Schuman 12, B-1049 Brussels, Belgium
EIPA	European Insolvency Practitioners' Association INSOL Studio, 7 Russell Pl, Nottingham NG1 5HJ, United Kingdom
EIPA	European Institute of Public Administration Onze Lieve Vrouweplein 22, PO Box 1229, NL-6201 BH Maastricht, Netherlands http://www.eipa.nl
EIPC	*See* ECPI

EIPG	Energy Investment Promotion Group
EIPPCB	European IPPC Bureau. Operates within the framework of Article 16(2) of Dir 96/61/EC on Integrated Pollution Prevention and Control (OJ L257/96) JRC, SEVILLE http:/eippcb.jrc.es
EIRENE	European Information Researchers' Network Secretariat: The Charnwood, Gas Research and Technology Centre, Ashby Rd, Loughborough, Leicestershire LE11 3GS, United Kingdom http://www.eirene.com
EIRO	European Industrial Relations OBSERVATORY at the EFILWC. *See also* EIROnline
EIROnline	Web database of industrial relations in Europe produced by EIRO http://www.eiro.eurofound.ie/
EIS	European Information Service. A monthly information bulletin produced by the Local Government International Bureau in the UK http://www.lgib.gov.uk
EIS	European Information System for customs purposes (OJ C316/95)
EISOSH	European Information System for Occupation Safety and Health (a Telematics for Healthcare project within the TELEMATICS APPLICATIONS programme) http://www.ehto.org/vds/projects/eisosh.html
EITC	European IT Conference
EJC	European Journalism Centre Boschstraat 60, NL- 6211 AX Maastricht, Netherlands
*EJT	Joint programme to encourage the exchange of young workers within the Community (3rd programme 1985-1991). *Continued as* PETRA

EKORN	EU/Korea R&D Network to link EuropaNET (an international network service) and KREONET (a Korean R&D Network)
ELADIS	European Local Administrative Data Integration Study (a Telematics for Integrated Applications for Digital Sites project within the TELEMATICS APPLICATIONS programme)
ELAN	ESPRIT/European Local Area Network (ESPRIT project)
ELARG	Enlargement DG of the European Commission
ELC	Employment and Labour Market Committee. Part of the consultative process for the implementation of employment guidelines across the Commission, Member State ministries and social partners
ELC	European Language Council. *See* CEL
ELCID	European Living Conditions Information Directory (compiled by the EFILWC) www.eurofound.eu.int/information/elcid.html
ELDONet	European Light Dosimeter Network (an Environmental Health and Chemical Safety Research project within the ENVIRONMENT AND CLIMATE programme)
ELDR	Group of the European Liberal Democrat and Reform Party (of the EP) http://eld.europarl.eu.int
ELDRED	European Lakes, Dams and Reservoirs Database (EEA project)
ELECTRA	Electronic Learning Environment for Continual Training and Research in Alma (Aachen, Liège, Maastricht and Diepenbeek/Hasselt) (a Telematics for Education and Training project within the TELEMATICS APPLICATIONS programme)

ELENA	Power range with fully integrated electronic control system for high efficiency low emission vehicles (EUREKA project)
ELGODIPINE	Anti-anginal calcium antagonist (EUREKA project)
ELIA	European League of Institutes of the Arts Waterlooplein 219, NL-1011 PG Amsterdam, Netherlands http://www.elia.ahk.nl/
ELINCS	European List of Notified Chemical Substances which supplements EINECS Access via EINECS-Plus
ELIS	Electrical Installation System (EUREKA project)
ELISE	Electronic Library Image Service for Europe (project within Area 5 of the TELEMATIC SYSTEMS programme)
ELISE	European Loan Insurance Scheme for Employment. Premiums are linked to loan guarantees from the EIF
ELO	Elusive Office (ESPRIT project)
ELOISE	European Land-Ocean Interaction Studies. Part of the EU initiative on integrated coastal zone management http://europa.eu.int/comm/dg12/eloise/eloise-p.html
ELPRO	Electronic Public Procurement System for Europe (a Telematics for Administrations project within the TELEMATICS APPLICATIONS programme)
ELRA	European Language Resources Association ave d'Italie 87, F-75013 Paris, France http://www.icp.grenet.fr/elra/home.html
ELSA	Electronic Library SGML Applications (project within Area 5 of the TELEMATIC SYSTEMS programme) http://www.cordis.lu/elsa/home.html

ELSA	Ethical, legal and social aspects of BIOMED
ELSA	European Laboratory for Structural Assessment at ISPRA
ELSA	European Law Students' Association rue Defacqz 1, B-1050 Brussels, Belgium http://www.ins.nl/elsa/
ELTIS	European Local Transport Information Service. An Internet guide to current transport measures, policies and practices http://www.eltis.org
ELVIL	European Legislative Virtual Library http://www.su.su.se/elvil.htm
ELWW	European Laboratory Without Walls
EM	European Movement European Action Centre, pl du Luxembourg 1, B-1050 Brussels, Belgium UK office: Dean Bradley House, Horseferry Rd, London SW1P 2AF
EM	*See* ME
EMAIL	Environmental Management Architecture for Information delivery (a Telematics for Environment project within the TELEMATICS APPLICATIONS programme) http://www.trentel.org/environment/research/projects/e-mail.html
EMAS	Reg 1836/93 to set up an Eco-Management and Audit Scheme (OJ L168/93)
EMBA	Management of technology in a European environment (COMETT project)
EMC	Dir 89/336/EEC on Electromagnetic Compatibility (OJ L139/89). Amended by Dir 92/31/EC (OJ L126/92) and Dir 93/68/EC (OJ L220/93)
*EMC	ESPRIT Management Committee

EMC	*See* CEC (European Managers' Confederation)
EMCDDA	European Monitoring Centre for Drugs and Drug Addiction. Set up by Reg 302/93 (OJ L36/93 with the latest amendment Reg 3294/94 in OJ L341/94) rua da Cruz de Santa Apólina 23-25, PT-1149-045 Lisbon, Portugal http://www.emcdda.org
EMCF	European Monetary Cooperation Fund
EMEA	European Agency for the the Evaluation of Medicinal Products. Set up by Reg 2309/93 (OJ L214/93). *See also* ETOMEP 7 Westferry Circus, Canary Wharf, London E14 4HB, United Kingdom http://www.eudra.org/emea.html
EMEP	Council Decision 86/277/EEC adopting the Protocol to the 1979 Convention on the Evaluation and Monitoring of European Pollution (OJ L181/86). The JRC at ISPRA operates a monitoring station http://www.unece.org/env/emep_h.htm
EMF	European Monetary Fund
*EMI	European Monetary Institute established under the TREATY ON EUROPEAN UNION. The forerunner of the ECB
EMIRE	An on-line database of European employment and industrial relations glossaries compiled by the EFILWC http://www.eurofound.ie/information/emire.htm
EMMA	European Marine Motorways (TRANSPORT project) http://www.cordis.lu/transport/src/emma.htm
EMMA	Integrated Environmental Monitoring, forecasting and warning systems in Metropolitan Areas (a Telematics for Environment project within the TELEMATICS APPLICATIONS programme) http://www.trentel.org/environment/research/projects/emma.html

122

EMMI	Euregional Multimedia Information Exchange (a Telematics for Administrations project within the TELEMATICS APPLICATIONS programme)
EMMIS	Evaluation of Man/Machine Interaction (DRIVE project)
EMOT	European masters programme in Management of Technology (COMETT project)
EMPL	Committee on Employment and Social Affairs (of the EP)
EMPL	Employment and Social Affairs DG of the European Commission
EMPLOY	Employment statistical domain on the NEW CRONOS databank
EMPLOY	European Multimedia Pedagogic LOcal support network organisation for the social integration of unemployed Young Europeans (a Telematics for Urban and Rural Areas project within the TELEMATICS APPLICATIONS programme)
*EMPLOYMENT	A COMMUNITY INITIATIVE on employment and the development of human resources (1994-1999) (Guidelines in OJ C180/94). Consists of four strands: HORIZON; INTEGRA; NOW and YOUTHSTART. *Continued by* EQUAL
EMPLOYMENT CONFIDENCE PACT	*See* EUROPEAN CONFIDENCE PACT
EMS	Enzymatic Modification of Soy proteins (EUREKA project)
EMS	European Monetary System. The first stage towards EMU, which came into being in March 1979 (OJ L379/78). *See also* ECU; ERM; ERM2; EURO

EMTF	Educational Multimedia Task Force. Set up by the Commission to study and develop educational and cultural products across Europe
EMU	Economic and Monetary Union. *See also* CONVERGENCE CRITERIA; CONVERGENCE REPORT; EMS; EMUNET; 'ins'; 'pre-ins'; STABILITY PACT; WERNER REPORTS
EMU	Economic and Monetary Union campaign (within PRINCE)
*EMUA	*See* ECU
EMUNET	Website on EMU http://www.euro-emu.co.uk
EN	English
EN	*See* EDN
EN	*See* EURONORM
ENABLE	Enabler for access to computer-based vocational tasks with language and speech (a Telematics for Disabled and Elderly People project within the TELEMATICS APPLICATIONS programme)
ENAM	European North Atlantic Margin: quantification and modelling of large-scale sedimentary processes and fluxes (MAST III project)
ENAR	European Network Against Racism http://www.enar-eu.org
ENCATA	European Network of Centres for the Advancement of Telematics in urban and rural Areas (a Telematics for Urban and Rural Areas project within the TELEMATICS APPLICATIONS programme)

ENCORE	European Network of Catchments Organised for Research on Ecosystems (STEP project)
ENDEF	European Non-Destructive Evaluation Forum. An expert group, managed by the Energy DG of the Commission
ENDHASP	European Network of Drug and HIV/AIDS Services in Prisons. Part of the five-year Community programme for the prevention of drug dependence (1996-2000)
*ENDOC	On-line directory of environmental information and documentation centres in the Member States. Ceased in June 1989
ENDS	European Nuclear Documentation System
*ENER	Committee on Energy, Research and Technology (of the EP)
ENER	Energy DG of the European Commission
ENERGIE	The Energy subprogramme within the EESD programme (1999-2002). *Successor to* the JOULE-THERMIE programme http://europa.eu.int/en/comm/dg17/prog5/index.htm
ENERGY	Regional Energy statistical domain on the REGIO database
ENERGY CHARTER	*See* EUROPEAN ENERGY CHARTER TREATY
Energy Star	The United States registered certification mark, owned by the United States Environmental Protection Agency. Adopted by the EU in an agreement with the United States on the coordination of energy-efficient labelling programmes (COM(99) 328)
ENGINEERS' Directive	Proposed Directive (first presented in 1969) for the mutual recognition of diplomas in engineering (and still on the table)
ENIG	Environment Information Group: a permanent Working Group

ENIP	European Neuroscience INDUSTRIAL PLATFORM http://europa.eu.int/comm/dg12/biotech/ip2.html#ENIP
ENIQ	European Network for Inspection validation or verification. A network established by the JRC on the verification of the effectiveness and performance of inspection techniques in nuclear plants. The IAM acts as Operating Agent and the Reference Laboratory
ENLARGEMENT	Term used for countries joining the original 6 Member States in 1973: Denmark; Ireland; United Kingdom 1981: Greece 1986: Portugal; Spain 1995: Austria; Finland; Sweden Now extended to any country applying to join the EU. *See also* APPLICANT COUNTRIES http://europa.eu.int/comm/enlargement/index.html
ENLIST	European Network for Legal Information, Study and Training (EMTF project)
ENN	European Neurological Network (a Telematics for Healthcare project within the TELEMATICS APPLICATIONS programme)
ENOS	European Network of Ocean Stations (COST action project)
ENOW	European Network of Women rue Blanche 29, B-1060 Brussels, Belgium
Enrich	European Network for Research Into global CHange. Part of the ENVIRONMENT AND CLIMATE programme to provide networking and to promote regional cooperation with developing countries in the global environment field (OJ C306/96)
ENS	European Nervous Systems (project within the TELEMATIC SYSTEMS programme)

ENS	European Network and Services projects (part of the INNOVATION programme) http://www.cordis.lu/innovation/src/projects.htm
ENSR	European Network for SME Research
ENTA	European Network for the Treatment of AIDS Contact: Prof N Clumeckk, Hôpital St Pierre, rue Haute 322, B-1000 Brussels, Belgium
ENTP	European Network of Training Partnerships (under the PETRA programme)
ENTR	Enterprise DG of the European Commission
ENV	Environment DG of the European Commission
ENV	See ENVIRONMENT AND CLIMATE programme
ENVI	Committee on the Environment, public health and consumer policy (of the EP)
ENVIB	Development of integrated systems for environmental mechanical vibration testing (EUREKA project)
ENVINET	Group of EUREKA projects
*ENVIREG	Regional Environment. A STRUCTURAL FUNDS Initiative to protect the environment and to promote economic development (1990-1993) (Guidelines in OJ C115/90)
ENVIROCITY	Public environmental information services (a Telematics for Environment project within the TELEMATICS APPLICATIONS programme) http://www.trentel.org/environment/research/projects/envirocity.html
ENVIRONET	Transfer of expertise in urban planning and environmental protection from developed cities to disadvantaged ones (RECITE project)

*ENVIRONMENT	Activity 3 of the (4th) RTD Framework programme). *See* ENVIRONMENT AND CLIMATE programme; MAST
*ENVIRONMENT AND CLIMATE programme	Council Decision 94/911/EC for an Environment and Climate programme (1994-1998) (OJ L361/94). *Replaced by* EESD. *Previously* EPOCH; STEP. *See also* ENVIRONMENT http://www.cordis.lu/env/home.html http://europa.eu.int/comm/dg12/envir1.html
EnviroWindows	EIONET's interface to external partners such as NGO's, companies and research groups http://www.eea.eu.int/frproj.htm
ENVISION	An EEA's Environmental Vision (part of the Agency's Annual Work Programme)
ENVISYS	Environmental Monitoring Warning and Emergency System (a Telematics for Environment project within the TELEMATICS APPLICATIONS programme) http://www.trentel.org/environment/research/projects/envisys.html
ENW	*See* ENOW
EOCS:HSC	European Occupational Case Studies in Health and Social Care (a Telematics for Healthcare project within the TELEMATICS APPLICATIONS programme)
EOD	*See* ODL
EODS	European Occupational Diseases Statistics. A pilot project to establish comparable EU statistics on occupational diseases Contact: Employment and Social Affairs DG of the European Commission
EOI	European Organ Index (RAPHAEL programme)
EoI	Expression of Interest. A service launched in 1999 by CORDIS to match partners with suitable projects http://www.cordis.lu/fp5

EON 2000	A research project to implement the HABITATS Directive
EOTA	European Organisation for Technical Approvals rue du Trône 12, B-1000 Brussels, Belgium
EOTC	European Organisation for Testing and Certification Egmont House, rue d'Egmont 15, B-1000 Brussels, Belgium UK contact: British Standards Institution, 2 Park Street, London W1A 2BS http://www.eotc.be/
EOU	Export Orientated Units. An export subsidy scheme. *See also* DEPB; EPCGS; EPZ; ITES
EP	European Parliament Alleé du Printemps, BP 1024/F, F-67070 Strasbourg Cedex, France Plateau du Kirchberg, BP 1601, L-2929 Luxembourg rue Wiertz, BP 1047, B-1047 Brussels, Belgium http://www.europarl.eu.int UK Information Office: 2 Queen Anne's Gate, London SW1H 9AA http://www.europarl.eu.int/uk
EPA	European Parents' Association rue du Champ de Mars 1A, B-1050 Brussels, Belgium
*EPADES	*See* EUROPARL
EPBN	European Plant Biotechnology Network. Launched in 1998 to promote the networking, exploitation and dissemination of the results of pan-European projects in this field (part of the BIOTECH programme)
EPC	Council Agreement 89/695/EEC on the European Patent Convention 1989 (OJ L401/89)
EPC	Economic Policy Committee

EPC	European Political Cooperation which was informally introduced in 1970 and adopted by the SEA
EPCGS	Export Promotion Capital Goods Scheme. An export subsidy scheme. *See also* DEPB; EOU; EPZ; ITES
EP DOC(UMENT)	Reports of the EP
EPE	Environmental Protection Expenditure
*EPHOS	*European Procurement Handbook for Open Systems*: version 7 published by the Commission, Directorate-General Telecommunications, Information Industries and Innovation. 1992. EUR 14021. *Replaced by* SPRITE-S2 http://www.ispo.cec.be/ephos
EPI	Institute of Professional Representatives before the EPO P.O.Box 260112, D-80058 München, Germany http://www.patentepi.com
EPIAM	Knowledge-based system for epidemiology (AIM project)
EPIC	Early Process Design Integrated with Controls (ESPRIT project)
EPIC	European Public Information Centre (in Public Libraries). *Previously* PIR. *See also* RELAYS
EPIC	A prototype for integrated care mainly focussed on elderly people (AIM project)
*EPICENTRE	Proposed centralised EP library service to be housed in the new EP building in Brussels. Once completed, however, it became known as the Parliamentary Documentation Centre
EPID COMAC	Epidemiology Concerted Action Committee

EPIOPTIC	European Project: Investigation of Optical Probe Techniques for Interface Characterisation (ESPRIT project)
EPI-RAID	Evaluation of Prototype and Improvement to RAID Workstation (TIDE project)
*Epistel	*See* OVIDE/Epistel
EPITELIO NETWORK	Excluded People Integration by the use of TELematic Innovative Opportunities – Network (a Telematics for Urban and Rural Areas project within the TELEMATICS APPLICATIONS programme)
EPLOT	Enhanced Performance Lasers for Optical Transmission (RACE project)
EPO	European Patent Office. Set up in 1973 Erhardtstrasse 27, D-80331 München, Germany http://www.european-patent-office.org
EPOC	Employee direct Participation in Organisational Change to stimulate debate between the social partners and the EU Institutions (EFILWC project)
*EPOCH	European Programme on Climatology and Natural Hazards (1989-1993) (OJ L359/89). *Continued as* ENVIRONMENT AND CLIMATE programme
EPOQUE	EP On-line QUEry. A documentary database covering the work of the EP and Sessional documents which *replaces* PARDOC and PARQ. *See also* EUROPARL Access only via the EP Intranet
EPOS	European PTT Open learning Service (DELTA project)
EPP/ED	European People's Party/European Democrats (of the EP). *Previously* PPE-DE
EPQ	European Parliamentary Question

EPRD	Council Decision 94/822/EC for a European Programme for Reconstruction and Development (1996-1999). An agreement between the EU and the Republic of South Africa for the support of specific projects (OJ L341/94)
EPROM	Study and development and industrialisation of integrated circuit non-volatile memory having storage capacity of 16 Mbit (EUREKA project)
EPSECC	Environmental Policy, Social Exclusion and Climate Change (ENVIRONMENT AND CLIMATE project)
EPSILON	Advanced knowledge base management system (ESPRIT project)
EPSP	European Peer Support Project. Part of the five-year Community programme for the prevention of drug dependence (1996-2000)
EPTA	European Parliamentary Technology Assessment network which links the STOA Unit with parliamentary technological assessment bodies in Denmark, France, Germany, the Netherlands and the United Kingdom. *See also* ETAN
*EPU	European Payments Union
EPU	European Political Union
EPZ	Export Processing Zones. An export subsidy scheme. *See also* DEPB; EOU; EPCGS; ITES
EQUAL	Electronic services for a better QUALity of life (a Telematics for Integrated Applications for Digital Sites project within the TELEMATICS APPLICATIONS programme) http://www.trentel.org/environment/research/projects/equal.html

EQUAL	Transnational cooperation to combat all forms of discrimination and inequalities in the labour market (2000-2006). A COMMUNITY INITIATIVE for human resources, under the ESF (COM(99) 476) *Continues* ADAPT; EMPLOYMENT
EQUALITY	Extending Quality Urban service for Added-value Living using Interactive Telematic sYstems (a Telematics for Urban and Rural Areas project within the TELEMATICS APPLICATIONS programme)
EQUAL OPPORTUNITIES FOR WOMEN programme	*See* ANIMA
EQUATOR	Environment for Qualitative Temporal Reasoning (ESPRIT project)
EQUICERA	Thermomechanical ceramic heating equipment (EUREKA project)
EQUUS	Efficient qualitative and quantitative use of KBSs in financial management (ESPRIT project)
ER	*See* DR
ERA	European Regions Association Baker Suite, Fairoaks Airport, Chobham, Woking, Surrey G024 8HX, United Kingdom http://www.eraa.org
ERA	*See* ARE (Group of the European Radical Alliance)
ERASMUS	European Community Action Scheme for the Mobility of University Students (1987-1994) (OJ L395/89). *Continued within* the SOCRATES programme
*ERB	ESPRIT Review Board
ERB	*See* BCC
ERC	European Radiocommunications Committee. Sub-committee of CEPT

*ERC	European Reference Centre
ERC	European Resource Centre for schools and colleges. An EU initiative in the UK to provide European information direct to schools and colleges. *See also* RELAYS
ERCOM	Solution to the recycling problems due to the use of reinforced plastics in the industry (EUREKA project)
ERDF	European Regional Development Fund (1975-) (Latest Reg 1783/99 in OJ L213/99)
ERDS	European Reliability Data System (JRC - reactor safety). *See also* AORS; CEDB; GRPDS; OUSR
Ergo	European Research Gateway On-line. R&D project involving the creation of a website covering around 71,000 research projects http://www.cordis.lu/ergo/
*ERGO II	European Community action programme for the long-term unemployed (1993-1996)
ERIS@	European Regional Information Society Association rue de l'Industrie 11, B-1000 Brussels, Belgium http://www.ispo.cec.be/risi
ERIT	Federation of European professionals working in the field of drug abuse. Part of the five-year Community programme for the prevention of drug dependence (1996-2000) rue de Vieux Pont de Sèvres 154, F-92100 Boulogne, France http://www.erit.org
ERLAP	European Reference Laboratory for Air Pollution. Part of the EI
ERM	Exchange Rate Mechanism (of the EMS)
ERM2	New Exchange Rate Mechanism

ERMES	European Radio Messaging System (OJ L310/90). *See also* DECT
EROMM	European Register of Microform Master (project within Area 5 of the TELEMATIC SYSTEMS programme)
EROS 2000	European River Ocean System (MAST/STEP programme)
ERT	European Round Table of Industrialists ave Henri Jaspar 113, B-1060 Brussels, Belgium http://www.ert.be
ERTICO	Intelligent Transport systems Europe. To support and promote the implementation of ITS in Europe http://www.ertico.com
ERTIS	European Road Transport Information Services (EUREKA project)
ERTMS	European Rail Traffic Management System (EURET project)
ERW	An office system Research Workstation for Europe (ESPRIT project)
ES	Spanish
ES2	Automatic design and production of custom chips using direct printing on silicon (EUREKA project)
ESA	Employment and Social Affairs. A series of periodicals which replace *Social Europe*
ESA	European Space Agency rue Mario Nikis 8-10, F-75738 Paris Cédex 15, France http://www.esa.int/
ESA 95	Reg 2223/96 for a European System of national and regional Accounts in the Community (OJ L310/96 with latest amendment in OJ L58/98)
ESAC	ECVAM Scientific Advisory Committee

ESATT	European Science and Technology Transfer Network (COPERNICUS project). *See also* RICE http://jukebox.isf.kiev.ua/rice/root/esatt-indis.html
ESAVS	European School for Postgraduate Veterinary Training and Continuing Education (COMETT project)
ESAW	European Statistics on Accidents at Work. A EUROSTAT and Employment and Social Affairs DG project to establish comparable EU statistics on accidents at work
ESB	European Soil Bureau Secretariat: c/o ISPRA
ESC	Economic and Social Committee rue Ravenstein 2, B-1000 Brussels, Belgium http://www.esc.eu.int/en/default.htm
ESCAPE	Entangled Sulphur and CArbon cycles in Phaeocystis dominated Ecosystems (ELOISE project)
ESCAPE	Group of EUREKA projects
ESCB	European System of Central Banks which comprises the ECB and NCBs http://www.ecb.int/
ESCF	European Seed Capital Funds for new or embryonic companies
ESD	Protection for submicron technologies (ESPRIT project)
ESDEP	European Steel Design Education Programme (COMETT project)
ESDP	European Spatial Development Perspective. Adopted by the informal Council of the European Union responsible for spatial planning, at its meeting in Potsdam in May 1999
ESF	EUREKA Software Factory (EUREKA project)

ESF	European Science Foundation quai Lezay Marnésia 1, F-67080 Strasbourg, France
ESF	European Social Fund (1972-) (Latest Reg 1784/99 in OJ L213/99)
ESIF	European Service Industries Forum Markt 26, B-9700 Oudenarde, Belgium
ESIMEAU	Information technologies for the modeling of water resources in semi-arid zones. Partly funded by INCO-DC and ESPRIT http://www-esimeau.inria.fr/
ESIS	European Survey of Information Society. An inventory of European Information Society projects and actions, initially running for two years from February 1997 (ISPO-led project) http://www.ispo.cec.be/esis/
*ESLA	Ethical, Social and Legal Aspects of human genome analysis. *Continued by* HEF
ESM-BASE	Author Support for Student Modelling in multimedia learning processes (DELTA project)
ESOP II	European Sub Polar Ocean Programme phase II: the thermohaline circulation in the Greenland sea (MAST III project)
ESP	Ebit Service Project (RACE project)
esp@cenet	EPO joint service to provide enterprises with free patent information http://www.european-patent-office.org/espacenet/
ESPITI	European Software Process Improvement Training Initiative (part of the ESSI project)
ESPO	European Sea Ports Organisation Michelangelolaan 68, B-1000 Brussels, Belgium http://www.espo.be
ESPOIR	European Shoe Programme on Instant Response (SPRINT project)

ESPON	European Spatial Planning Observatory Network (part of the ESDP)
ESPRIT	A database of information on ESPRIT projects http://www.cordis.lu/esprit/home.html
*ESPRIT IV	Council Decision 94/802/EC for a European Strategic Programme for R&D in Information Technology (1994-1998) (OJ L334/94). *See also* ICT. *Continued as* IST
*ESRO	European Space Research Organisation. *Replaced by* ESA
ESS	European Statistical System (OJ C47/92) Contact: EUROSTAT
ESSEN Priorities	Proposal for analysis, research, cooperation and action in the field of employment (COM(95) 250)
ESSENTIAL	European Systems Strategy for Evolution of New Technology in Advanced Learning (DELTA project)
ESSI	European Software and Systems Initiative (ESPRIT project)
ESSN	European Senior Service Network which is designed to help the management of enterprises in TACIS countries
*ESSOR	Complex at ISPRA
ESSPROS	*See* SESPROS
ESTA	European Science and Technology Assembly to assist the European Commission in the implementation of EU research http://europa.eu.int/comm/dg12/esta/index.html
ESTAT	Eurostat DG of the European Commission

Ester	European Source Term Code system. A Community initiative in the analysis of LWR to stimulate collaboration between laboratories. Coordinated by the JRC
ESTI	European Society of Transport Institutes rue Archimède 5-11, B-1000 Brussels, Belgium
ESTI	European Solar Test Installation at ISPRA
ESTO	European Science and Technology Observatory. Developed by IPTS and part of the JRC http://esto.jrc.es/
ESTPER	European Severe Trauma Perspective (EMTF project)
ESU	European Size Unit
E.T.	Education in the Transport Sector (COMETT project)
ETA	Decision 94/23/EC on European Technical Approval for construction products (OJ L17/94)
ETAG	EURONET Technical Aspects Working Group
ETAN	European Technology Assessment Network to bring together EPTA; IPTS and STOA http://www.cordis.lu/etan/home.html
ETAP	A programme of desk research relating to energy policy within the EU (1998-2002)
ET-ASSIST	European Telemedicine for medical ASSISTance (a Telematics for Healthcare project within the TELEMATICS APPLICATIONS programme)
ETC	European Technology Community

ETC	European Topic Centre. Contracted by the EEA to lead the development in European environmental information. *See* ETC/AEM; ETC/AQ; ETC/CDS; ETC/IW; ETC/LC; ETC/MC; ETC/NC; ETC/S; ETC/W http://www.eionet.eu.int/
ETC	*See* Eurotech Capital
ETC/AEM	ETC on Air EMissions http://www.aeat.co.uk/netcen/corinair/corinair.html
ETC/AQ	ETC on Air Quality. *See also* EUROAIRNET http://www.etcaq.rivm.nl/
ETC/CDS	ETC on Catalogue of Data Sources. *See also* GEMET http://etc-cds.eionet.eu.int/
ETC/IW	ETC on Inland Waters. *See also* EURO-WATERNET; WRC http://etc-iw.eionet.eu.int http://www.eionet.eu.int/
ETC/LC	ETC on LandCover http://mdc.kiruna.se/projects/etc/
ETC/MC	ETC on Marine and Coastal environment http://estaxp.santateresa.enea.it/wwww/etc/etc-mc.html
ETC/NC	ETC on Nature Conservation. *See also* EUNIS http://www.mnhn.fr/ctn/
ETC/S	ETC on Soil http://eionet.eu.int/
ETC/W	ETC on Waste. *See also* WASTEBASE http://www.eionet.eu.int/
ETEE	Educational Technologies for European Enterprises (DELTA project)
ETEMA	European Terrestrial Ecosystem Modelling Activity (TERI project)

ETF	European Technology Facility for SMEs, set up by the EIB under the ASAP and managed by the EIF (1998-2002) (OJ C302/98)
ETF	European Training Foundation. Set up by Reg 1360/90 (OJ L131/90 with latest amendment in OJ L206/98) to give technical assistance under PHARE and TACIS Villa Gualino, Viale Settimio Severo 65, I-10133 Turin, Italy http://www.etf.it/
ETHEL	European Tritium Handling Experimental Laboratory (JRC project)
ETHOS	European Telematics Horizontal Observatory Service (a Programme Support Actions project within the TELEMATICS APPLICATIONS programme)
ETIS	European Telecommunications Informatics Services bringing together 25 European telecommunications companies focusing on key IT issues http://www.etis.org/
ETK	Exchange of Technology Know-how conference. Organised by EUROSTAT and ISIS http://europa.eu.int/en/comm/eurostat/research/conferences/etk-99
ETL	European Test Laboratory at PETTEN
ETMO	See CTMO
ETOMEP	European Technical Office for Medicinal Products at the EMEA
ETOP	European Technology for Optical Processing
ETP	Executive Training Programme for young EU executives in Japan (1979-)
ETR	ElecTrothermal Ribbon (ESPRIT project)

ETS	European Trust Services. Set up by the Commission to establish security of information services http://www.cordis.lu/infosec/src/ets.htm
ETSA	European Textiles Services Association rue Montoyer 24, B-1000 Brussels, Belgium
ETSI	European Telecommunications Standards Institute route de Lucioles 650, F-06921 Sophia Antipolis Cédex, France http://www.etsi.fr/
ETTI	European Technology Transfer Initiative. Launched in 1998, it is designed to accelerate the exploitation of research results emerging from the JRC
ETTN	European Technology Transfer Network coordinated by the JRC
ETUC	European Trade Union Confederation. *Previously* ECFTU bd Emile Jacqmain 155, B-1210 Brussels, Belgium http://www.etuc.org
ETUCO	European Trade Union College bd Emile Jacqmain 155, B-1210 Brussels, Belgium http://www.etuc.org/etuco/default.cfm
ETUDE	European Trade Union Distance Education (EMTF project)
ETUE-Net	European Trade Union Education Network (a Telematics for Education and Training project within the TELEMATICS APPLICATIONS programme)
ETUI	European Trade Union Institute bd du Roi Albert II 5, B-1210 Brussels, Belgium http://www.etuc.org/ETUI/default.cfm
ETV	Electronic Training Village. A CEDEFOP initiative launched in 1998 http://www.trainingvillage.gr
*ETY	European Tourism Year (1990)

EU	European Union. The term introduced in the TREATY ON EUROPEAN UNION which will be used for matters which concern the 'external' functions of the European Communities ie the Second and Third Pillars of the Three PILLARS
EU	*See* EURONORM
*EUA	European Unit of Account. *See* ECU
EUAM	Council Decision 94/308/CFSP to set up the EU Administration Mostar (OJ L134/94)
EUBIMA	Mass spectrometric analysis of biologically active macromolecules (EUREKA project)
EUC	An ISPO funded project concentrating on developing school networks (part of the EUN programme)
EU-CHIP	Euro-Chinese Information Point. An on-line information service for Chinese and European IT companies (partly funded by the European Commission) http://www.esi.es/EU-CHIP/
EUCLID	European and International information, news and analysis for the arts and cultural sector http://www.euclid.co.uk
EUCLID	*See* IUCLID
EUCLIDES	EUropean standard for Clinical Laboratory Data Exchange between independent information Systems (AIM project)
EUCOFEL	European Union of the Fruit and Vegetable Wholesale, Import and Export Trade rue Jenneval 29, B-1000 Brussels, Belgium
EUCOLAIT	European Union of Importers, Exporters and Dealers in Dairy Products ave Livingstone 26, Boîte 5, B-1000 Brussels, Belgium

EUCREA	European Association for Creativity by Disabled People sq Ambiorix 32, Boîte 47, B-1000 Brussels, Belgium
EUCREX	European Cloud and Radiation EXperiment (EPOCH project)
EUDAT	European Association for the Development of Databases in Education and Training Centre INFFO, Tour Europe, F-92049 Paris La Défense Cedex 07, France
EUDIF	European Documentation and Information Network for Women Sentier du Presbytère 8, B-1630 Linkebeek, Belgium
EU Direct	A current awareness service on EU informatiom Access via BUTTERWORTHS http://www.butterworths.co.uk
EUDISED	EUropean Documentation and Information System for EDucation Access via ESA-IRS and EINS (password required)
EUDOR	EUropean DOcument Repository. An on-line document delivery service covering the OJ and COM DOCS. Free searching but costs associated with downloading documents http://eudor.com
EudraLex	A multilingual lexicon of technical vocabulary used in pharmaceutical legislation. *See also* EudraNet
EudraMat	A database of economic information on pharmaceutical products. *See also* EudraNet
EudraNet	A network to disseminate information on pharmaceutical products, consisting of EudraLex; EudraMat; EudraTrack http://www.eudra.org
EudraTrack	A tracking system for regulatory procedures for pharmaceutical products. *See also* EudraNet

EUDUG	EU Databases User Group. *Formerly* the UK Eurobases User Group Contact: Jill Speed at http://www.eudug.org
EUI	European University Institute Badia Fiesolana, Via dei Roccettini 5, I-50016 San Domenico di Fiesola, Florence, Italy http://www.iue.it
EU INFODISK	An electronic bibliographical index listing journal articles on EU policy and official EU documents Available on CD-ROM from ILI and on the Internet at http://www.ili.co.uk (subscription required)
EU interactive	An indexed database providing official EU documents within 24 hours of release Access via LAWTEL http://www.EUinteractive.com
EUKIOSK	A service for citizens via information kiosks (ISIS multimedia systems project) http://www.ispo.cec.be/isis/95eukios.htm
EUL	*See* CG
EULEGIS	European User views to LEGislative Information in Structured form (a Telematics for Administrations project within the TELEMATICS APPLICATIONS programme)
EULIT	Effects of EUtrophicated seawater on rocky shore ecosystems studied in large LITtoral mesocosms (ELOISE project)
EUL/NGL	Confederal Group of the European United Left - Nordic Green Left (of the EP)
EUMED	EU - Mediterranean countries
EUMEDIS	Euro-MEDiterranean Information Society (part of MEDA's regional cooperation programme)

EUN	European schoolNet project to establish a European school information network. Funded by the Educational Multimedia Task Force and coordinated by the SOCRATES programme http://www.en.eun.org/front/actual/
EUNET	European Organisation for Packaging and the Environment ave de Tervuren 113, Boîte 35, B-1040 Brussels, Belgium
EUNET	Experimental Network funded by INNOVATION, linking national technology transfer schemes to transfer technology from research institutions to industry
EU NET ART	EUropean NETwork of ART organisations for children and young people
EUNIS	European Nature Information System. Database developed by ETC/NC containing information on species, habitats and sites to assist the Commission on NATURA 2000 and the EEA
EU-OSHA	European Agency for Safety and Health at Work. Set up under Reg 2062/94 (OJ L216/94 with amendment in OJ L156/95) Gran Via 33, E-48009 Bilbao, Spain http://europe.osha.eu.int
EUPEPT	Synthetic PEPTides for clinical nutrition (EUREKA project)
EUPHORE	EUropean PHOto-REactor (EI project)
EUPRIO	Association of European University Public Relations and Information Officers Contact: Wim Janssen, Rijksuniversiteit Groningen, Postbus 72, NL-9700 AB Groningen, Netherlands
EU PUBLISHERS' FORUM	*See* FORUM
EUR	Series of scientific and technical reports published by EUR-OP and other commercial publishers

EUR1	*See* EUROSTATUS
EUR2	*See* EUROSTATISTICS
EUR 15 (12; 10; 9)	Fifteen (Twelve; Ten; Nine) countries of the EU
EURADA	European Association of Development Agencies ave des Arts 12, Boîte 7, B-1210 Brussels, Belgium
EURAM	*See* BRITE/EURAM
EURAMIS	European Advanced Multilingual Information System. A computer system to develop and integrate multilingual tools into multilingual services for translators
EURASHE	European Association for Institutions of Higher Education rue de la Concorde 57, B-1050 Brussels, Belgium
*EURATHLON	A programme to encourage sports projects and programmes with a European dimension 1995-1999 (OJ C222/96)
EuRaTIN	European Research and Technology Information Network http://www.euratin.net/
EURATN	European Aeronautical Telecommunication Network (EURET project)
EURATOM	European Atomic Energy Community rue du Luxembourg 46, B-1000 Brussels, Belgium
EURATOM TREATY	signed by Belgium, France, Germany, Italy, Luxembourg and the Netherlands on 25th March 1957. Came into force 1st January 1958
EUREAU	Union of the Water Supply Associations from Countries of the EC ch de Waterloo 255, Boîte 6, B-1060 Brussels, Belgium

EUREED-II	Dynamics and stability of reed-dominated ecosystems in relation to major environmental factors that are subject to global and regional anthropogenically-induced changes (ENVIRONMENT AND CLIMATE project)
EUREGIO	Trans-frontier Cooperation Associations Postfach 11 80, Enscheder Strasse 362, D-48590 Gronau, Germany
EUREKA	A database of projects financed under the EUREKA programme http://eureka.belspo.be
EUREKA	European Research and Coordination Agency. A French initiative for non-military industrial research in advanced technology in Europe (1985-) Secretariat: ave des Arts 19H, Boîte 5, B-1000 Brussels, Belgium http://www3.eureka.be
EURENEW	European Sustainable Energy Charter. In a Resolution of 18 June 1998, the EP called for a charter on RES to be drawn up (OJ C210/98)
EURES	EURopean Employment Services. Council Decision 93/569/EEC on European Employment Services. A network to liaise the public employment services of the Member States to exchange data relating to employment opportunities (OJ L274/93). *Previously* SEDOC http://europa.eu.int/jobs/eures http://europa.eu.int/comm/dg05/elm/eures/en/index_en.htm
EURESCO	European Research Conferences. This programme is co-sponsored by the European Science Foundation and the Euroconferences activity of the EU http://www.esf.org/euresco/active_c.htm
EURESPOIR	*See* EUROPE AGAINST CANCER

*EURET	European Research and Technical Development programme in the field of Transport (1990-1993) (OJ L8/91). *Continued as* TRANSPORT
EUREX	EUREKA Research Expert System (EUREKA project)
EURHISTAR	An on-line database of EU historical archives http://www.iue.it
EURILIA	European Initiative in Library and Information in Aerospace (project within Area 5 of the TELEMATIC SYSTEMS programme)
EURISLE	Economic Integration of Islands (RECITE project)
Euristote	On-line directory of University theses and studies on research into European integration http://europa.eu.int/ecsa/eurist.html
EUR-Lex	European Commission web service giving free search access to EU legislation and case law with full text access to the OJ 'C' and 'L' for 45 days after publication Available on CD-ROM from EUR-OP or on the Internet http://europa.eu.int/eur-lex
EURO	EU currency from 1 January 1999 which replaces the ECU. Reg 974/98 on the introduction of the Euro (OJ L139/98). *See also* EMS; STABILITY PACT http://europa.eu.int/euro/html/home5.html?lang=5
EURO	Statistics for the EU from quarterly national statistics. A statistical domain on the NEW CRONOS databank
Euro-11	The eleven EU Member States which are members of the EMU (Austria; Belgium; Finland; France; Germany; Ireland; Italy; Luxembourg; Netherlands; Portugal; Spain). *Also known as* Euroland; Eurozone

EURO<26 card	A European youth card giving access to discounts, services and information throughout Europe to promote youth mobility and access to culture and information. *See also* EYCA
EuroACE	European Association for the Conservation of Energy Prins Boudewijnlaan 41, B-2650 Edegem, Belgium
EURO-AIM	European Organisation for an Audiovisual Independent Market rue Stévin 112, B-1000 Brussels, Belgium
EUROAIRNET	European Air Quality Monitoring Network which is currently being established under the coordination of the ETC/AQ
EUROBAROMETER	A periodical publication issued by EUR-OP which gives the results of opinion polls on EU issues http://europa.eu.int/comm/dg10/epo/eb.html
*EUROBASES	Former database distribution service of the European Commission operated by EUR-OP
EUROBIO	Group of EUREKA projects
EUROBORDER	The port as a hub in the intermodal transport chain (TRANSPORT project)
EUROBOT	Group of EUREKA projects
EUROCARE	Group of EUREKA projects
EUROCASE	European Case initiative (EUREKA project)
EUROCAT	A co-produced CD-ROM containing records from CATDIFF and selections from the CELEX database Available from: CHADWYCK-HEALEY; ELLIS and EUR-OP
EUROCAT	European Registration of Congenital Anomalies http://www.iph.fgov.be/eurocat/
EUROCERAM	Ceramics Industry regions (RECITE project)

EUROCHAMBRES	Association of European Chambers of Commerce and Industry rue d'Archimède 5, Boîte 4, B-1000 Brussels, Belgium http://www.eurochambres.be
EUROCHEMOMETRICS	Chemometrics and qualimetrics for the chemical, pharmaceutical and agro-alimentary industry (COMETT project)
EUROCIEL	Observatory networks comprising wide-field visible and infra-red sensing instruments (EUREKA project)
EUROCIM	Flexible automated factory for electronic cards, including preparation of circuits and quality control of products (EUREKA project)
EUROCITIES	European Association of Metropolitan Cities. A network set up in 1986 to bring together major municipal authorities in Europe to share ideas and resources bd de Waterloo 27, B-1000 Brussels, Belgium http://www.edc.eu.int/eurocities
EUROCODES	Reference documents for the preparation of product standards in the construction field
EUROCOM	Group of EUREKA projects
EUROCOMP	EUROpean structural polymeric COMPosites group (EUREKA project)
EUROCONTROL	European Organisation for the Safety of Air Navigation. *See also* ADEXP; OLDI rue de la Fusée 96, B-1130 Brussels, Belgium http://www.eurocontrol.be
EURO COOP	European Community of Consumer Cooperatives rue Archimède 17, Boîte 2, B-1000 Brussels, Belgium
EUROCORPS	European army operational from October 1993 which was set up in Strasbourg as a first step towards the creation of a European army

EUROCOTON	Committee of the Cotton and Allied Textile Industries of the EEC rue Montoyer 24, B-1000 Brussels, Belgium
EUROCOUNSEL	Action research programme focusing on ways to improve guidance and employment counselling services for the long term unemployed (an EFILWC programme)
*EUROCRON	A EUROSTAT databank containing general economic statistics (EUROSTATISTICS), some regional data (REGIOSTAT) and some farm structure survey information
Eurodac	A system for fingerprinting asylum applicants (COM(99) 260)
EURODELPHES	Device for Electronic Learning and Pedagogy of History in European Schools (EMTF project)
EURODEMO	EUROpean telematics DEMOnstration centre (a Telematics for Research project within the TELEMATICS APPLICATIONS programme)
EURODESK	A European network for the dissemination of EU information to young people and those who work with them. Set up within the framework of the YOUTH FOR EUROPE programme Eurodesk Brussels Link: Scotland House, Rond-Point Schuman 6, B-1040, Brussels, Belgium UK contact: Youth Exchange Centre, British Council, 10 Spring Gdns, London SW1A 2BN http://www.eurodesk.org
EURODICAUTOM	On-line terminology databank of the EU http://eurodic.ip.lu
EURO DISC Directive	*See* EUROVIGNETTE Directive
EURODOC	An electronic discussion group of DEPs and EDCs Contact: eurodoc.request@mailbase.ac.uk
EURODYN	High technology gas turbine engine demonstrator programme (EUREKA project)

EUROEDUCA	Group of EUREKA projects
EUROENERGY	Group of EUREKA projects
EUROENVIRON	Group of EUREKA projects
EUROFAN	EUROpean network for the Functional ANalysis of yeast genes discovered by systematic sequencing (BIOTECH project)
EUROFAR	Group of EUREKA projects
EUROFARM	A database on the structure of agricultural holdings developed by EUROSTAT Magnetic tapes, diskettes and CD-ROM available from EUROSTAT
EUROFARM	Structure of agricultural holdings statistical domain on the NEW CRONOS databank (a summary of the EUROFARM database)
EUROFER	European Confederation of Iron and Steel Industries rue du Noyer 211, B-1030 Brussels, Belgium
EUROFILE	European legislation and standards service which combines SEM legislation and British Standards Institution transpositions of CEN/CENELEC standards and pre-standards CD-ROM available from TECHNICAL INDEXES
Eurofinas	European Federation of Finance House Associations ave de Tervuren 267, B-1150 Brussels, Belgium
EUROFLUX	The study of exchanges of carbon dioxide, water and energy in 17 forests throughout Europe (ENVIRONMENT AND CLIMATE project)
EUROFOR	Automation and computerisation of a drilling apparatus for the petroleum industry (EUREKA project)

*EUROFORM	The improvement of employment opportunities and new qualifications through vocational training and employment. A STRUCTURAL FUNDS Initiative (1990-1993) (Guidelines in OJ C327/90). *Continued under* EMPLOYMENT
EUROFRET	European system for international road Freight Transport operation (DRIVE project)
EUROGAME	EUROpean regions Game (EMTF project)
EUROGATHERER	Personalised information Gathering system (a Telematics Information Engineering project within the TELEMATICS APPLICATIONS programme)
EUROGI	European Umbrella Organisation for Geographic Information ave Blaise Pascal 6-8, Cité Descartes, Champs-sur-Marne, F-77455 Marne-la-vallée Cedex 2, France http://www.eurogi.org
Eurogroup	Informal group within the North Atlantic Treaty Organisation consisting of European Defence Ministers
EUROGUICHET	European Consumer Information Centre. *See also* RELAYS
EUROHELP	Intelligent help for information systems users (ESPRIT project)
EUROHOT	Design, development, evaluation and dissemination of an open, flexible, distance learning scheme...for the European highway construction and maintenance industry (COMETT project)
EUROINFOCENTRE	*See* EIC
EURO INFO POINT	*See* EIP
EURO-JUS	A service of practical information provided by a lawyer through European Commission Representation offices in the Member States UK Contact: The AIRE Centre

EUR OK	Slogan of a Northern Ireland initiative to give a new image to Europe in Northern Ireland
EUROKOM	Electronic mail and computer conferencing service established in 1983 as an ESPRIT project EUROKOM, Dale House, 30 Dale Rd, Stillorgan, Co Dublin, Ireland http://www.eurokom.ie/
Euroland	*See* Euro-11
EUROLASER	Group of EUREKA projects
EUROLAW	An electronic database of European law Access on CD-ROM or Internet from ILI: http://www.ili.co.uk (subscription required)
EUROLEADERS	Training programme for young European entrepreneurs to study the management implications of the SEM European Business and Innovation Centre Network, A.S.B.L., ave de Tervuren 188A, B-1150 Brussels, Belgium
EUROLIB	European Community and Associated Institutions Library Cooperative Group http://europa.eu.int/comm/dg10/libraries/eurolib/basic_en.htm
EUROLIB-PER	An on-line database of periodicals in the libraries of the EUROLIB group
EUROLIBRARIES	*See* PIR
EUROLILIA	European Initiative in Library and Information in Aerospace (TELEMATICS APPLICATIONS project)
EUROLIST Directive	Dir 80/390/EEC on the drawing up, scrutiny and distribution of the listing particulars to be published for the admission of securities to official stock exchange listings (OJ L100/80 with latest amendment in OJ L135/94)

EUROLITH	New protective coatings for the protection of marbles and carbonate stones of ancient monuments and statues (EUREKA project)
EUROMAISERS	Maize Industry Association Group of the EEC countries ave des Gaulois 9, B-1040 Brussels, Belgium
Euromanagement	A pilot action of standardisation, certification, quality and safety: measures to provide advisory services to SMEs in the SEM Contact: Enterprise DG of the European Commission
EUROMAR	Group of EUREKA projets
EUROMARFOR	*See* EUROFOR
EUROMART	*European Cooperative Measures for Aeronautical Research and Technology.* A report on the European aeronautical industry requested by the Commission and published in November 1988
EUROMAT	Group of EUREKA projects
EUROMATERIAUX	A university/enterprise network for materials set up in 1988 under the COMETT programme
EUROMATH	Communications software between mathematicians (SCIENCE project)
EUROMATIC	Group of EUREKA projects
EUROMECUM	An information package containing data on European Higher Education and Research Institutions Available in looseleaf format or CD-ROM from RAABE-FACHUERLAG

EUROMED	Euro-Mediterranean Partnership. Established by the Conference of Foreign Ministers held in Barcelona in November 1995. It is a joint initiative by the 27 Partners on both sides of the Mediterranean: the 15 member States of the EU plus Algeria, Cyprus, Egypt, Israel, Jordan, Lebanon, Malta, Morocco, Syria, Tunisia, Turkey and the Palestinian territories. Financed under the MEDA programme. *See also* EUROMED HERITAGE http://www.euromed.net/
EUROMED	Standards for processing and visualising medical images (ISIS bioinformatics project) http://narcisus.esd.ece.ntua.gr/~www/euromed.html
EUROMED HERITAGE	Regional programme for a EURO-MEDiterranean cultural HERITAGE. Financed under the MEDA programme. *See also* EUROMED
EUROMET	EUROpean Meteorological Education and Training (a Telematics for Education and Training project within the TELEMATICS APPLICATIONS programme)
EURO-METHWORK	Forum of exchange of expertise between providers of methadone in European countries. Part of the five-year Community programme for the prevention of drug dependence (1996-2000)
EUROMOD	An integrated European benefit-tax Model (TSER project)
EUROMODEL	Hydrodynamic Modelling of the Western Mediterranean (MAST project)
EUROMOTOR	Training modules for innovation in motor vehicle design and manufacture (COMETT project)
EURONAID	A food aid and food security network created by 24 European NGOs

EURONETT	Evaluating User Reaction On New European Transport Technologies (DRIVE project)
EURONICE	Database for the translation of descriptions of goods and services into eleven languages (OHIM project) http://oami.eu.int/en/marque/euronice.htm
EURONORM	Basic European Standard, published by CEN and CENELEC
EUR-OP	Office for Official Publications of the European Communities rue Mercier 2, L-2985 Luxembourg http://europa.eu.int/
EUROPA	Main public-access European Commission Internet information site. *See also* EUROPAplus; EuropaTEAM http://europa.eu.int
EUROPA CAMPUS	A Commission website of information on education and training in the EU http://europa.eu.int/campus
EUROPAGATE	European SR-Z39.50 Gateway (project within Area 5 of the TELEMATIC SYSTEMS programme)
EUROPAplus	European Commission internal website which is only available to staff of the European Commission. It consists of EUROPA, plus internal Commission information. *See also* EuropaTEAM
EUROPARI	Group of EUREKA projects
EUROPARL	Main EP Internet information site. *Previously* EPADES http://www.europarl.eu.int
EUROPARTENARIAT	An EU initiative to stimulate and create cooperation and partnership agreements between companies in the Member States. Held in different locations each year

Europass	Council Decision 99/51/EC on the promotion of European pathways in work-linked training, including apprenticeship (OJ L17/99) http://europa.eu.int/en/comm/dg22/europass/index-en.html
EuropaTEAM	An internal European Commission website which is available to all the EU Institutions and which consists of selected information from EUROPAplus
EUROPATH	EUROpean PATHology assisted by Telematics for health (a Telematics for Healthcare project within the TELEMATICS APPLICATIONS programme)
EUROPE 2000	Document on land use and physical planning (COM(91) 452). *See also* EUROPE 2000+
EUROPE 2000+	*Europe 2000+: cooperation for European territorial development*. Published in 1994 by EUR-OP. This publication continues the EUROPE 2000 theme
EUROPE AGAINST AIDS	Council and EP Decision 647/96/EC for a programme of action on the prevention of AIDS (1996-2000) (OJ L95/96)
EUROPE AGAINST CANCER	Council Decision 646/96/EC for a programme of action against cancer (1996-2000) (OJ L95/96). *Previously* EURESPOIR
EUROPEAN COAL AND STEEL COMMUNITY TREATY	*See* PARIS TREATY
EUROPEAN CONFIDENCE PACT	Launched in June 1996 by Jacques Santer to create jobs. It is centred around 4 pillars: macro-economic policy; the single market; employment systems and structural polices (COM(96) 507)

EUROPEAN COUNCIL	Meetings of Heads of State which usually take place twice yearly at the end of the rotating 6-month Presidency of each Member State
European Digital Cities	The provision of an open cooperation network for a concerted urban development through Telematics (a Telematics for Urban and Rural Areas project within the TELEMATICS APPLICATIONS programme)
EUROPEAN DOCUMENTATION	A series of information pamphlets issued by EUR-OP and partly replaced by the more substantial booklets in the EUROPE ON THE MOVE SERIES
EUROPEAN ENERGY CHARTER TREATY	Council Decision 94/998/EC to join Western technology and capital with resources in Eastern Europe (OJ L380/94). The Treaty entered into force in 1998 http://www.encharter.org
European Fast-Stream	A scheme to encourage recruitment into the EU from the British civil service
EUROPEAN OMBUDSMAN	*See* OMBUDSMAN
EUROPEAN RELAYS	*See* RELAYS
EUROPEAN SUMMIT	Meetings of the Heads of government in the EU Member States (known as the European Council)
EUROPEAN UNION	*See* EU
EUROPEAN UPDATE	A database produced by Deloitte Touche Europe Services which gives a series of reports to provide an in-depth analysis of EU policy areas in the business sector Access via DATASTAR; THOMSON FINANCIAL SERVICES; WESTLAW Available on CD-ROM (which includes DTI SPEARHEAD and INFO 92) from CONTEXT

European Voluntary Service	*See* EVS
European Youth Forum	An organisation representing young people rue Joseph II 129, B-1040 Brussels, Belgium
EUROPECHE	Association of National Organisations of Fishing Enterprises of the EEC rue de la Science 23-25, Boîte 15, B-1040 Brussels, Belgium
Europe Direct	An information service set up by the Commission in 1996 to answer enquiries about the EU http://europa.eu.int/europedirect Freephone in the UK: 0800 581 591
EUROPE MMM	Remote and On-line Publication of Multimedia (a Telematics Information Engineering project within the TELEMATICS APPLICATIONS programme)
EUROPEN	*See* EUNET
EUROPE ON THE MOVE	A series of information pamphlets issued by EUR-OP which began in 1991
Europe's 500	A programme launched by EFER to promote entrepreneurship in the EU
EUROPIC	EUROpean development of Post-secondary training of students and trainers in Integrated Circuit fabrication techniques (COMETT project)
EUROPICON	EUROpean Process Intelligent CONtrol (EUREKA project)
EUROPINION	Contains results of the CTS (European Continuous Tracking Survey) http://europa.eu.int
EUROPMI	European Committee for Small and Medium-Sized Independent Companies. Merged Secretariats with UEAPME in 1997 rue de Toulouse 43, Boîte J-E2, App J, B-1040 Brussels, Belgium

EUROPOL	European Police Office. *See also* EDU; EUROPOL CONVENTION
	Radweg 47, NL-2509 The Hague, Netherlands
	http://www.europol.eu.int/home2.htm

| EUROPOL CONVENTION | The Convention setting up EUROPOL (OJ C316/95) |

| EUROPOLIS | New intelligent control systems to aid urban and inter-urban traffic and advanced metropolitan information control and monitoring (EUREKA project) |

| EUROPROMS | EUROSTAT database for comparing European production and market statistics |
| | Access on-line via NEW CRONOS and CD-ROM from EUROSTAT |

| EUROQUALIFICATION | A joint initiative to establish a permanent partnership of training organisations in the Member States (1989-) |
| | Permanent Transnational Technical Assistance Team, rue Duquesnoy 38, Boîte 13, B-1000 Brussels, Belgium |

| Euroquest | An information system on sources of European finance produced by EBN |
| | http://www.citizen.be/euroquest |

EUROREF	A database containing SCAD, EU Documents and European legal literature
	Access via ELLIS
	http://www.epms.nl/ellis

| EUROROUTES | Road routes designated by the ECE |

| EUROS | EC shipping register (OJ C19/92) |

| EUROSCOLA | Programme of meetings between sixth-form classes from Community countries. An EP initiative |

| EUROSIDA | A BIOMED study to assess the impact of antiretroviral drugs on the outcome of the general population of HIV-infected patients living in Europe |
| | http://inet.uni2.dk/home/chip/eurosidaindex.htm |

| EUROSILVA | Cooperation on tree physiology research (EUREKA project) |

EUROSSAM	EUROpean SAlt Marshes modelling (ELOISE project)
EUROSTARS	System for the thematic analysis of remote sensed data (EUREKA project)
EUROSTAT	Statistical support service for the EU. EUROSTAT collects statistics from each Member State government and presents them in a consolidated, harmonised format. *Previously* known as SOEC Jean Monnet Building, rue Alcide de Gasperi, L-2920 Luxembourg. http://europa.eu.int/eurostat.html
EUROSTATISTICS	Paper copy of the main economic and social statistics domains published monthly by EUROSTAT and also loaded on the NEW CRONOS databank
EUROSTATUS	Main indicators statistical domain on the NEW CRONOS databank
EUROSTEP	European Association of Satellites in Training Education Programmes (DELTA project)
EUROSYNET	Cooperation in public procurement and promotion of SMEs (RECITE project)
EUROTALK	An electronic discussion group for EU information professionals Contact: The Manager, EIA
Euro-TAP-Viet	A technical assistance programme to assist Vietnam towards a market economy
EuroTechAlert	European Information Service for the Results of Public Research. Set up under the SPRINT programme

Eurotech Capital	European Technology Private Capital. A financial device for SMEs to promote THTPs (OJ C192/89). *See also* INNVEST Contact: European Commission Enterprise DG, Bâtiment Wagner, L-2920 Luxembourg UK contacts: Biotechnology Investments Ltd, Five Arrows House, St Swithin's Lane, London EC4N 8NR and Alta Berkeley Associates, 9-10 Savile Row, London W1X 1AF
*EUROTECNET II	European Technical Network: Community action programme in the field of vocational training and technological change (1990-1994) (OJ L393/89). *Continued as* part of the LEONARDO DA VINCI programme
EUROTEXT	A web-based teaching and learning resource of key EU documents. A joint project of the Universities of Hull and Ulster http://eurotext.ulst.ac.uk
EUROTOLL	EUROpean project for TOLL effects and pricing strategies (TRANSPORT project)
EUROTOPP	European Transport Planning Process (DRIVE project)
EUROTRA	Council Decision 90/664/EEC for a European Translation System of advanced design (1990-1992) (OJ L358/90)
EUROTRAC	European experiment on transport and transformation of environmentally relevant trace constituents in the troposphere over Europe (EUREKA project)
EUROTRANS	Group of EUREKA projects
EURO-TRIANGLE	Transl/retrieval-oriented information base adapting data from 'native speaking' grammmatical/lexicograph (EUREKA project)
EUROTRIP	European Trip planning system (DRIVE project)

EUROTUNNEL	Standardised segmental lining for fully mechanised continuous tunnel operation with new waterstop system (EUREKA project)
EURO UNITS	A UK national network to support practitioners in education and training to deliver the European curriculum and develop projects in the EU. *See also* RELAYS Contacts: http://www.cec.org.UK/relays.educ.htm
Euro Velo	A network of 12 trans-European cycle routes promoted by the ECF with the help of the EU
EURO VIEW	Pilot directory service for European telematics applications (a Telematics for Administrations project within the TELEMATICS APPLICATIONS programme)
EUROVIGNETTE Directive	Directive 93/89/EEC relating to the charges paid by Heavy Goods Vehicles for using road networks (OJ L279/93). Annulled by the ECJ in 1995 but in force until a new Proposed Directive is in place (OJ C59/97)
EUROVISE	European Vision System Economic (EUREKA project)
EUROVOC	*Multilingual thesaurus of standardised terms for indexing documents held by the EU Institutions.* 3rd ed published as a Annex to the OJ in 3 vols in 1995 Also available on CD-ROM from EUR-OP
EURO-WATERNET	A water resources information and monitoring network for Europe, designed and tested by the ETC/IW
Eurozone	*See* Euro-11
EURYCLEE	Network of national information centres specialising in new information technologies and education in the Member States Contact: European Commission Education and Culture DG

EURYDICE

Education Information Network in the European Community. *Continued as* part of the SOCRATES programme
EURYDICE European Unit, rue d'Arlon 15, B-1050 Brussels, Belgium
UK contact: National Foundation for Educational Research, The Mere, Upton Park, Slough, Berkshire SL1 2DQ
http://europa.eu.int/en/comm/dg22/euryen.html

EU-SEASED

Internet database of seafloor samples held at European research institutions (product of a MAST III project)
http://www.eu-seased.net/

EUSIDIC

European Association of Information Services
c/o Instant Library Recruitment, 104b St John St, London EC1M 4EH, United Kingdom

EUSIS

European Soil Information System (ESB project)

EUSTAT

Empowering USers Through Assistive Technology (a Telematics for Disabled and Elderly People project within the TELEMATICS APPLICATIONS programme)

EUVAS

Environmental UltraViolet Action Spectroscopy (an Environmental and Chemical Safety Research project within the ENVIRONMENT AND CLIMATE programme)

EUW

European Union of Women
c/o The Auklands, Gloucester Road, Thornbury, Bristol BS12 1JH, United Kingdom

EVA

Evaluation Process for Road Transport Informatics (DRIVE project)

EVALUE

EVALuation and self-evaluation of Universities in Europe (TSER project)

EVCA

European Venture Capital Association
Keibergpark Minervastraat 6, Boîte 6, B-1930 Zaventem, Belgium
http://www.evca.com/

EVE	Environmental Valuation in Europe (within the ENVIRONMENT AND CLIMATE programme)
EVE	Espace Video Européen (MEDIA project) Contact: Irish Film Institute, 6 Eustace St, Dublin 2, Eire
EVENET	EuroVillage on the European information infrastructure (a Telematics for Urban and Rural Areas project within the TELEMATICS APPLICATIONS programme)
EVEREST	Three dimensional algorithms for robust and efficient semiconductor simulator (ESPRIT project)
EVIDENT	European Versatility in Deaf Education using New Technologies (EMTF project)
*EVS	European Voluntary Service for young people. An informal education programme providing young people with work opportunities abroad (1998-1999). *Replaced by* YOUTH
EWC	Dir 94/45/EC to set up European Works Councils (OJ L254/94 with latest amendment in OJ L10/98)
EWC	European Waste Catalogue (OJ L5/94)
EWGRB	European Working Group on Research and Biodiversity (within the ENVIRONMENT AND CLIMATE programme)
E-Windows	*See* EnviroWindows
EWL	European Women's Lobby rue du Méridien 22, B-1210 Brussels, Belgium http://www.womenlobby.org/
EWON	European Network on Work Organisation. Set up by the Commission to support and speed up the modernisation process in EU enterprises http://europa.int/comm/dg05/soc-dial/workorg/news/workorg_en.htm

EWS	EuroWorkStation (ESPRIT project)
EXCISE	Excise Control. Automation of access to SEED (System for Exchange of Excise Data) (IDA project)
EXCLUSION I	*See* POVERTY 4
EXE	Extranet Education (EMTF project)
EXLIB	Expansion of European systems for the visually disadvantaged (project within Area 5 of the TELEMATIC SYSTEMS programme)
EXMAN	Experimental Manipulations of forest ecosystems in Europe (STEP project)
EXPERTS	EDI/XML (Extensible Markup Language) Procurement Enabling Real Trade Standards (ISIS Electronic Commerce project) http://www.ispo.cec.be/isis/98expert.htm
*EXPLOSIVE ATMOSPHERES' Directives	Dirs 76/117/EEC and 79/196/EEC on electrical equipment for use in potentially explosive atmospheres (OJ L24/76; OJ L43/79). *Replaced by* ATEX Directive
EXPOLIS	Air pollution exposure distribution of adult urban population in Europe (an Environmental Health and Chemical Safety Research project within the ENVIRONMENT AND CLIMATE programme)
EXPROM	Promotion of Community Exports to Japan. *See also* ETP Contact: European Commission Trade DG
EXTENSIFICATION	A policy of farming less intensively in order to balance lower output by savings in expenditure on feedingstuffs, fertilisers and pesticides
EXTRA2	Euromethodologies X TRavel Assessment to assess European travel behaviour (a TRANSPORT project)

EXTRACOM	Telematics in foreign trade statistics (IDA project)
EXTRAMINT	EXTRAnet, Multicast INTranet (a Telematics Information Engineering project within the TELEMATICS APPLICATIONS programme)
EXVOC	EXpert system contribution to VOCational training (DELTA project)
EYCA	European Youth Card Association. *See also* EURO<26 card Weteringschans 53, NL-1017 RW Amsterdam, Netherlands http://www.eyca.org
*EYE	European Year of the Environment (1987-1988) (OJ C63/86)
EYE	European Youth Exchange network Tiefendorfergasse 11/32, A-1140 Vienna, Austria
*EYLL	European Year of Lifelong Learning (1996). Set up by EP and Council Decision 2493/95/EC (OJ L256/95)
*EYT	European Year of Tourism (1990) (OJ L17/89)
F	France
FABULA	Bilingual multimedia educational material for children (EMTF project)
FAC	Foreign Affairs Council of the European Union
FACE	Federation of Field Sports of the EEC rue F Pelletier 82, B-1030 Brussels, Belgium
FACE	Framework for Academic Cooperation in Europe (ERASMUS project)

FACILE	Support tools for housing design and management, integrated with telematics systems and services (a Telematics for Disabled and Elderly People project within the TELEMATICS APPLICATIONS programme)
FACIT	Fast Automatic Conversion with Integrated Tools (project within Area 5 of the TELEMATIC SYSTEMS programme)
FACT	Feasibility studies for the creation of global cardiovascular multimedia databases (a Telematics for Healthcare project within the TELEMATICS APPLICATIONS programme)
FACT Fund	Created by DG VIII and approved by the CDI in 1996, it aims to support the development of ACP companies
FADN	Farm Accountancy Data Network set up in 1965 (OJ 1859/65)
FAEP	Federation of Associations of Periodical Publishers in the EEC ave de Tervuren 142-144, B-1150 Brussels, Belgium http://www.faep.org
FAIP	Farm Animal INDUSTRIAL PLATFORM http://europa.eu.int/comm/dg12/biotech/ip2.html#FAIP http://www.faip.dk/
*FAIR	Council Decision 94/805/EC for Fisheries, Agriculture and agro-Industrial Research (1994-1998) (OJ L334/94). *Previously* AIR. *See also* LST
FAIR	Forecast and Assessment of socio-economic Impact of advanced communications and Recommendations (part of the ACTS programme) http://www.databank.it/dbc/fair/page04.htm

Falcone	Council Joint Action 98/245/JHA on a programme of exchanges, training and cooperation for persons responsible for action to combat organised crime(1998-2002) (OJ L99/98) http://europa.eu.int/comm/sg/tfjai/project/falcone_en.htm
FAME	Fate and Activity Modelling of Environmental pollutants using structure-activity relationships (an Environmental Health and Chemical Safety Research project within the ENVIRONMENT AND CLIMATE programme)
FAMIMO	Fuzzy Algorithms for the control of Multi-Input, Multi-Output processes (supported by the ESPRIT programme) http://iridia.ulb.ac.be/~famimo/index.html
FAMOS	Group of EUREKA projects
FANS	Finland, Austria, Norway and Sweden
FAOR	Functional Analysis of Office Requirements (ESPRIT project)
FAP	Final Abandonment Premium
*FAP	Forestry Action Programme (within the Renewable Raw Materials programme) (1989-1992) (OJ L359/89). *Continued in* AIR
*FAR	Fisheries and Aquaculture Research (1988-1992) (OJ L314/87). *Continued in* AIR
FARO	Fuel Melting and Release Oven (JRC - reactor safety programme)
FASDE	Future Alarm and awareness Services for the Disabled and Elderly (TIDE project)
*FASE	Committee on Foreign Affairs, Security and Defence policy (of the EP)

FASP	Flexibile Automation in Ship Prefabrication (EUREKA project)
FASS	Fast Ships Safety (TRANSPORT project)
FASSEL	Diagnostic procedure through selective and specific filtration of antigens on labelled antibodies (EUREKA project)
*FAST	Forecasting and Assessment in the Field of Science and Technology (part of the MONITOR programme)
FASTCAT	High speed multilingual computer assisted translation system (EUREKA project)
FASTDOC	Fast Document ordering and document delivery (project within Area 5 of the TELEMATIC SYSTEMS programme)
Fast-Stream	*See* European Fast-Stream
FATHTS	Fatigue-based design rules for the Application of High-Tensile Steels in ships (BRITE/EURAM project)
FAUDIT	EAGGF auditing system (CADDIA project)
FBF	A database of EAGGF budget forecasting (CADDIA project)
FBS	*Family Budget Survey*. The 1988 survey was published for EUROSTAT by EUR-OP in 6 vols 1991-1994, plus *Methodology* in 1993
FCB	Fuel Cell Bus (EUREKA project)
FCPN	Factory Customer Premise Network (ESPRIT project)
FEANTSA	European Federation of National Organisations Working with the Homeless rue Defacqz 1, B-1000 Brussels, Belgium
FED	*See* EDF (European Development Fund)

FEDARENE	European Federation of Regional Energy and Environment Agencies rue du Beau-Site 11, B-1000 Brussels, Belgium
FEDER	*See* ERDF
FEDIOL	EC Seed Crushers' and Oil Processors' Federation ave de Tervuren 168, Boîte 12, B-1150 Brussels, Belgium
Fédolive	Federation of the Olive Oil Industry of the EEC ave Achille Peretti 118, F-92200 Neuilly-sur-Seine, France
FEE	Federation of European Publishers ave de Tervuren 204, B-1150 Brussels, Belgium
FEE	*See* EFA (Federation of European Accountants)
FEEE	Foundation for Environmental Education in Europe Friluftsrådet, Olof Palmes Gade 10, DK-2100 København, Denmark
FEFAF	European Federation of Women Working in the Home ave Père Damien 76, B-1150 Brussels, Belgium
FEIP	Front-end for Echograph Image Processing (AIM project)
FELICITA	Development of FErroelectric LIquid Crystal devices for Information Technology Applications (ESPRIT project)
FEMIRC	*See* IRC
FEMISE	Euro-Mediterranean Forum of Economic Institutes. *See also* EUROMED http://www.euromed.net/information-notes/old/In34e.htm
FEMM	Committee on Women's rights and equal opportunities (of the EP)
FEOGA	*See* EAGGF

FEOPAY	A project to review the payment system for the Guidance section of the EAGGF (CADDIA project)
FEORI	A project to establish a database for aid applications under the Guidance section of the EAGGF (CADDIA project)
FEPF	European Federation of the Industries of Earthenware and China Tableware and Ornamental Ware c/o Ceramie Unie, rue des Colonies 18-24, Boîte 17, B-1000 Brussels, Belgium
FESAT	European Foundation of Drug Help Lines. Part of the five-year EU programme for the prevention of drug dependence (1996-2000) rue Dulong 11, F-75017 Paris, France
FESTIVAL	Functional Electrical Stimulation to Improve Value Ability and Lifestyle (TIDE project)
FFI	Family Farm Income
FIABCI	International Real Estate Federation ave Bosquet 23, F-75007 Paris, France
FIABEX	Expert system for the automatic calculation and presentation of Fault Tree Analysis (EUREKA project)
FICHE D'IMPACT	A brief note attached to an EU proposal for legislation, which indicates the likely effect of that proposal on a small firm or on the environment
FIDE	Formally Integrated Data Environment (ESPRIT project)
FIDES	Fisheries Data Exchange System. The Telematic exchange of catch reports, fleet register data and fishing licences (IDA project)
FIDESY	Fire Detection System based on intelligent processing of infrared and visible images (EUREKA project)

FIELDBUS	Communications architecture based on local area networks for real time control of industrial processes and machines (EUREKA project)
FIESTA	Facility for the Implementation of Effective Sectoral and Technical Assistance (a Polish programme set up under PHARE)
FIFG	Financial Instrument for Fisheries Guidance (1994-) (Latest Reg 1263/99 in OJ L161/99)
FINATLANTIC	Development of a Risk Capital Fund in the Atlantic region (RECITE project)
FINET, Paul	*See* PAUL FINET FOUNDATION
FINREAD	FINancial transactional IC card READer (ISIS Electronic Commerce project) http://www.ispo.cec.be/isis/98finrea.htm
FIORE	Funding and Investment Objective for Road transport informatics in Europe (DRIVE project)
FIP	Fungal INDUSTRIAL PLATFORM http://europa.eu.int/comm/dg12/biotech/ip2.html#FIP
FIRES	Facility for Investigating Runaway Events Safety (JRC project)
FIRST	Friendly Interactive Robot for Service Tasks (EUREKA project)
FIRST	Fundamentals of Intelligent reliable Robot SysTems (ESPRIT project)
FIRST	Project to merge the Web for Schools project and the EUN (supported by the ESPRIT programme)
FIS	FAST Information System to establish a computer infrastructure for the horizontal utilisation of the AMIS database (CADDIA project)

FISCALIS	EP and Council Decision 888/98/EC for a multiannual programme of Community action to reinforce the functioning of the indirect taxation systems of the INTERNAL MARKET (1998-2002) (OJ L206/98). *Previously* MATTHAEUS TAX
FISH	Annual catches by Fishing zone statistical domain on the NEW CRONOS databank
*FISH	Committee on Fisheries (of the EP). *See* PECH
FISH	Fisheries DG of the European Commission
FIS-IDES	Fast Information System - Interactive Data Exchange System. A telematic application for the management of the CAP (IDA project)
FIT	Finance for Innovative Technology
FITCE	Federation of Telecommunications Engineers in the EC c/o Belgacom, Tour TBR, bd E Jacqmain 166, B-1210 Brussels, Belgium
FIWG	Financial Issues Working Group. Part of the Electronic Commerce actions of the Information Society DG of the European Commission and the G8-10 pilot project http://www.ispo.cec.be/fiwg/
*FLAIR	Food-linked Agro-Industrial Research (1989-1993) (OJ L200/89). *See also* ECLAIR. *Continued as* AIR
FLEET	Freight and Logisitics Efforts for European Traffic (DRIVE project)
FLEX	FLEXible learning environment experiment (EMTF project)
FLEXPLAN	Knowledge-based planning and control in manufacturing environments (ESPRIT project)

FLUIDS	Future Lines of User Interface Decision Support (a Telematics Engineering project within the TELEMATICS APPLICATIONS programme)
FLUSTRIN	FLUid STRucture INteraction (EUREKA project)
FNVA	Farm Net Value-Added
Fob	Friends of Bruges. A group which was formed after Mrs Thatcher's speech in Bruges in September 1988 Chairman: Mr W Cash MP, c/o House of Commons, Westminster, London SW1, United Kingdom
FOCUS	Front-ends for Open and Closed User Systems (ESPRIT project)
FOD	French Overseas Departments
FOF	Towards an integrated theory for design, production and production management of complex, one of a kind products in the factory of the future (ESPRIT project)
FOOTBRIDGE	*See* PASSERELLE
FOPS	Falling-Object Protective Structures relating to wheeled agricultural or forestry tractors
FORATOM	European Atomic Forum rue Belliard 15-17, 8e étage, B-1040 Brussels, Belgium http://www.foratom.org
*FORCE	Formation Continue en Europe (Development of continuing vocational training in the EC) (1990-1993) (OJ L156/90). *Continued as* part of the LEONARDO DA VINCI programme
FORES	Forestry statistical domain on the NEW CRONOS databank

*FOREST	Forestry sector research and technology (Subprogramme of the Raw Materials and Recycling programme) (1990-1992) (OJ L359/89). *Continued as* AIR
Forest Trees	The study of genetic diversity in forest species (a BIOTECH project)
FORFUN	Formal description of arbitrary systems by means of functional languages (ESPRIT project)
FORMAST	FORmal Methods for Asynchronous System Technology (ESPRIT project)
FORMENTOR	Expert system for dealing with major plant failures and security control (EUREKA project)
FOR-ME-TOO	Formalisms, Methods and Tools (ESPRIT project)
FORMEX	*Formalised Exchange of Electronic Publications.* An OOPEC programme to store multi-lingual publications in machine-readable format. Details published by OOPEC in 1984
FORTUNE	FORum of user-organisations Training for Usability and Networking in Europe (a Telematics for Disabled and Elderly People project within the TELEMATICS APPLICATIONS programme)
FORTY EIGHT HOUR Directive	*See* WORKING TIME Directive
FORUM	EU Publishers' Forum http://eur_op.eu.index.htm
FORUM	A pan-European network for language courses (a Telematics for Education and Training project within the TELEMATICS APPLICATIONS programme)
FOURCOM	Network for information exchange on competition policy (IDA project)

FOUR FREEDOMS	*See* FREE MOVEMENT
FOWM	Fibre Optic Well Monitoring system (EUREKA project)
FP	Flash Profile (within BC-NET)
FP	*See* FRAMEWORK PROGRAMME
FP5	Fifth RTD FRAMEWORK PROGRAMME consisting of HORIZONTAL and THEMATIC PROGRAMMES and the Fifth (EURATOM) FRAMEWORK PROGRAMME for the nuclear sector (1998-2002) (OJ L26/99). *See* EESD; GROWTH; IMPROVING; INCO II; INNOVATION/SMEs; IST; QUALITY http://cordis.lu/fp5/home.html http://europa.eu.int/comm/dg12/fp5.html
FR	French
FRAMES	European agreement on the radio access system for third generation multi-media mobile communications (ACTS project)
FRAMEWORK PROGRAMME	A broad EU programme from which further specific programmes will emerge, for example FP5
FRCC	Fast Reactors Coordinating Committee
FREE MOVEMENT	The four 'freedoms' on which the SEM is based are to be found in the *Consolidated version of the Treaty establishing the EC*. Goods, Title I; Persons, services and capital, Title III; plus the addition of visas, asylum, immigration and other relevant policies, Title IV. *See also* HLP
Free Mover	Student who does not participate in an ICP of the ERASMUS and SOCRATES programmes, but who may apply for a grant under the programme
FRESCO REPORT	on the general considerations of the problems of Enlargement. Published in the *Bulletin of the EC Supplement 1/78*

FRIDA	FRamework for Integrated Dynamic Analysis of travel and traffic (DRIVE project)
FRIENDS	Farming and Rural Information, Expertise and News Dissemination Service (a Telematics for Urban and Rural Areas project within the TELEMATICS APPLICATIONS programme)
FRSWG	Fast Reactor Safety Working Group
FRUCTUS	Orchards statistical domain on the NEW CRONOS databank
FSA-HSC	Formal Safety Assessment of High-Speed Craft. Project in the field of design, production and operation for safer, more efficient, environmentally friendly and user-friendly ships (coordinated by NETS)
FSE	*See* ESF (European Social Fund)
FSGP	Financial Services Policy Group of personal representatives of EU Finance Ministers
FSSRS	*See* EUROFARM
FSU	Forward Studies Unit. A Commission unit which was set up in 1989 to monitor and evaluate European integration http://www.europa.eu.int/comm/cdp/index_en.htm
FTSC	Fusion Technology Steering Committee
FUNCODE	Coding, service and interoperability for high-quality vidcotelephones and high-definition television (RACE project)
FURS	Functional Urban Regions
FUSION	Council Decision 1999/175/Euratom adopting a KEY ACTION RTD programme in the field of nuclear energy (1998-2002) (OJ L64/99) http://europa.eu.int/comm/dg12/fusion1.html

FVA	Food and Veterinary Agency. An amalgamation of the FVO and OVPIC Belfield Office Park, Beech Hill Road, IRL-Dublin 4, Eire http://europa.eu.int/comm/dg24/
FVO	Food and Veterinary Office. *See* FVA
FWP	*See* FRAMEWORK PROGRAMME
FYROM	Former Yugoslav Republic of Macedonia
G	Greece
G7 GLOPHIN	GLObal Public Health Information Network feasibility study/accompanying measure (a Telematics for Healthcare project within the TELEMATICS APPLICATIONS programme)
GAC	General Advisory Committee of the JRC
*GAEIB	Group of Advisers on the Ethical Implications of Biotechnology. *Replaced by* EGE
GAG	General Affairs Group of the Council of the European Union
GALA	Global Access to Local Applications and services (a Telematics for Integrated Applications for Digital Sites project within the TELEMATICS APPLICATIONS programme)
GALENO 2000	Development of automatic non-invasive medical diagnostic equipment based on new sensors and AI (EUREKA project)
GALILEO	Satellite navigation technology project (a project within the GNSS programme)
GAMES	General Architecture for Medical Expert Systems (AIM project)

GAMMA-EC	Gaming And MultiMedia Applications for Environmental Crisis management training (EMTF project)
GAP	Analysis and Forecasting Group. A sub-group of SOG-T
GASTER	Gastrointestinal endoscopy applications for standards in telecommunications and research (a Telematics for Healthcare project within the TELEMATICS APPLICATIONS programme)
GATS	General Agreement on Trade in Services
*GATT	General Agreement on Tariffs and Trade (1948-1994). *See* WTO
GAUCHO	General distributed Architecture for Unified Communication in Heterogeneous OSI-Environments (ESPRIT project)
GCAC	General Concerted Action Committee
GEEL	JRC establishment Steenweg op Retie, B-2440 Geel, Belgium
GEIE	*See* EEIG
GELOS	Global Environmental Information Locator Service http://www.eea.eu.int/frdb.htm
GEMET	GEneral Multilingual Environmental Thesaurus developed by ETC/CDS http://www.mu.niedersachsen.de/cds/etc-cds_neu/software.html#GEMET
GEN	Global European Network agreement for digital telecommunication links between the Member States
GENEDIS	Real-time generation of the 2.5D sketch for moving scenes (ESPRIT project)
GENELEX	Generic Lexicon (EUREKA project)

GENESIS	Development of distributed memory MIMD system for very high performance numerical computing (ESPRIT project)
GENESIS	A General Environment for Formal Systems Development (ESPRIT project)
GENIS	Standardisation Support for GEN (an Electronic Commerce project within ISIS) http://www.ispo.cec.be/isis/98genis.htm
GENIUS ZEUS	Integrated system to promote advanced tourist services in Europe (a Telematics for Urban and Rural Areas project within the TELEMATICS APPLICATIONS programme)
GEO	Application of robotics to the construction industry to eliminate laborious and dangerous tasks as well as improving productivity (EUREKA project)
GEOMED	GEOgraphical MEDiation System (a Telematics Information Engineering project within the TELEMATICS APPLICATIONS programme)
GEONOM	Geonomenclature. Country nomenclature for external trade statistics. The latest separate vol was published by EUR-OP for EUROSTAT in the trade statistics theme in 1998
GEOSERVE	GEO-data access SERVicEs (a Telematics for Administrations project within the TELEMATICS APPLICATIONS programme)
GEOSTAR	Geophysical and Oceanographic STation for Abyssal Research. A deep sea observatory (MAST III project)
GEOTEL	Application pilot in the petroleum and chemicals industry (RACE project)
GESMES	Generic Statistical Message: an Edifact message

GETS	Global Emergency Telemedicine Service (a Telematics for Healthcare project within the TELEMATICS APPLICATIONS programme)
GFCF	Gross Fixed Capital Formation
GIDS	Generic Intelligent Driver Support system (DRIVE project)
GINGER 2000	Improvement of communications between European public engineering works sites... (EUREKA project)
GIPE	Generation of Interactive Programming Environments (ESPRIT project)
GIRP	International Group for Pharmaceutical Distribution in Europe PO Box 170326, D-60075 Frankfurt am Main, Germany
GISCO	Geographic Information System of the European Commission (topographical data from EUROSTAT)
GISEDI	Electronic trade for Geographical Information (a Telematics Information Engineering project within the TELEMATICS APPLICATIONS programme)
GISELA	Interservice Group on Enlargement
GLOBAL HORIZON	Feasibility study on the implementation of the European component of the G7 global cancer network sub-project (a Telematics for Healthcare project within the TELEMATICS APPLICATIONS programme)
GLOBE	Global Legislators Organisation for a Balanced Environment. A group of European and American MPs formed to improve the global environment

GLOBIS	GLOBal change and biodiversity In Soils (TERI project)
GLP	Good Laboratory Practice
GMM	Dir 90/219/EEC on the continued use of Genetically Modified Micro-organisms (OJ L117/90) with the latest amendment in OJ L330/98)
GMO	Dir 90/220/EEC on Genetically Modified Organisms released into the environment (OJ L117/90 with the latest adaptation to technical progress in OJ L169/97)
GNP	Gross National Product
GNSS	Global Navigation Satellite Systems. A programme which forms part of the trans-European transport network Contact: European Commission Transport DG
GO EAST/GO WEST	An EP initiative to enable researchers from the West to spend time in CEEC and vice versa (EP Doc A3 174/90)
GOLDPLATING	A term used in the UK to describe the over-zealous interpretation by UK officials of EU legislation
GOV	Government accounts statistical domain on the NEW CRONOS databank
*GPIC	CADDIA Policy Interservice Group
GPPC	General Purpose Portable Communicator (TIDE project)
GPRMC	European Organisation of Reinforced Plastics Associations - Composite Materials c/o Fabrimetal, rue des Drapiers 21, B-1050 Brussels, Belgium
GR	Greek
GRADIENT	GRAphics and knowledge-based DIalogue for dynamic systems (ESPRIT project)

GRAMINAE	Biosphere atmosphere interactions of ammonia with grasslands across Europe (TERI project)
GRASP	Global Retrieval Access and information System for Property items (a Telematics for Administrations project within the TELEMATICS APPLICATIONS programme)
GRASPIN	Personal workstation for incremental Graphic Specialisation and formal Implementation of Non-sequential systems (ESPRIT project)
GRECO	Groupement Européen pour la Circulation des Oeuvres (MEDIA project) Contact: Widenmayerstrasse 32, D-80538 München, Germany
GREEN	General Research on Environment for Eastern European Nations. An EP own-initiative proposal (EP Doc A3 174/90)
GREEN CURRENCY	*See* GREEN RATE
GREEN PAPER	A discussion paper which is widely circulated for comment. *See also* WHITE PAPER http://europa.eu.int/comm/off/green/index_en.htm
GREEN POUND	*See* GREEN RATE
GREEN RATE	The term to denote the system used to convert CAP support prices into national currencies
GREENS/EFA	Greens and European Free Alliance group (of the EP). *Previously* EFA; GREENS; V
GREEN WASTES	*See* WASTES
GRETA	Co-fired green-tape ceramics as a three-dimensional hybrid component (CC-3D) (EUREKA project)

GREY LIST	of dangerous substances discharged into the aquatic environment. Dir 76/464/EEC (OJ L129/76 - List 2). *See also* BLACK LIST
GRIM	Groupe Réglementation, Information et Management set up by DG III of the Commission in 1987 for construction products
GRIP	Greenland Ice Core Project (EPOCH project)
GRIPS	General Relation-based Information Processing Software
GROTIUS	Joint Action 96/636/JHA on training for judges (1996-2000) (OJ L287/96 with latest amendment in OJ C12/99) http://europa.eu.int/comm/sg/tfjai/project/grotius_en.htm
GroupDesk	A CSCW project to provide support for cooperation and awareness in distributed working groups http://orgwis.gmd.de/projects/GroupDesk/
Groupeuro	Network of conference speakers specialising in EMU affairs in the EU
GROUPISOL	Association of the European Manufacturers of Technical Ceramics for Electronic, Electrical, Mechanical and other Applications rue des Colonies 18-24, Boîte 17, B-1000 Brussels, Belgium
GROW	Global Real Order Web (a Telematics for Urban and Rural Areas project within the TELEMATICS APPLICATIONS programme)
GROWTH	Council Decision 1999/169/EC adopting a specific programme for RTD and demonstration on competitive and sustainable growth (1998-2002) (OJ L64/99). One of the THEMATIC PROGRAMMES which form part of FP5. *Previously* BRITE/EURAM III; SMT

GRPDS	Generic Reliability Parameter Data System which forms part of ERDS
GRULA	Group of Latin American countries
GRUNDTVIG	Adult education and lifelong learning programme (within the SOCRATES programme)
GSP	Generalised System of Preferences. Preferential import duties into the EU from Developing countries (Latest in OJ L357/98 which covers July 1999-December 2001)
GUE/NGL	*See* EUL/NGL
GUIB	Textual and Graphical User Interfaces for Blind people (TIDE project)
GUIDE	Telematics applications for education and training documentation GUIDE support (a Telematics for Education and Training project within the TELEMATICS APPLICATIONS programme)
*GUTENBERG	A programme to promote access to books and reading (OJ C183/89 and OJ C160/93)
GVA	Gross Value Added
HAA	Development of Hybrid Antibodies of the Anthracycline group (EUREKA project)
HABITATS Directive	Dir 92/43/EEC on the conservation of natural habitats and of wild fauna and flora (OJ L206/92 with latest adaptation to technical and scientific progress in OJ L305/97). *See also* NATURA 2000
HAE2000	Healthy Ageing Europe INDUSTRIAL PLATFORM http://europa.eu.int/comm/dg12/biotech/ip2.html#HAE
HAGUE REPORT	on the Common Fisheries Policy July 1976. Not published, but Council Resolution published in OJ C105/81

HALIOS	Development of technologies for future fishing vessels (EUREKA project)
HALOMAX	Mid and high latitude stratospheric distribution of long and short lived HALOgen species during the MAXimum chlorine loading (THESEO project)
HAMPIIS	Hearing Aids and Mobile Phones Immunity and Interference Standards (ISIS Multimedia Systems project) http://www.ispo.cec.be/isis/98hampis.htm
*HANDYAIDS	An index of technical aids available in Europe for disabled people. A module of HANDYNET
*HANDYCE	An EU information system for disabled people consisting of HANDYLEX and HANDYCOM. Not developed
*HANDYCOM	Any document of EU origin relating to disabled people which does not appear in HANDYLEX. Not operational
*HANDYLEX	EU and national legislation concerned with the disabled. Not operational
*HANDYNET	An EU information system containing descriptions of technical aids for disabled people set up by Council Decision 89/658 (OJ L393/89). *See also* HANDYAIDS; HANDYTEC; HANDYWHO
*HANDYSEARCH	Index of current research on technical aids for disabled people in the EU. Not operational
*HANDYTEC	An information system on technical aids for the disabled within HANDYNET
*HANDYVOC	A multi-lingual thesaurus on technical aids for the disabled. Not operational
*HANDYWHO	A European index of organisations associated with technical aids for the disabled within HANDYNET

HANSA	Healthcare Advanced Networked System Architecture (a Telematics for Healthcare project within the TELEMATICS APPLICATIONS programme)
HARD	Hardware Resources for Development (CADDIA project)
HARDIE	HARmonisation of Roadside and Driver Information in Europe (DRIVE project)
HARP	An Autonomous speech rehabilitation system for hearing impaired people (TIDE project)
*HASS	Home Accident Surveillance System (1976-1986). *Continued as* EHLASS
HASTE	*Health and Safety in Europe.* A report and off-line database published in 1995 by EFILWC
HATS	Hands Assessment and Treatment System (a Telematics for Disabled and Elderly People project within the TELEMATICS APPLICATIONS programme)
HAWK	Knowledge-based open publication model for intelligent media services (a Telematics Information Engineering project within the TELEMATICS APPLICATIONS programme)
HBS	Household Budgets Survey statistical domain on the NEW CRONOS databank
*HCM	Human Capital and Mobility programme (1990-1994) (OJ L107/92). *Previously* SCIENCE. *Continued as* TMR
HCPI	Harmonised Consumer Price Index which is produced by each Member State (OJ C84/95)

HC-REMA	Health Care REsource MAnagement (a Telematics for Healthcare project within the TELEMATICS APPLICATIONS programme)
HD	A Harmonised Document issued by CEN/CENELEC when details of an EU Standard cannot be agreed
HDG	Horizontal Drugs Group which coordinates the drugs activities of the EU. Set up in 1997 by COREPER
HDTV	Compatible High-Definition Television system (EUREKA project)
HEALTHBENCH	HEALTH information and decision support workBENCH (AIM project)
HEALTHLINE	Securing the success of health telematics projects implementation of the telehealth through information dissemination and training (a Telematics for Healthcare project within the TELEMATICS APPLICATIONS programme) http://www.ehto.org/vds/projects/healthline.html
HEALTHPLANS	A concerted action to support national and regional health authorities in developing plans for the introduction of healthcare telematics (a Telematics for Healthcare project within the TELEMATICS APPLICATIONS programme)
HEALTHWATCH	Healthwatch database (a Telematics for Healthcare project within the TELEMATICS APPLICATIONS programme)
HEARDIP	Hearing Aid Research with Digital Intelligent Processing (TIDE project)
HEART	Horizontal European Activities in Rehabilitation Technology (TIDE project)

HECTOR	Health Emergency management and Coordination through Telematics Operational Resources (a Telematics for Healthcare project within the TELEMATICS APPLICATIONS programme)
HEF	Human Embryo and Foetus group. Working group in the field of Bioethics. *Replaces* ESLA and HER
HELEN	Investigation into Greek language transliteration problems (project within Area 5 of the TELEMATIC SYSTEMS programme)
*HELENA PRIZE	EP prize for women achievers in art; industry and commerce; science and scientific research and for outstanding contributions to public life
HELIOS	Hospital Environment Language within an Information Object System (AIM project)
*HELIOS II	Council Decision 93/136/EEC on Handicapped people in the European Community Living Independently in an Open Society (1993-1996) (OJ L56/93)
HELP'ME	Handicapped Elderly Lonely Person's Multimedia Equipment (TIDE project)
HELSINKI CONVENTION	on the protection of the marine environment of the Baltic Sea area (OJ L73/94)
HEPATITIS C	Development of diagnostic screening and confirmation assays for detection of Hepatitis C virus infection: Cloning (EUREKA project)
*HER	*See* HEF
HERCULE	Application of robotics to the construction industry (EUREKA project)

HEREIN	Heritage Information Network (a Telematics for Administrations project within the TELEMATICS APPLICATIONS programme)
HERITAGE	Historic Environment for Integrated Telematics Application programmes in Europe (a Telematics for Integrated Applications for Digital Sites project within the TELEMATICS APPLICATIONS programme)
HERMES	Harmonised European Research on Models of Energy Systems. A European Model which analyses the inter-relationships between energy and the economy (Research DG of the European Commission)
HERMES	Message handling survey and trends for the IES user community (ESPRIT project)
HERMES	Telematic Healthcare, Remoteness and Mobility factors in common European Scenarios (a Telematics for Healthcare project within the TELEMATICS APPLICATIONS programme)
HERODE	Handling of mixed text/image/voice documents based on a standardised office document architecture (ESPRIT project)
HESSILSIL	Heterostructure of semiconducting silicides on silicon-applications to SI compatible optoelectronic devices (ESPRIT project)
HFR	High Flux Reactor at PETTEN
HICP	*See* HCPI
HIDCIM	Holographic labelling techniques for automatic IDentification in CIM-environments (ESPRIT project)
HIEMS	Health Information Exchange and Monitoring System (IDA project). *See also* CARE

HIPACS	Hospital Integrated Picture Archiving and Communication System (AIM project)
HIPM-FAMILY	Publishing Model for FAMILY home entertainment (a Telematics Information Engineering project within the TELEMATICS APPLICATIONS programme)
HISTA 3	Therapeutic development of Histamine H3 receptor agonist (EUREKA project)
HIVITS	High-quality Videophone and HDTV Systems (RACE project)
HLEG	High Level Expert Group on social and societal aspects of the IS http://www.ispo.cec.be/hleg/hleg.html
HLP	High Level Panel, set up in 1996 to pinpoint areas where FREE MOVEMENT legislation is lagging behind or lacking
HOME	Highly Optimised Microscope Environment (AIM project)
HOME	Home applications Optimum Multimedia/multimodal system for Environment control (a Telematics for Disabled and Elderly People project within the TELEMATICS APPLICATIONS programme)
HOMEBRAIN	Design for all (a Telematics for Disabled and Elderly People project within the TELEMATICS APPLICATIONS programme)
HOMER-D	HOME Rehabilitation treatment and Dialysis (a Telematics for Healthcare project within the TELEMATICS APPLICATIONS programme)
HONLEA	Heads Of National drugs Law Enforcement Agencies-Europe

HOPE	Humanitarian Aid Office Programme Environment. ECHO's financial management database which monitors contracts and financial information
HOPES	HOrizontal Project for the Evaluation of traffic Safety and man-machine interaction (DRIVE project)
Horeca/ta	HOtels, REstaurants, CAfés, Travel Agents
*HORIZON	Promotion of the social and professional integration of the disabled and disadvantaged person. Part of EMPLOYMENT, the COMMUNITY INITIATIVE (1994-1999) (Amended guidelines in OJ C200/96). *See* INTEGRA; NOW; YOUTHSTART
HORIZON 2000	on development cooperation in the run-up to 2000 (SEC(92) 915)
HORIZON ACTION	HORIZONtal accompanying measure for the ACTION cluster for telematics-assisted cooperative work for healthcare professionals (a Telematics for Healthcare project within the TELEMATICS APPLICATIONS programme)
HORIZONTAL PROGRAMMES	Wide-ranging programmes to ensure coordination, support and coherence within the EU's research policy. A component of FP5. *See* IMPROVING ; INCO II; INNOVATION/SMEs. *See also* THEMATIC PROGRAMMES
HOSCOM	HOSpitals COMparisons: medical and financial data (AIM project)
HPC-Vision	Interconnection of broadband sites in France and Germany: a fibre interconnection initiative to prepare for TEN-TELECOMMUNICATIONS
HPPWB	High Performance Printing Wiring Boards (EUREKA project)

HPV	Diagnosis of Human Papilloma Virus infection (EUREKA project)
HRTP	Japan industry insight programme
HS	Harmonised System Nomenclature. A 6-digit Harmonised commodity description and coding System of statistics (OJ L198/87). *Previously* CCCN. *See also* SIMONE
HS-ADEPT	Home Systems-Access for Disabled and Elderly People to this Technology (TIDE project)
HSD	Human and Social Development
HSPRO-EU	Health and Safety PROmotion in the European Union (a Telematics for Healthcare project within the TELEMATICS APPLICATIONS programme)
HSR COMAC	Health Service Research Concerted Action Committee
HSSCD	Health Surveillance System for Communicable Diseases (IDA project). *See also* CARE
HTCOR-DB	A High Temperature Corrosion Database Access via the JRC at PETTEN
HTDS	Host Target Development System (ESPRIT project)
HTM-DB	High Temperature Materials Databank containing information on engineering materials with high temperature applications Access via the JRC at PETTEN
HTPV	Group of EUREKA projects
HUFIT	Human Factor Laboratories in Information Technologies (ESPRIT project)

HUMAN CAPITAL AND MOBILITY	*See* HCM
HYACE	HYdrate Autoclave Coring Equipment system (MAST III project)
HYDRE	Improved water facilities in the Mediterranean area (RECITE project)
HYETI	High Yield and high reliability ULSI system (ESPRIT project)
HYPDOC	HYPermedia publishing and cooperation (a Telematics Information Engineering project within the TELEMATICS APPLICATIONS programme)
HYPERLIB	HYPERtext interfaces to LIBrary information systems (project within Area 5 of the TELEMATIC SYSTEMS programme)
HYPERMUSEUM	The European cultural network (a Telematics for Administrations project within the TELEMATICS APPLICATIONS programme) http://www.h2000.be/horizon2000
HYPIT	Human resources and management product interface (TIDE project)
HYPRO	Establishment of new, advanced treatment of waste water... (EUREKA project)
I	Italy
I4C	Integration and Communication for the continuity of cardiac care (a Telematics for Healthcare project within the TELEMATICS APPLICATIONS programme)
*I&T Magazine	Industry and Telecommunications Magazine which ceased publication in 1997. *Previously* XIII Magazine

IACIS	Intelligent Area Communication and Information System (ESPRIT project)
IADS	Integrated Applications for Digital Sites (TELEMATICS APPLICATIONS project)
IAEVA	A distributed multimedia database and environment for virtual walks of 3D models of human organs (a Telematics for Healthcare project within the TELEMATICS APPLICATIONS programme)
IAM	Institute for Advanced Materials. Part of the JRC at PETTEN and ISPRA
IAP	Integrated Action Programme
IBASS	Intelligent Business Applications Support System (ESPRIT project)
IBBS	Electronic Identification of Blood BagS in connection with autologous blood banking (EUREKA project)
IBC	Integrated Broadband Communications (RACE project)
ICAN	Integrated Communication and control for All Needs (a Telematics for Disabled and Elderly People project within the TELEMATICS APPLICATIONS programme)
ICARE	Industrial Characterisation of an Advanced Resonant Etcher (ESPRIT project)
ICARE 9000	ISO9000 on-demand Consulting And Remote Electronic training for SMEs in urban and rural areas (a Telematics for Urban and Rural Areas project within the TELEMATICS APPLICATIONS programme)
ICARUS	EDI project under the TEDIS programme

ICARUS	Incremental Construction and Reuse of Requirements Specifications (ESPRIT project)
ICARUS	Interurban Control and Roads Utilisation Simulation (DRIVE project)
ICD	Multiview VLSI-design system (ESPRIT project)
ICE-CAR	Interworking public key CErtification infrastructure for Commerce Administration and Research (a Telematics for Research project within the TELEMATICS APPLICATIONS programme)
ICE-TEL	Interworking public key infrastructure for Europe (a Telematics for Research project within the TELEMATICS APPLICATIONS programme)
ICI	Intelligent Communication Interface (ESPRIT project)
ICP	Inter-University Cooperation Programmes (within the ERASMUS programme)
ICSIC	Integrated Communication System for Intensive Care (AIM project)
*ICT	Information and Communication Technologies. Activity 1.1 of the (4th) RTD Framework programme. *See* ACTS; ESPRIT IV; TELEMATICS APPLICATIONS programme
ICTDAS	Integrated CAE Techniques for Dynamic Analysis of Structures (ESPRIT project)
IDA	Council Decision 95/468/EC for the implementation of trans-European networks for the Interchange of Data between Administrations (1995-1997) (OJ L269/95 and extended until 2004 in OJ L203/99) http://www.ispo.cec.be/ida/ida.html

IDEA	Indicators and Data for European Analysis (funded by the TSER programme)
IDEA	Integrated Development Environment for ADA (EUREKA project)
IDEA	Inter-institutional Directory of the EU. Available in paper copy and on the Internet http://europa.eu.int.ideaen.html
IDEAL	Interactive Dialogues for Explanation And Learning (ESPRIT project)
IDEAL-IST	Information Dissemination and European Awareness Launch for the IST programme
IDEALS	Integration of DEdicated for Advanced training Linked to Small and medium enterprises and Institutes of Higher Education (sic)(a Telematics for Education and Training project within the TELEMATICS APPLICATIONS programme)
IDEE	Social insertion in urban regions (RECITE project)
IDEHA	Integrated Electric Drive for Automation (EUREKA project)
IDES	Interactive Data Entry System (CADDIA project)
IDMS	Integrated Data Management System
*IDO	Integrated Development Operations in urban and industrial areas (within the framework of the STRUCTURAL FUNDS) (1979-1999). See also IDP; SPD
*IDP	Integrated Development Programmes in rural areas (within the framework of the STRUCTURAL FUNDS) (1979-1999). See also IDO
IDPS	Integrated Design and Production System (ESPRIT project)

IDRIS	Intelligent Drive for shop floor Systems (ESPRIT project)
IDST	Scientific and Technical Information and Documentation
*IEAR	European Communities Institute for Economic Analysis
IEEP	Institute for European Environmental Policy c/o STEM, Jansbuitensingel 7, NL-6800 AA Arnhem, Netherlands UK Contact: Dean Bradley House, 52 Horseferry Road, London, SW1P 2AG
*IES-DC	ECHO database on Information Exchange Systems - Data Collections. Directory and reference services on European Information Technology projects
IESERV2	Information Engineering support SERvices (a Telematics Information Engineering project within the TELEMATICS APPLICATIONS programme)
IETM	Informal European Theatre Meeting to facilitate information exchanges amongst people working in the performing arts (KALEIDOSCOPE project) sq Sainctelette 19, B-1000 Brussels, Belgium
IGC	Inter-Governmental Conference: *First*: (1950-1951) resulting in the PARIS TREATY; *Second*: (1955-1957) resulting in the Treaties establishing the EEC and EURATOM; *Third*: (1985) resulting in the SEA; *Fourth/Fifth*: (1990-1991) resulting in the TREATY ON EUROPEAN UNION; *Sixth*: (1996-1997) resulting in the AMSTERDAM TREATY. *See also* THREE WISE MEN REPORT on the Institutional implications of enlargement http://europa.eu.int/en/agenda/igc-home/index.html
IGLO	*See* EuRaTIN
IGO	Intergovernmental Organisation

IGOS	Image Guided Orthopaedic Surgery (a Telematics for Healthcare project within the TELEMATICS APPLICATIONS programme)
IGS	Inspectorate General DG of the European Commission
IHCP	Institue of Health and Consumer Protection. Created by the JRC in 1998 and based at ISPRA
IHS	Integrated Home Systems: development of a communications system for use inside the home (EUREKA project)
IIP	*See* ECIP (European Communities Investment Partners)
IKAROS	Intelligence and Knowledge Aided Recognition of Speech (ESPRIT project)
ILE	Isotopic Lead Experiment (environmental research programme)
I'M	Information Market
IMACE	Association of the Margarine Industry of the EC countries ave de Tervuren 168, Boîte 12, B-1150 Brussels, Belgium
IMAGINE	Integrated Multimedia Applications Generating Innovative Networks in European digital towns (a Telematics for Integrated Applications for Digital Sites project within the TELEMATICS APPLICATIONS programme)
IMATE	Innovative Multimedia Application for Textile Education (EMTF project)
IMAURO	Integrated Model for the Analysis of Urban Route Optimisation (DRIVE project)

I*M EUROPE	Information Market Europe. Information and initiatives relating to the Information Society DG http://158.169.50.95:10080/home.html
I*M FORUM	A database which gives details of organisations and individuals specialising in consultancy on the electronic information market and the identification of partners for Calls for research proposals related to the I'M. *See also* NAP http://158.169.50.95:10080/imforum/
IMG	Individual Mobility Grants to fund individual visits by higher education staff, senior Ministry Officers and education planners within Europe (part of the PHARE programme)
I*M GUIDE	Information Market Guide database. *Previously* BROKERSGUIDE and DIANEGUIDE http://158.169.50.95:10080/imguide/
IMMUNITY	Impacts of Increased and Multiple Use of inland Navigation and Identification of Tools to reduce negative impacts (TRANSPORT project)
IMMUNOSCREEN	Development of two categories of rapid Immunoassays based on membrane technology (EUREKA project)
IMO	European Information Market OBSERVATORY to increase knowledge of the EU information market. Attached to the Information Society DG of the European Commission
*IMP	Integrated Mediterranean Programmes (1985-1993) (OJ L197/85)
IMP	Telematic exchange of Information on Medicinal Products (IDA project)
IMPACS	Integrated Manufacturing Planning and Control System (ESPRIT project)

IMPACT	Implementation Aspects Concerning planning and legislation (DRIVE project)
IMPACT	Increasing the IMPACT of assistive technology (a Telematics for Disabled and Elderly People project within the TELEMATICS APPLICATIONS programme)
*IMPACT II	Programme for an Information Services Market (1992-1995) (OJ L377/91). *Continued by* INFO 2000
IMPACT Directive	Dir 85/337/EEC on Environmental Impact Assessment (OJ L175/85 with latest amendment in OJ L73/97). (COM(93) 28 vol.12 contains the annex for the UK)
IMPEL	Implementation and enforcement of Environmental Law: an informal EU network
IMPLUS	Improved plastic pipe systems (EUREKA project)
IMPPACT	Integrated Modelling of Products and Processes using Advanced Computer Technologies (ESPRIT project)
IMPRIMATUR	Intellectual Multimedia Property Rights Model And Terminology for Universal Reference (ESPRIT project)
IMPROFEED	Development of new methods for the improvement of the feed value of raw materials and feeds (EUREKA project)
IMPROVING	Council Decision 99/173/EC adopting a specific programme for Improving Human Research Potential and the Socio-Economic Knowledge Base (1998-2002) (OJ L64/99). One of the HORIZONTAL PROGRAMMES which form part of FP5. *Formerly* TMR; TSER

IMPULSE	Interoperable Modular Pilot plants Underlying Logistic System in Europe (TRANSPORT project) http://www.cordis.lu/transport/src/impulse.htm
IMPW	Integrated Management Process Workbench (ESPRIT project)
IMRI	Improved Magnetic Resonance Imaging System (EUREKA project)
IMSE	Integrated Modelling Support Environment (ESPRIT project)
*IMT	Industrial and Materials Technologies programme. *See* BRITE/EURAM III
IMTs	Innovation Management Techniques. A strand of the INNOVATION programme http://www.cordis.lu/imt/home.html
IMU	Image and Movement Understanding (ESPRIT project)
INCA	Integrated Network Architecture for office Communications (ESPRIT project)
INCA	Standardised Interface for sensors and Actuators (EUREKA project)
INCARNATION	Efficient inland navigation information system (TRANSPORT project)
INCIPIT	Bibliographic records and images: a CD-ROM of incunabula editions (project within Area 5 of the TELEMATIC SYSTEMS programme)
INCLUDE	INCLUsion of Disabled and Elderly in telematics (a Telematics for Disabled and Elderly People project within the TELEMATICS APPLICATIONS programme)

INCO II	Council Decision 99/171/EC adopting a specific programme confirming the international role of Community research (1998-2002) (OJ L64/99). One of the HORIZONTAL PROGRAMMES which form part of FP5. *Previously* COPERNICUS-PECO; *See also* INCO-COPERNICUS; INCO-DC; INCOPOL http://www.cordis.lu/inco2/home.html
INCO-COPERNICUS	Scientific & Technical cooperation with the CCE and with the NIS (1994-1998). *See also* COPERNICUS; INCO II
INCO-DC	Cooperation with THIRD COUNTRIES and International organisations-Developing Countries. *See* also INCO II
INCOPOL	INternational COoperation POLicies. A series of seven studies commissioned by INCO on the cooperation activities of the 18 EEA countries (15 Member States plus Iceland, Liechtenstein and Norway) in the field of international RTD cooperation
IND	Non-attached group (of the EP). *Previously* NI
*INDAC	Integral Nuclear Data Information Centre
INDICES	INterfacing Disabled people with Industry standard Computing EnvironmentS (TIDE project)
INDIS	Information Dissemination in European RTD (PHARE project). *See also* RICE
INDOC	INtelligent DOCuments production demonstrator (ESPRIT project)
INDUSTRIAL PLATFORM	Industrial groupings established on the initiative of industry around biotechnology RTD. *See* ACTIP; BACIP; BBP; EBIP; ENIP; FAIP; FIP; HAE2000; IPM; IVTIP; LABIP; PIP; SBIP; TSE IP; YIP http://europa.eu.int/comm/dg12/biotech/ip1.html

IN-EMERGENCY	INtegrated incident management, EMERGENCY healthcare and environment monitoring in road networks (a Telematics for Integrated Applications for Digital Sites project within the TELEMATICS APPLICATIONS programme)
INFEO	Earth Observation data and INFormation Exchange system. Launched by the CEO in 1998
INFO 92	A database produced by the Secretariat-General of the European Commission which covers progress on the legislation contained in the SEM and the SOCIAL CHARTER. *Now within* SCADPlus
INFO 2000	Council Decision 96/339/EC for a multiannual programme to stimulate the development of a European multimedia content industry (1996-1999) (OJ L129/96). *Previously* IMPACT II
InfoCARE	Interactive INFOrmation system for health/social CARE (a Telematics for Healthcare project within the TELEMATICS APPLICATIONS programme)
INFODISK	See EU INFODISK
INFOEURO ACCESS	European wide Access to Information about the EU and its Member States (IMPACT project)
INFOGRANT	Database which provides details of the grants and other financial assistance schemes available to businesses in the UK. *Successor to* AIMS Available on subscription on the Internet and CD-ROM via EPRC www.eprcltd.strath.ac.uk
INFOLOG	Intermodal INFOrmation link for improved LOGistics (TRANSPORT project)

INFOMALL	Full-Cycle Information Mall (a Telematics Information Engineering project within the TELEMATICS APPLICATIONS programme)
InfoPoint EUROPE	*See* EIP
Inforegio	EU's web site on the regions http://inforegio.cec.eu.int/
INFORM	Information management and decision support in high dependency environments (AIM project)
INFORMATION RELAYS	*See* RELAYS
INFORMATION SOCIETY	*See* IS
INFORMATION TECHNOLOGY	*See* IST
InfoRules	Database which provides details of business regulations and services. *Successor to* STARS Available on subscription on the Internet and CD-ROM via EPRC www.eprcltd.strath.ac.uk
INFOS	Assessment of policy instruments for efficient ozone abatement strategies in Europe (ENVIRONMENT AND CLIMATE project)
INFOSAFE	Information system for road user Safety and traffic performance (DRIVE project)
INFOSOND	INFOrmation and Service ON Demand (a Telematics for Urban and Rural Areas project within the TELEMATICS APPLICATIONS programme)
INFOSTAT	Information Systems project to prepare ETIS (TRANSPORT project)
Infosys	INFOrmation and communication SYStem. A gateway to the European databases on agronomic research for development established by the EIARD http://www.dainet.de/eiard/infosys/

INFSO	Information Society DG of the European Commission
INITIATIVES	*See* COMMUNITY INITIATIVES
INJURY-PREV C	EP and Council Decision 372/1999/EC adopting a programme of Community action on injury prevention in the framework for action in the field of public health (1999-2003) (OJ L46/99). *See also* EHLASS
INLANDWW	Inland Waterways transport statistical domain on the NEW CRONOS databank
INNOVAT	Survey on innovation in EU enterprises statistical domain on the NEW CRONOS databank
*INNOVATION	Council Decision 94/917/EC for the dissemination of the results of RTD activities: Activity 3 of the (4th) RTD Framework programme (1994-1998) (OJ L361/94). *Previously* SPRINT; VALUE. *Replaced by* INNOVATION/SMEs. *See also* IMT; IRC http://www.cordis.lu/innovation/home.html
INNOVATION RELAY CENTRES	*See* IRC
INNOVATION/SMEs	Council Decision 1999/172/EC adopting a programme of research, technological development and demonstration to promote innovation and encourage the participation of SMEs (1998-2002) (OJ L64/99). One of the HORIZONTAL PROGRAMMES which form part of FP5. *Previously* INNOVATION http://www.cordis.lu/innovation-smes/home.html
INNOVEX	Study and analysis of five INNOVATION projects dealing with the management of water in urban and rural regions http://www.euweb.de/innotec

INNVEST	A confidential database to provide commercial and technical information on high-tech projects to EUROTECH CAPITAL members
INOGATE	INterstate Oil And GAs Transport to Europe. A TACIS programme in the field of energy to stimulate cooperation and help ensure the security of supplies of oil and gas from the Caspian and Central Asia regions to European markets
INPART	INclusion through PARTicipation (TSER project)
'ins'	Member States participating in the EMU. *See also* 'pre-ins'
INSCAD	Development of a CADCAM system for manufacturing customised insoles for shoes (TIDE project)
INSEM	Inter-institutional Service of Electronic Mail
*INSIS	Inter-institutional Integrated Services Information System (1983-1992) (OJ L368/82)
INSPIRE	INnovation Ship PIlot REsearch (TRANSPORT project)
*INST	Committee on Institutional Affairs (of the EP)
INSTIL	Integration of Symbolic and Numeric Learning Techniques (ESPRIT project)
INTAS	International Association for the Promotion of Cooperation with Scientists from the NIS. It consists of the Member States, the 12 NIS, Switzerland, Norway and Israel ave des Arts 58, Boîte 8, B-1000 Brussels, Belgium http://www.cordis.lu/intas/home.html
INTEGRA	European manufacturing interface (EUREKA project)

*INTEGRA	One of the four strands of the COMMUNITY INITIATIVE, EMPLOYMENT. It covered the homeless, long-term unemployed, gypsies, ex prisoners and drug abusers (1994-1999) (Guidelines in OJ C200/96). *See also* HORIZON; NOW; YOUTHSTART
INTEGRATION	Integrating the foundations of functional, logic and object-orientated programming (ESPRIT project)
IN-TELE	Internet-based Teaching and Learning (EMTF project)
IN#TEL#EC	Integrated Telecommunications Training for the European Community (COMETT programme)
INTER	Project to develop a communications network in the interests of harmonising European railways (within the TELEMATICS APPLICATIONS programme)
*INTERACT	An EC information system to coordinate measures at local level to achieve the social and economic integration of disabled and old people. Now part of the HELIOS network
INTERCARE	The Interworking and interoperability of networked services for healthcare using Internet-based technology (a Telematics for Healthcare project within the TELEMATICS APPLICATIONS programme) http://www.ehto.org/vds/projects/intercare.html
INTERCONNECTION Directive	Dir 97/33/EC on interconnection in telecommunications with regard to ensuring universal service and interoperability through application of the principles of ONP (OJ L199/97 with latest amendment in OJ L268/98)

| INTERLAINE | Committee of the Wool Textile Industries in the EEC |
| | rue du Luxembourg 19, Boîte 14, B-1000 Brussels, Belgium |

| INTERMAPS | Interactive Multimedia Access Publishing Services (DELTA project) |

| INTERNAL MARKET | *See* SEM (Single European Market) |

| INTERPRISE | Council Decision 93/379/EEC for Initiatives to Encourage Partnerships between Industries and Services in Europe (1993-1996) (OJ L161/93). *Continued within* SMEAP |
| | http://europa.eu.int/en/comm/dg23/interpri/project.htm |

| INTERREG | A COMMUNITY INITIATIVE to assist border areas (2000-2006) (COM(99) 479). *Incorporates* RECITE; *See also* LACE |

| INTERSUDMED | An IPTS activity involving cooperation with countries around the Mediterranean in the field of renewable energies |

| INTERVENTION PRICE | The minimum guaranteed price for agricultural produce. Intervention Boards in each EU country buy farm produce from the market at this agreed price and store it. Prices are published for individual commodities in the OJ |

| INTRA-SEAS | Integrated management of multimodal traffic in ports (TRANSPORT project) |

| INTRASTAT | Reg 3330/91 relating to statistics for the trading of goods between Member States 1 January 1993- . INTRASTAT links trade statistics to VAT (OJ L316/91 with latest amendment in OJ L307/92) |

| INUSE | INformation engineering Usability Support centres (a Telematics Information Engineering project within the TELEMATICS APPLICATIONS programme) |

INVAID	INtegration of computer Vision techniques for Automatic Incident Detection (DRIVE project)
IOANNINA compromise	on voting rules within the Council of the European Union. Council Decision in OJ C105/94 with amendment in OJ C1/95
IOLE	IBC On-Line Environment (RACE project)
IOP	Integrated Operational Programme
IOT	Input-Output Tables of the national accounts. *See* TES/IOT
IP	Indicative Programme(s)
IP	A series of Press releases issued by the European Commission Access via RAPID
IP	*See* INDUSTRIAL PLATFORM
IPCES	Intelligent Process Control by means of Expert Systems (ESPRIT project)
IPDES	Integrated Product Design System (ESPRIT project)
IPE	Info Point Europe. *See* EIP
IPM	INDUSTRIAL PLATFORM for Microbiology http://europa.eu.int/comm/dg12/biotech/ip2.html#IPM http://www.tech-know.be/
IPPC	Dir 96/61/EC on Integrated Pollution Prevention and Control (OJ L257/96)
IPR	Inward Processing Relief (in relation to customs matters)
IPSI	Improved Port/Ship Interface (TRANSPORT project)
IPSNI	Integration of People with Special Needs by the IBC (RACE project)

IPTS	Institute for Prospective Technological Studies. Part of the JRC at SEVILLE. *See also* ETAN http://www.jrc.es/extprojects
IQ	Intelligent Quattro to develop intelligent mechatronic automation and a remote control system for hydraulically operated vehicles which gives possibilities to wide range applications (EUREKA project)
IRC	Innovation Relay Centre. A network of Centres set up originally under the VALUE programme to promote innovation and the exchange of research results. *Contined under* the INNOVATION and INNOVATION/SMEs programmes. *See also* RELAYS http://www.cordis.lu/irc/home.html
IRDAC	Industrial R&D Advisory Committee. *Previously* CORDI http://europa.eu.int/comm/dg12/irdac.html
IRDSS	Integrated Regional Development Support System (a Telematics for Urban and Rural Areas project within the TELEMATICS APPLICATIONS programme)
IREFREA	A European network for research and evaluation on drug prevention http://www.irefrea.org
IRELA	Institute for Relations between Europe and Latin America Pedro de Valdivia 10, E-28006 Madrid, Spain http://www.irela.org/
IRENA	Industrial Requirements Engineering based on Nets for Added Applications (EUREKA project)
IRENE	Integrated Modelling of Renewable Natural Resources (FAST project)

IRENIE	Improved Reporting of ENvironmental Information using EIONET (a Telematics for Environment project within the TELEMATICS APPLICATIONS programme) http://www.trentel.org/environment/research/projects/irenie.html
IRHIS	Intelligent adaptive information Retrieval systems as Hospital Information System front end (AIM project)
IRIMS	ISPRA Risk Management Support System (JRC project)
IRIS	European network for the training of women (1987-). From July 1995 it became an independent association. *See also* NOW rue Capouillet 25, B-1060 Brussels, Belgium
*IRIS	Initiative pour Régions isolées. *Continued as* REGIS
IRIS	Integrated Road Safety Information and Navigation System (within the DRIVE programme)
IRISI	Inter-Regional Information Society Initiative. An Inter-Member State network set up with European Commission support to define the establishment of the information society
IRL	Ireland
IRMM	Institute for Reference Materials and Measurements. Part of the JRC at GEEL
IRNU	Information Relays and Networks Unit of the Education and Culture DG of the European Commission. *See also* RELAYS
IRSA	Institute for Remote Sensing Applications. Part of the JRC at ISPRA

IS	Council Decision 98/253/EC for a multiannual programme to stimulate the establishment of the Information Society (1998-2002) (OJ L107/98). *See also* IS ACTION PLAN; ISPO; IST
ISA	Integrated Systems Architecture (ESPRIT project)
ISAAC	Integration System Architecture for Advanced primary Care (AIM project)
ISABEL	Interconnected broadband islands between Spain and Portugal: a fibre interconnection initiative to prepare for TEN-TELECOMMUNICATIONS
ISAC	Information Society Activity Centre European Commission BU24 2/78 rue de la Loi 200, B-1049 Brussels, Belgium
IS ACTION PLAN	*Europe's way to the information society* (COM(94) 347). *See also* IS
ISAEUS	Speech training for deaf and hearing-impaired people (a Telematics for Disabled and Elderly People project within the TELEMATICS APPLICATIONS programme)
ISAM	Integrated system for Small Airport Management (a Telematics for Integrated Applications for Digital Sites project within the TELEMATICS APPLICATIONS programme)
ISAR-T	Integration System ARchitecture Telematics (a Telematics for Healthcare project within the TELEMATICS APPLICATIONS programme)
ISCONIS	Improving Scientific COoperation with the NIS (INCO programme) http://www.cordis.lu/isconis/home.html
IS-CORE	Information Systems: COrrectness and REusability (ESPRIT project)

ISD	Dir 93/22/EEC on Investment Services in the securities field (OJ L141/93 with latest amendment in OJ L84/97)
ISDN	Recommendation 86/659 for an Integrated Services Digital Network (OJ L382/86 with guidelines in OJ L282/95)
ISEI	Institute for Systems Engineering and Informatics. Part of the JRC at ISPRA. *Previously* CITE
ISEM	IT Support for Emergency Management (ESPRIT project)
ISG	Internal Steering Group
ISHTAR	Implementing Secure Healthcare Telematics Application in Europe (a Telematics for Healthcare project within the TELEMATICS APPLICATIONS programme)
ISIDE	Advanced model for integration of DB and KB management systems (ESPRIT project)
ISIS	Implementation and feasibility Study for Integrated Services (a Telematics for Integrated Applications for Digital Sites project within the TELEMATICS APPLICATIONS programme)
ISIS	Information Society Initiative in Standardisation. Set up under Council Decision 87/95/EC (OJ L36/87) http://www.ispo.cec.be/isis/
ISIS	Institute for Systems, Informatics and Safety. Part of the JRC at ISPRA
ISLAND	Information System Linking Applications in a Network Demonstrator (a Telematics for Administrations project within the TELEMATICS APPLICATIONS programme)

ISLED	Influence of rising Sea Level on Ecosystem Dynamics of salt marshes (ELOISE project)
ISLIL	Integrated System for Long Distance Intercultural Learning (EMTF project)
ISMAP	Integrated System for Management of Agricultural Production (EUREKA project)
ISOTOPE	Improved Structure and Organisation for urban Transport Operations of Passengers in Europe (TRANSPORT project)
ISPA	Instrument for Structural Policies for Pre-Accession. Reg 1267/99 for Structural Policies to provide financial assistance for transport infrastructure measures and environmental measures, enabling applicant countries to comply with EU standards (2000-2006) (OJ L161/99)
ISPO	Information Society Project Office. A one stop shop for Commission information on the IS http://www.ispo.cec.be
ISPRA	JRC establishment I-21020 Ispra (VA), Italy
ISSUE	IBCN Systems and Services Useability Engineering (RACE project)
IST	Council Decision 1999/168/EC adopting a specific Information Society Technologies programme (1998-2002) (OJ L64/99). One of the THEMATIC PROGRAMMES which form part of FP5. *Previously* ACTS; ESPRIT; TELEMATICS APPLICATIONS programme. *See also* IS; ISPO http://www.cordis.lu/ist/eoi http://www.cordis.lu/ist/home.html IST conference and exhibition:http://www.ist99.fi/
IST	Institute for Safety Technology. Part of the JRC at ISPRA
ISTAG	IST programme Advisory Group

ISTC AGREEMENT	Reg 500/94 for an Agreement to establish an International Science and Technology Centre (OJ L64/94) http://www.istc.ru/
*IT	Industrial Technologies: Activity 1.2 of (4th) RTD Framework programme. *See* BRITE/EURAM III; SMT
IT	Information Technology
IT	Italian
ITACA	IBCN Testing Architecture for Conformance Assessment (RACE project)
ITCG	Illegal Traffic of Cultural Goods. Protecting the cultural heritage of Member States through telematics (IDA project)
ITDNS	Integrated Tour operating Digital Network Service (IMPACT project)
ITEA	Information Technology European Awards to recognise innovative products which have market potential (under the ESPRIT programme)
I-TEC 2	Innovation and Technology Equity Capital. A scheme to help private capital investment in SMEs. It is managed by the EIF http://www.cordis.lu/finance/src/i-tec.htm
IT EDUCTRA	Information Technologies Education and Training (a Telematics for Healthcare project within the TELEMATICS APPLICATIONS programme)
ITER	Council Decision 92/439/Euratom for the International Thermonuclear Experimental Reactor, the successor to JET (EURATOM with participation by Japan; the United States of America and the Union of Soviet Socialist Republics) (OJ L244/92). *See also* DEMO

ITES	Income Tax Exemption Scheme. An export subsidy scheme. *See also* DEPB; EOU; EPCGS; EPZ
ITEX	Information Technology for the textile and clothing industry (ESPRIT project)
ITHACA	Integrated Toolkit for Highly Advanced Computer Applications (ESPRIT project)
ITHACA	Telematics for integrated client centred community care (a Telematics for Healthcare project within the TELEMATICS APPLICATIONS programme)
ITIS	IBC Terminal for Interactive Services (RACE project)
ITMA	*See* I&T Magazine
ITRE	Committee on Industry, External Trade, Research and Energy (of the EP)
ITS	Evaluation: Intelligent Tutoring System shell for industrial/office training (ESPRIT project)
ITS	Intelligent Transport Systems
ITSAEM	Integrated Telematics System for Administrations Environmental Management (a Telematics for Environment project within the TELEMATICS APPLICATIONS programme) http://www.trentel.org/environment/research/projects/itsaem.html
ITS City Pioneers	Planning for Intelligent TranSport in Europe's Cities project to support the deployment of telematics applications in cities and to manage links with systems on the Trans-European Transport Network (ERTICO initiative)

ITSEC	Council Recommendation 95/144/EC on common Information Technology Security Evaluation Criteria (OJ L93/95)
ITSIE	Intelligent Training Systems in Industrial Environments (ESPRIT project)
ITU	Institute for Transuranium Elements. Part of the JRC at KARLSRUHE
ITUC 99	Integrated Territorial & Urban Conservation workshop (RAPHAEL programme)
IUCLID	A database covering the classification and evaluation of existing chemical substances CD-ROM available from the JRC at ISPRA
IUE	See EUI
IUI	Prospects for construction techniques creation of an industrialised urban infrastructure applicable on an identified site, using building techniques for the years 2000 to 2020 (EUREKA project)
IULA	International Union of Local Authorities Laan Copes van Cattenburch 60A, NL-2585 GC The Hague, Netherlands UK Office: 35 Great Smith Street, London SW1P 3BJ (where it is known as the Local Government International Bureau)
IVICO	Integrated Video Codec (RACE project)
IVIS	Integrated Vacuum Instrumentation System... (EUREKA project)
IVTIP	In Vitro Testing INDUSTRIAL PLATFORM http://europa.eu.int/comm/dg12/biotech/ip2.html#IVTIP
IWS	Intelligent Workstation (ESPRIT project)
JAF	COST working party on legal, administrative and financial questions
JAI	Justice and Home Affairs DG of the European Commission

JAMES-RN	Joint AtM Experiment on European Services (a Telematics for Research project within the TELEMATICS APPLICATIONS programme)
JANUS	Community information system for health and safety at work (OJ C28/88) Cives Europe, bd Clovis 12A, B-1000 Brussels, Belgium
JANUS	Joint Academic Network using Satellite for European distance education and training (DELTA project)
JEAN MONNET PROJECT	to develop European studies, courses and modules in Universities (1994-1997 and extended to CEEC 1998-) Contact: European Commission Education and Culture DG, rue de la Loi 200, B-1049 Brussels, Belgium
JEN	Joint European Networks (within the TEMPUS programme)
JENDRPC	Joint EURATOM Nuclear Data and Reactor Physics Committee
JEP	Joint Educational Project (under Action IV and E of the LINGUA programme)
JEP	Joint European Project (under the TEMPUS and TACIS programmes). *See also* Pre-JEP
JEPS	Bootstrap project for Joint European Print Server (ESPRIT project)
*JESSI	Joint European Submicron Silicon Initiative (EUREKA project). *Continued as* MEDEA
JESSI-JTTT	JESSI Transnational Technology Training (COMETT project)
JET	Joint European Torus at Abingdon in the UK (OJ L151/78). *See also* ITER
JETDLAG	Joint European Development of Tunable Diode Laser Absorption (EUREKA project)
JET-SB	Joint European Supervisory Board

JEV	Joint European Venture scheme. Commission Decision 97/761/EC for financial support to SMEs for transnational joint ventures (1998-2000) (OJ L310/97 and incorporated into Council Decision 98/347/EC in OJ L155/98)
JHA	Justice and Home Affairs
JI	Joint Implementation
JMPA	Joint Production and Marketing Agreement
*JNRC	Joint Nuclear Research Centre
JOP	Joint venture Phare and TACIS Programme. Project to help companies to establish joint ventures in Eastern and Central Europe Contact: European Commission Enterprise DG, Wagner Building, rue Alcide de Gasperi, L-2920 Luxembourg
*JOULE II	Joint Opportunities for Unconventional or Long-term Energy Supply (1990-1994) (OJ L257/91). The Biomass Area was continued within the AIR programme. *See* JOULE-THERMIE
*JOULE-THERMIE	Council Decision 94/806/EC for research in non-nuclear energy (1994-1998) (OJ L334/94). *Replaced by* ENERGIE http://europa.eu.int/comm/dg12/joule1.html http://europa.eu.int/en/comm/dg17/thermie.htm
JRC	Joint Research Centre rue de la Loi 200, B-1049 Brussels, Belgium Establishments at: GEEL (Belgium); ISPRA (Italy); KARLSRUHE (Germany); PETTEN (Netherlands) and SEVILLE (Spain) http://www.jrc.org
JSP	Joint Study Programme (established under the ERASMUS programme)
JSTCC	Joint Science and Technology Cooperation Committee to be set up to administer the EU/Canada Agreement for scientific and technological cooperation

JTMP	Joint Technology Management Plan. A contract concluded between participants involved in joint research
JUKE-BOX	Applying telematics technology to improve public access to audio/archives (project within Area 5 of the TELEMATIC SYSTEMS programme)
JUMBO COUNCIL	ECO/FIN and Social Affairs Council of Ministers joint meeting of 16th November 1982 on the economic and social situation in the EC
JURI	Committee on legal affairs and the internal market (of the EP)
JV	Joint Venture
JWP	Joint Working Party
KADS	A methodology for the development of knowledge-based systems (ESPRIT project)
KALANKE	Case C-450/93 in the ECJ on quotas in favour of employment for women (Case reported in ECR I-1995/9-10)
*KALEIDOSCOPE	Council Decision 719/96/EC to support artistic and cultural activities with a European dimension (1996-1998) (OJ L99/96). *Previously* PLATFORM EUROPE. *Replaced by* CULTURE 2000 http://europa.eu.int/en/comm/dg10/culture/en/action/kaleidos-gen.html
KALIMEDIA	Regional promotion of electronic commerce standards for SMEs (ISIS project) http://www.ispo.cec.be/isis/95kalim.htm
KAMP	Knowledge Assurance in Multimedia Publishing (a Telematics for Education and Training project within the TELEMATICS APPLICATIONS programme)

KANGAROO GROUP	Movement for free movement. An EP initiative EP LEO6C18, rue Belliard 97-113, B-1047 Brussels, Belgium
KARLSRUHE	JRC establishment Linkenheim, Postfach 2340, D-76125 Karlsruhe, Germany
KAROLUS	Council Decision 92/481/EEC for an action plan for the exchange between Member State administrations of national officials engaged in the implementation of the SEM (1993-1997 and extended to 1999) (OJ L286/92 and OJ L8/93 with latest amendment in OJ L126/98)
KAU	Kind-of-Activity-Unit
KAUDYTE	Acquisition and use of knowledge in the control of dynamic systems (ESPRIT project)
KAVAS	Knowledge Acquisition Visualisation and Assessment Study (AIM project)
KB-MUSICA	Knowledge-Based MUlti-sensors Systems In CIM Applications (ESPRIT project)
KBS-SHIP	Shipboard Installation of Knowledge-Based Systems - Conceptual Design (ESPRIT project)
KESO	A CSCW project to construct a data mining system that satisfies the needs of providers of large-scale databases (partially funded under the TELEMATICS APPLICATIONS programme) http://orgwis.gmd.de/projects/KESO/
KEY ACTIONS	Groupings of research projects directed towards common European challenges or problems. A component of FP5. *See also* THEMATIC PROGRAMMES

KEYCOP	KEY COastal Processes in the mesotrophic Skagerrak and the oligotrophic Northern Aegean: a comparative study (ELOISE project)
KEYMARK	A voluntary quality mark launched by CEN in 1995
KIMSAC	Kiosk based Integrated Multimedia Service Access for Citizens (ACTS project)
KISS	Knowledge-based Interactive Signal monitoring System (AIM project)
KIWI	KBS user friendly system for information bases (ESPRIT project)
KLEX	Development of a knowledge-based system to support operators of waste water treatment plants (EUREKA project)
KNOSOS	KNOwledge-base environment for SOftware System configuration reusing components (ESPRIT project)
KnowEurope	An on-line information service for EU information, incorporating *European Access Plus* Access via CHADWYCK-HEALEY http://www.knoweurope.net
KNOW-HOW LICENSING	Reg 240/96/EC on BLOCK EXEMPTIONS for certain categories of technology transfer agreements including know-how licences (OJ L31/96)
KOMBLE	Communication aids for the handicapped (TIDE project)
*KONVER	A COMMUNITY INITIATIVE to assist regions affected by the Conversion of the defence industry and military bases (1994-1997) (Guidelines in OJ C180/94). *Successor to* PERIFRA
KOPERNICUS	*See* COPERNICUS-PECO

KRITIC	Knowledge Representation and Inference Techniques in Industrial Control (ESPRIT project)
KWICK	Knowledge Workers Intelligently Collecting/coordinating /consulting Knowledge (ESPRIT project)
L	Luxembourg
LAA	Latin American and Asian Countries
LAB	Legal Advisory Board. Set up under the IMPACT programme to advise the Commission on legal issues raised by the development of the I'M
LABIP	Lactic Acid Bacteria INDUSTRIAL PLATFORM http://europa.eu.int/comm./dg12/biotech/ip2.html#LABIP
LABORTEL	Latin American Business OppoRtunities for TELematics applications projects (a Telematics for Education and Training project within the TELEMATICS APPLICATIONS programme)
LACE	Linkage Assistance and Cooperation for the European border regions (within the INTERREG programme). *See also* LACE-PHARE http://www.lace.aebr-agcg.de/lacebr/htm/lframbrx.htm
LACE-PHARE	A programme relating to border regions in CEEC. *See also* LACE
LACOSTS	Labour Costs statistical domain on the NEW CRONOS databank
LAG	Local Action Group (within the LEADER programme)
LAHYSTOTRAIN	Integration of virtual environments and intelligent training systems for LAparoscopy/HYSTerOscopy surgery TRAINing (EMTF project)

LAKES	Long distance dispersal in Acquatic KEy Species (TERI project)
LAMA	Large Manipulators for CIM (ESPRIT project)
LAMA	Very large optical telescopes (EUREKA project)
LAMP	Laser Mouse (TIDE project)
LAPIN	LAbour Policies Information Network (a Telematics for Administrations project within the TELEMATICS APPLICATIONS programme)
LASCAR	LArge SCAle Reprocessing project. A joint EURATOM; International Atomic Energy Agency; French; German; UK; Japanese; United States of America project
LASFLEUR	Remote sensing of vegetation by monitoring laser-induced chlorophyll fluorescence (EUREKA project)
LAT	Learning by Advanced Telecommunications (DELTA project)
LATMIC	Lateral Microstructures (ESPRIT project)
LDA	See LFA
LDC	Less-Developed Countries
LDEIs	Local Development and Employment Initiatives
*LDR	Liberal, Democratic and Reformist Group (of the EP)
LDS	MBE and VPE growth of Low Dimensionality Structure for future quantum semiconductor devices (ESPRIT project)
LDTF	Large Dynamic Test Facility (JRC - reactor safety programme)

LEA	Local Enterprise Agency to provide technical assistance to SMEs as part of the PHARE 1997 programme in Hungary
LEADER +	Links between Actions for the Development of the Rural Economy. A COMMUNITY INITIATIVE (2000-2006) (COM(99) 475) LEADER Coordinating Unit, AEIDL, ch St Pierre 260, B-1040 Brussels, Belgium http://www.rural-europe.aeidl.be/
LEASED LINES Directive	Dir 92/44/EEC on the application of the ONP to leased lines (OJ L165/92 with latest amendment in OJ L14/98)
LEAST	Learning systems standardisation (DELTA project)
LEAST PRIVILEGED GROUPS	*See* POVERTY IV
*LEDA	Local Employment Development Action research programme set up by DG V of the European Commission
*LEGA	Committee on Legal Affairs and Citizen's Rights (of the EP)
LégiChim	Legislative database of chemical substances cited in the OJ. *See* RISC Access via the Internet (password required)
*LEI	*See* ANIMA
LEMMA	Methods and architectures for logic engineering in medicine (AIM project)
LEONARDO DA VINCI	Council Decision 1999/382/EC for an action programme on vocational training policy (2000-2006) (OJ L146/99). *Combines* COMETT; EUROTECNET; FORCE; LINGUA; PETRA LEONARDO Technical Assistance Office, ave de l'Astronomie 9, B-1210 Brussels, Belgium UK contact: Central Bureau for Educational Visits and Exchanges, 10 Spring Gdns, London SW1A 2BN http://europa.eu.int/en/comm/dg22/leonardo.html

LEPE	European Reference Laboratory for Water Pollution. Established by the EI in 1998. It aims to consolidate the scientific and technical support to the Community policy in the field of water Contact: EI at ISPRA
LET'S GO EAST	*See* GO EAST/GO WEST
LFA	Less-Favoured Area
LFR	Less-Favoured Region designated as having high unemployment, low domestic product per capita and low levels of economic prosperity
LFS	Labour Force Survey statistical domain on the NEW CRONOS databank
LFS-R	Regional Labour Force Survey statistical domain on the REGIO database
LG	Liaison Group
LGIB	Local Government International Bureau 35 Great Smith Street, London, SW1P 3BJ, United Kingdom http://www.lgib.gov.uk
LIB-2	Studies on the impact of new information technologies in libraries
LIBE	Committee on citizens' freedoms and rights, justice and home affairs (of the EP)
LIBER	League of European Research Libraries Skindergarde 27 I, DK-1159 København, Denmark
LIDAR	Light Detection and Ranging (environmental research programme)
LIEN	Link Inter-European NGOs. *See* PHARE LIEN; TACIS LIEN

LIFE II	Reg 1404/96 for a financial instrument for environmental protection (OJ L181/96 with amended proposal for extension 2000-2004 in COM(99) 305). LIFE will consist of three components: LIFE-Environment; LIFE-Nature; LIFE-Third Countries. *Replaces* ACNAT; MEDSPA; NORSPA
LIFT	Linking Innovation Finance and Technology. A helpdesk to guide high tech entrepreneurs to obtain funding. Set up under the INNOVATION/SMEs programme http://www.cordis.lu/lift/src/about.htm
LILIENTHAL	Multimedia off- and on-line distance learning for European pilot training (EMTF project)
LINAC	Linear Accelerator at GEEL. A JRC establishment
LINES	Learning Information support Networks in Europe for SOCRATES (a Telematics for Education and Training project within the TELEMATICS APPLICATIONS programme)
LINGUA	Community action programme to promote foreign language competence in the EU (1990-1994) (OJ L239/89). *Continued as* part of the LEONARDO DA VINCI and SOCRATES programmes
LION	Local Integrated Optical Network (ESPRIT project)
LIRN	Library Information enquiry and Referral Network (project within Area 5 of the TELEMATIC SYSTEMS programme)
LISCOM	LIStening COMfort System for hearing-instruments and telephone (a Telematics for Disabled and Elderly People project within the TELEMATICS APPLICATIONS programme)

LISTEC	Database of the technical services in the Member States having the competence to carry out testing of motor vehicles in accordance with the type approval framework Directive 70/156/EEC with latest amendment in OJ L11/99 http://www.listec.lu
LIUTO	Low Impact Urban Transport water Omnibus. Project in the field of design, production and operation for safer, more efficient, environmentally friendly and user-friendly ships (BRITE-EURAM III project)
LOADS Directive	*See* MANUAL HANDLING Directive
LOBI	LOop Blowdown Investigation (JRC - reactor safety programme)
LOCAL CONTENT	Regs 384/96 and 2026/97 which specify the amount of work carried out by a non-EU firm which has been set up in an EU country to assemble imported components into a finished article (OJ L56/96 and L288/97)
local KAU	Local Kind-of-Activity Unit
local UHP	Local Unit of Homogeneous Production
LOCIN	Database on LOCal INitiatives to combat social exclusion in Europe (TSER project) http://www.dur.ac.uk/~dgg0www6/
LOCSTAR	Technological development programme for a system of radio determination by satellites with European coverage (EUREKA project)
LOGIMAX	Development of a 2nd generation information and transport network throughout Europe (EUREKA project)
LOKI	Logic Oriented approach to Knowledge and databases supplying natural use Interaction (ESPRIT project)

LOME CONVENTION	An Agreement between the EU and 69 African, Caribbean and Pacific States for trade, industrial cooperation and so on. (*Lomé I* published in OJ L25/76; *Lomé II* published in OJ L347/80; *Lomé III* published in OJ L86/86; *Lomé IV* (1990-2000) published in OJ L229/91 with amendment in OJ L156/98). *See also* EDF
LONDON REPORT	on *European political cooperation* 1981. Published by HMSO as Cmnd 8424
LOOP	Low-Cost Optical Components (RACE project)
LORAN - C	LORAN - C radionavigation system (OJ L59/92)
LORINE	Limited Rate Imagery Network Elements (RACE project)
LOW VOLTAGE Directive	Dir 73/23/EEC relating to electrical equipment designed for use within certain voltage limits (OJ L77/73 with latest amendment in OJ L220/93)
LRE	Linguistic Research and Engineering (Area 6 of the TELEMATIC SYSTEMS programme)
LRRD	Linkages between Relief, Rehabilitation and Development actions and programmes carried out by EU Member States in THIRD COUNTRIES
LSIF	Large Scale Infrastructure Facility. Part of the PHARE investment strategy for Central Europe
*LST	Life Sciences and Technologies: Activity 1.4 of the (4th) RTD Framework programme. *See* BIOMED II; BIOTECH II; FAIR
LSVI	Large Size Visual Interface design for multimedia workstation terminals (ESPRIT project)

LU	*See* CG
LUCIFER	Land Use Change Interactions with FiRE in Mediterranean landscape (TERI project)
LUCIOLE	Multi-function integrated optical circuits and fibres for sensors and sensor arrays (EUREKA project)
LUGANO CONVENTION	on jurisdiction and the enforcement of judgments in civil and commercial matters 1988 (OJ L319/88). *See also* LUXEMBOURG CONVENTION
LUIC	Local Urban Initiative Centre to provide EU information for sustainable development in cities. *See also* RELAYS
LUPINPUR	Processing of better lupins into high protein feed components (EUREKA project)
LUXEMBOURG AGREEMENT (COMPROMISE)	on majority voting, agreed by the Six Member States in 1966. Published by HMSO as House of Lords Papers 1984-85 (236)
LUXEMBOURG CONVENTION	on jurisdiction and enforcement of judgments in civil and commercial matters (OJ L304/78). *See also* LUGANO CONVENTION
LUXEMBOURG REPORT	on political union, approved in 1970. Published in the *Bulletin of the EC 11/1970*
M3S	Intelligent interface for the rehabilitation environment (TIDE project)
MAAS Group	An independent expert group appointed in 1994 to examine practical issues relating to the EURO
MAASTRICHT TREATY	*See* TREATY ON EUROPEAN UNION

MAC	Multi-purpose Anti-pollution Craft (EUREKA project)
MACPOP	Modelling and Automatic Control of the POlishing Process (BRITE project)
MACRO	Multimedia Application for Clinical Research in Oncology (a Telematics for Healthcare project within the TELEMATICS APPLICATIONS programme)
MACS	Maintenance Assistance Capability for Software (ESPRIT project)
MADMUD	Digital Museums ADministration and MUseumsDidaktik (a Telematics Information Engineering project within the TELEMATICS APPLICATIONS programme)
MADRAS	Modular Approach to Definition of RACE Subscriber premises network (RACE project)
MADS	Message passing Architectures and Description Systems (ESPRIT project)
MAF	Multimedia Applications in Furniture (a Telematics Information Engineering project within the TELEMATICS APPLICATIONS programme)
MAGEC	Modelling Agroecosystems under Global Environmental Change (TERI project)
MAGHREB countries	Algeria; Libya; Mauritania; Morocco and Tunisia
MAGIC	Methods for Advanced Group Technology Integrated with CAD/CAM (ESPRIT project)

MAGICA	Multimedia AGent-based Interactive CAtalogues (a Telematics Information Engineering project within the TELEMATICS APPLICATIONS programme)
MAGNETS	Museum And Galleries NEw Technology Study (a Telematics for Administrations project within the Telematics Application programme)
MAGP	Multi-Annual Guidance Programme
MAHB	Major Accident Hazards Bureau. Based in the JRC at ISPRA
MAID	Multimedia Assets for Industrial Design (a Telematics Information Engineering project within the TELEMATICS APPLICATIONS programme)
MAIL ORDER SALES Directive	*See* DISTANCE SELLING Directive
MALTED	Multimedia Authoring for Language Tutors and Educational Development (EMTF project)
MANICORAL	Multimedia And Network In COoperative Research And Learning (a Telematics for Research project within the TELEMATICS APPLICATIONS programme)
MANSEV	Market Authorisation by Network Submission and EValuation (a Telematics for Healthcare project within the TELEMATICS APPLICATIONS programme)
MANSHOLT PLAN	on the reform of agriculture 1970-1980. Published in the *Bulletin of the EC Supplement 1/1969*

MANUAL HANDLING Directive	Dir 90/269/EEC on the minimum health and safety requirements for manual handling of heavy loads where there is a risk of…back injury to workers (OJ L156/90)
MANUS	Modular ANthropomorphous USer-adaptable hand prosthesis with enhanced mobility and force feedback (a Telematics for Disabled and Elderly People project within the TELEMATICS APPLICATIONS programme)
MAP	Mediterranean Action Plan
MAP	Multi-Annual Programme
MAPS	Mobile Applications Pilot Scheme (RACE project)
MAP-TV	Memory-Archives-Programmes TV (MEDIA project) pl de Bordeaux 3, F-67015 Strasbourg Cédex, France
MARCU	Manipulative Automatic Reaction Control and User supervision (TIDE project)
MARGRITE	MARrow GRaft: Integrated Telematics in Europe (a Telematics for Healthcare project within the TELEMATICS APPLICATIONS programme)
MARIA	Methods for Assessing the Radiological Impact of Accidents (AIM project)
MARIA	Multimedia Applications for Regional and International Access (AIM project)
MARIE	Mobile Autonomous Robot in an Industrial Environment (ESPRIT project)
MARIN	MARine INdustry applications of broadband communications (RACE project)
MARKT	Internal Market DG of the European Commission

MARLIA REPORTS	A device whereby the President of the Council of the European Union presents the General Affairs Council with a progress report on outstanding business from other Councils
MARNET	Inter-regional MARitime information NETwork (TRANSPORT project)
MARNET CFD	Computational Fluid Dynamics for the Marine industry (BRITE/EURAM III project)
MAROPT	MARine OPTical recording system (EUREKA project)
MARPOWER	Concepts of advanced marine machinery systems with low Pollution and high efficiency (BRITE/EURAM III project)
Marques	Association of European Trade Mark Owners 840 Melton Rd, Thurmaston, Leicester LE4 8BN, United Kingdom http://www.martex.co.uk/marques/index.htm
MARS	Highly secure office information systems - Definition phase (ESPRIT project)
MARS	Major Accident Reporting System based at ISPRA
MARS	Monitoring Agriculture with Remote Sensing (ISPRA project)
MARS	Multimedia Access Relying on Standards (ISIS multimedia project) http://www.ispo.cec.be/isis/96mars.htm
MARSIS	MArine Remote Sensing Information System for regional European seas (EUREKA project)
MART	Definition of an environment to maximise the MARket for Telecommunications-based RT (TIDE project)

MARTRANS

Part of the Marine information society to establish a real-time information system for cargoes and vessels
Contact: European Commission Transport DG

MASCOT

Multi-environment Advanced System for COlour Treatment (ESPRIT project)

MASHREQ countries

Egypt; Jordan; Lebanon and Syria

MASIS

Human factors in the man/ship system for the European fleets (EURET project)

MASQUES

Medical Application Software QUality Enhancement by Standards (AIM project)

*MAST III

Council Decision 94/804/EC for a Marine Science and Technology R&D programme (1994-1998) (OJ L334/94). *See also* ENVIRONMENT. *Replaced by* EESD
http://www.cordis.lu/mast/home.html

MATER

One of the four major regional RTD projects of MAST III. MATER covers the Mediterranean. *See also* BASYS; CANIGO; OMEX

MATHS

Mathematical Access for technology and science for visually disabled users (TIDE project)

MATIC

Multi-strategy Authoring Toolkit for Intelligent Courseware (DELTA project)

MATISSE2000

Metropolitan Area Tourist Information Support System for Europe 2000 (a Telematics for Integrated Applications for Digital Sites project within the TELEMATICS APPLICATIONS programme)

MATTHAEUS

Council Decision 91/341/EEC for a multiannual programme for the vocational training of customs officials (OJ L187/91)

*MATTHAEUS-TAX	Council Decision 93/588/EEC for an action programme for the vocational training of indirect taxation officials (1993-1997) (OJ L280/93). *Replaced by* FISCALIS
MAUVE	Mini Autonomous Underwater VEhicle (MAST III project) http://www.mumm.ac.be/docs_en/projects/mauve/
MAWP	Multiannual Work Programme
MAX	Metropolitan area communication system (ESPRIT project)
MBLN	Multimedia as Business option for Local Newspapers (a Telematics Information Engineering project within the TELEMATICS APPLICATIONS programme)
MC	Management Committee
MCA	Monetary Compensatory Amounts
MCAC	Management and Coordination Advisory Committee
MCACE	Measurement Characterisation and control of Ambulatory Care in Europe (AIM project)
MCBRIDE	Development of a Multi-Chamber Batch Reactor for the production of multilayer Interpoly DiElectrics (ESPRIT project)
MCE	Main Component Elements. National environmental information bodies appointed as units in the EIONET by Member States
MCPR	Multi-media Communication Processing and Representation (RACE project)
ME	European Mutual Society (Amended Proposal in OJ C236/93)
M-E	*See* MERCATOR-EDUCATION

MEANS	Methods and tools for evaluating structural assistance from the Community in order to ensure greater effectiveness in the use of EU funds
*MEASUREMENTS AND TESTING	Research and technological development programme in the field of measurements and testing (1990-1994) (OJ L126/92). *Continued as* SMT
MEC	Special committee of inquiry
MECANO	Mechanism of automatic comparison of CD-ROM answers with OPACs (project within Area 5 of the TELEMATIC SYSTEMS programme)
MECCANO	Multimedia Education and Conferencing Collaboration over ATM Networks and Others (a Telematics for Research project within the TELEMATICS APPLICATIONS programme)
MECCS	Modular Environmental Control and Communications System (TIDE project)
MECDIN	Expert system on portable CD-ROM terminal (EUREKA project)
*MECU	Million European Currency Units
MEDA	Reg 1488/96 for a Mediterranean Special programme (1995-1999) (OJ L189/96 with guidelines in OJ L325/96). *See also* EUMEDIS; EUROMED; EUROMED HERITAGE; MED-Campus; MED-Invest; MED-Media; MED-Techno; MED-Urbs
MEDALUS	Mediterranean Desertification and Land Use Impacts (EPOCH project)
Med-Avicenne	*See* AVICENNE INITIATIVE

MED-Campus	Cooperative networks between Higher Education Institutions in the EC and Mediterranean Third countries (1992-) (Information in OJ C161/95). *See also* MEDA
MEDEA	Micro Electronics Development for European Applications (EUREKA project). *Previously* JESSI
MEDIA II	Council Decisions 95/563/EC and 95/564/EC for the implementation of a programme to promote the development of the European Audiovisual Industry (1996-2000) (OJ L321/95) http://europa.eu.int/en/comm/dg10/avpolicy/media/en/home-m2.html
Mediaage	Electronic European news service on ageing issues http://www.mediaage.net/
MEDIAKIDS	MultiMEDIA for KIDS (EMTF project)
MEDICA	Multimedial Medical Diagnostic Assistant (AIM project)
MEDICI Framework	Multimedia for EDucation and employment through Integrated Cultural Initiative (IS initiative) http://www.medicif.org
MEDICINE	MEdical Data InterChange IN Europe (EUREKA project)
MEDICO	Multimedia Education Datasystem In Clinical Oncology (a Telematics for Healthcare project within the TELEMATICS APPLICATIONS programme)

MEDIMEDIA	Medical Images Integration for Multimedia European Databases Interconnection and common Access (a Telematics for Healthcare project within the TELEMATICS APPLICATIONS programme) http://www.ehto.org/vds/projects/medimedia.html
MED-Invest	Cooperation for the development of SMEs in the EU and Mediterranean Third countries (1992-) (Information in OJ C150/94). *See also* MEDA
MED-Media	A programme to enhance and create networks between media professionals in the EU and Mediterranean Third countries (1992-) (Information in OJ C128/95). *See also* MEDA
MED-Migration	A sub-topic of MED-Urbs (1995-) (Information in OJ C180/95)
*MEDREP	ECHO database of biomedical and health care research projects in the EC
MEDSEC	Healthcare security and privacy in the information society (ISIS healthcare networks project) http://www.ispo.cec.be/isis/96medsec.htm
*MEDSPA	Mediterranean Special Programme of Action for the protection of the environment (1991-1996) (OJ L63/91). *Replaced by* LIFE
MED-Techno	Improvement of efficient technologies in 12 Mediterranean countries (1996-) (Information in OJ C161/95). *See also* MEDA
MED-Urbs	Cooperation between local authorities in the EU and Mediterranean Third countries (1992-) (Information in OJ C128/95). *See also* MEDA; MED-Migration
MEET	MEthodologies for Estimating air pollutant emissions from Transport (TRANSPORT project)

MEGATAQ	MEthods and Guidelines for the Assessment of Telematics Applications Quality (a Telematics Engineering project within the TELEMATICS APPLICATIONS programme)
MEIP	Market Economy Investor Principle
*MEL	Microelectronics Technology programme (1982-1985) (OJ L376/81)
MEMCARE	Development of mobile self-supporting emergency hospitals for immediate medical attendance for victims of calamities (EUREKA project)
MEMO	Background information on EU events Access via RAPID
MENTOR	Expert system for dealing with major plant failures and security control (EUREKA project)
MENTOR	Multimedia Education Network for Teaching, Output and Research (EMTF project)
MEP	Member of the EP
MERA	Mars-monitoring of agriculture by remote sensing (PHARE project)
MERCATOR-EDUCATION	European network for regional or minority languages and education Contact: Fryske Akademy, PO Box 54, Coulonhus, NL-8900 DX, Leeuwarden, Netherlands http://www.troc.es/mercator/
MERCHANT	Methods in Electronic Retail Cash Handling (RACE project)
MERCI	Multimedia European Research Conferencing Integration (a Telematics for Research project within the TELEMATICS APPLICATIONS programme)

MERCOSUR countries	Mercado Comun del Sur (Southern cone countries) consisting of Argentina; Brazil; Paraguay and Uruguay
MERGE	Media Economic Research Group of Europe (EUREKA project)
MERGER CONTROL Regulation	Reg 4064/89 on the control of concentrations between undertakings (OJ L257/90 with latest amendment in OJ L180/97)
MERGER TREATY	establishing a single Council and a single Commission. Signed by Belgium, France, Germany, Italy, Luxembourg and the Netherlands on 8th April 1965. Came into force 1st July 1967
MERIT	Municipal Economic and social Reform Initiative of Tacis (TACIS project)
MERMAID	Marine Environmental Remote-controlled Measuring And Integrated Detection (EUREKA project)
MERMAID	Medical emergency aid through telematics (a Telematics for Healthcare project within the TELEMATICS APPLICATIONS programme)
MERMAID	MEtrication and Resource Modelling AID (ESPRIT project)
MERMAIDS	Mediterranean Eddy Resolving Modelling And InterDisciplinary Studies (MAST project)
MESA group	Mutual ECU Settlement Account. Financial agencies operating in ECUs
MESH	Possible mechanisms for High-TC superconductivity and phenomenological approaches (ESPRIT project)

META	Multimedia Educational Telematics Applications (a Telematics for Education and Training project within the TELEMATICS APPLICATIONS programme)
METAP	Mediterranean Environmental Technological Assistance Programme financed by the EIB and the World Bank
METARAIL	METhodologies and Actions for RAIL noise and vibration control (TRANSPORT project) http://www.cordis.lu/transport/src/metarail.htm
METASA	Digital Towns: Multimedia European experimental Towns with A Social pull Approach (a Telematics for Urban and Rural Areas project within the TELEMATICS APPLICATIONS programme)
METEOR	An integrated formal approach to industrial software development (ESPRIT project)
METKIT	Metrics Education Tool Kit (ESPRIT project)
METRE	Measurements, standards and reference techniques (JRC research programme)
METR-ICS	High precision (ESPRIT project)
*MEUA	Million Units of Accounts. *See also* MECU
*MFA	Multi-Fibre Agreement (1974-1994). *MFA I* published in OJ L118/74; *MFA II* published in OJ L348/77; *MFA III* published in OJ L83/82; *MFA IV* published in OJ L341/86 and extended to December 1994 in OJ L124/94. *Replaced by* the WTO Agreement on Textiles and Clothing (1995-2004)
MGP	Mediterranean Guidance Programme
MGS	Multi Guarantee Scheme

MIAC	Multipoint Interactive Audiovisual Communication (ESPRIT project)
MIAS	Multipoint Interactive Audiovisual System (ESPRIT project)
*MIC	Mobile Information Centre of the European Commission Representation Office in London
MICA	Met Improvements for Controller Aids (TRANSPORT project)
MICOFF	MIcrowave COnservation of Fast Food (EUREKA project)
MICROMARE	Development of MICRO-sensors for use in the MARine Environment (MAST III project) http://www.dmu.dk/LakeandEstuarineEcology/Micromare/
MIDAS-NET	Multimedia Information, Demonstration And Support NETwork. Operational since 1997 (INFO2000 initiative)
MIF	Maritime Industries Forum Contact: European Commission, rue de la Science 15, B-1000 Brussels, Belgium
MIGRAT	International Migration statistical domain on the NEW CRONOS databank
MILIEU	Environment statistical domain on the NEW CRONOS databank
MIME	Development of Emulators and Simulators (RACE project)
MIMEH	Models of Innovative Management of European Heritage (RAPHAEL project)
MIMI	Medical workstation for Intelligent interactive acquisition and analysis of digital Medical Images (AIM project)
MINE	Microbial Information Network Europe (BAP project)

MINERVA	Education and multimedia initiative (part of the SOCRATES programme)
MINIFLOATER	Low cost oil and gas production facility in deep water (EUREKA project)
MINSTREL	New information models for office filing and retrieval (ESPRIT project)
MINT	Managing the Integration of New Technology (SPRINT project)
MINTOUR	Multimedia Information Network for TOURists (a Telematics for Administrations project within the TELEMATICS APPLICATIONS programme)
MINWAGES	Minimum Wages statistical domain on the NEW CRONOS databank
MIOCA	Monolithic Integrated Optics for Customer Access Applications (RACE project)
MIP	Multi-annual Indicative Programme
MIPEX	Message based Industrial Property (a Telematics for Administrations project within the TELEMATICS APPLICATIONS programme)
MIRAGE	Combined multimedia development environment for TV, radio and on-line production and delivery (a Telematics Information Engineering project within the TELEMATICS APPLICATIONS programme)
Mirage	Migration of Radioisotopes in the Geosphere (Radioactive waste programme)
*MIRIAM	Model Scheme for Information on Rural Development Initiatives and Agricultural Markets. *See* CARREFOUR

MIRS	Musical Information Retrieval System (project within Area 5 of the TELEMATIC SYSTEMS programme)
MIRTI	Models of Industrial Relations in Telework Innovation (a Telematics Engineering project within the TELEMATICS APPLICATIONS programme)
MIRTO	Multimedia Interaction with Regional and Transnational Organisations (a Telematics for Administrations project within the TELEMATICS APPLICATIONS programme)
MIS	Multilingual Information System (ESPRIT project)
MISEP	Mutual Information System on Employment Polices in Europe. A database on employment policy and unemployment measures IAS Institute for Applied Socio-Economics, Novalisstrasse 10, D-10115 Berlin, Germany UK contact: Department of Employment, Caxton House, Tothill Street, London SW1H 9NF
*Miss Model	Term used to calculate the benefits (or otherwise) of an EC/GATT Agreement
MISSOC	Mutual Information System on Social Protection in the EU http://europa.eu.int/comm/dg05/soc-prot/missoc98/english/f_main.htm
MITHRA	Development, industrialisation and the sale of mobile robots for tele-surveillance (EUREKA project)
MITI	Multilingual Intelligent Interface (IMPACT project)
MLIS	Council Decision 96/664/EC on the adoption of a multiannual programme to promote the Multi-Lingual Information Society (1997-1999) (OJ L306/96). *See also* ELRA

MLT	Machine Learning Toolbox (ESPRIT project)
MLTS	Medium and Long-term Translation Service
MM12	A multi-modal interface for man-machine interaction with knowledge-based systems (ESPRIT project)
MMOMS	Multi-Modal Organ Modelling System (AIM project)
MNC	Mediterranean Non-Member Countries (Algeria; Cyprus; Egypt; Israel and the Occupied Territories; Jordan; Lebanon; Malta; Morocco; Syria; Tunisia; Turkey)
MNE	MultiNational Enterprise
MNY	Banking and financial statistical domain on the NEW CRONOS databank
MOBCARE	Home/ambulatory healthcare services based on mobile communication (a Telematics for Healthcare project within the TELEMATICS APPLICATIONS programme) http://www.ehto.org/vds/projects/mobcare.html
MOBIC	Mobility of Blind and elderly people Interacting with Computers (TIDE project)
MOBIDICK	Multivariable On-line BIlingual DICtionary Kit (EUREKA project)
MOBIL	Intelligent MOBILity and transportation aid for elderly people with combined motor and mental impairment (a Telematics for Disabled and Elderly People project within the TELEMATICS APPLICATIONS programme)
MOBILE	Extending European information access through Mobile libraries (project within Area 5 of the TELEMATIC SYSTEMS programme)

MODA SPECTRA	MOtor Disability Assessment SPECialists TRAining (EMTF project)
MODEM	MODelling of EMission and consumption in urban areas (DRIVE project)
MODEM	Multimedia Optimisation Demonstration for Education in Microelectronics (a Telematics for Education and Training project within the TELEMATICS APPLICATIONS programme)
MODEMA	Modelling for the disabled in working environments (TIDE project)
MODESTI	Mould design and manufacturing optimisation by development, standardisation and integration of CAD/CAM procedures (BRITE project)
MODULATES	Multimedia Organisation for Developing the Understanding and Learning of Advanced Technologies in European Schools (EMTF project)
MOHAWC	Models of Human Actions in Work Context (ESPRIT project)
MOLCOM	Exploration of electronic properties in conducting organic materials as a function of structural modifications (ESPRIT project)
MOLSWITCH	Evaluation of MOLecular SWITCH type devices… (ESPRIT project)
MOMEDA	Mobile Medical Data (a Telematics for Healthcare project within the TELEMATICS APPLICATIONS programme) http://www.ehto.org/vds/projects/momeda.html
MONICA	System integration for incident-congestion detection and traffic monitoring (DRIVE project)

*MONITOR	Strategic analysis, forecasting and evaluation in matters of research and technology programme (1989-1993) (OJ L200/89). *See also* FAST; SAST; SPEAR. *Continued as* TSER
MONNET PROJECT	*See* JEAN MONNET PROJECT
MONOFAST	Monolithic integration beyond 26.5 GHZ (ESPRIT project)
MONTI REPORT	on taxation in the EU (COM(96) 546)
MONTREAL PROTOCOL	Council Decision 88/540/EEC on substances that deplete the ozone layer (OJ L297/88; First amendment OJ L377/91; Second amendment OJ L33/94)
MOP	Multifund Operational Programme
MORE	Marc Optical Recognition (project within Area 5 of the TELEMATIC SYSTEMS programme)
MORE	MObile REscue phone (a Telematics for Disabled and Elderly People project within the TELEMATICS APPLICATIONS programme)
MOSAIC-HS	MOdular System for Application Integration and Clustering in Home System (a Telematics for Disabled and Elderly People project within the TELEMATICS APPLICATIONS programme)
MOSDT	MOMBSE for III-V Semiconductor Devices and Technology (ESPRIT project)
MOSES	Development of a new generation of multi-media database services with integration of the multi-media features in the whole chain of equipment (EUREKA project)
MOU	Memorandum of Understanding
MOU	*See* EUAM

MOVAID	MObility and actiVity AssIstance systems for the Disabled (TIDE project)
MPD	Multi-lingual Product Description (EUREKA project)
MPP	Multi-annual Policy Programme
MS	Member States of the EU
MST	Manufacturing Science and Technology for ICs production (within the JESSI programme)
MTC	Mediterranean Third Countries
MTFA	Medium-Term Financial Assistance
MTFS	Medium-Term Financial Support
MTN-T	Multimodal Trans-European transport Network
MTP	Managers Training Programme. A TACIS project developed in 1998 to continue the PIP programme for NIS managers
MTP-II MATER	Mediterranean Targeted Project phase II (MAST III project)
*MUA	Million Units of Account. *See* MECU
MUCOM	Multisensory Control of Movement (ESPRIT project)
MUCPI	Monetary Union Consumer Price Index which is based on the HCPIs of the Member States and produced by EUROSTAT (OJ C84/95)
MUICP	*See* MUCPI
Multi-APEL	Accreditation of Prior Experience and Learning (LEONARDO DA VINCI project)
MULTICRAFT	Industrial fettling cell (EUREKA project)

MULTIFIBRE AGREEMENTS	*See* MFA
MULTIMED	Demonstration of functional service integration in support of professional user-groups (RACE project)
Multimedia Broker	Critical support tools for Multimedia publishing (a Telematics Information Engineering project within the TELEMATICS APPLICATIONS programme)
MULTIPLE	Multimedia education and training system (a Telematics for Disabled and Elderly People project within the TELEMATICS APPLICATIONS programme)
MULTOS	Multimedia filing system (ESPRIT project)
MUNICIPIA	Multilingual Urban Network for the Integration of CIty Planners and Involved local Actors (a Telematics for Urban and Rural Areas project within the TELEMATICS APPLICATIONS programme)
MUREX	Multi-purpose Underwater Remote EXpert system (EUREKA project)
MURIM	Multi-dimensional Reconstruction and Imaging in Medicine (AIM project)
MUS	Monetary Unit Sampling. A method of statistical sampling undertaken by the Court of Auditors to ensure that errors affecting the reliability of accounts do not exceed the reference amount selected by the Court of Auditors
MUSA	MUltilingual multimedia Speech Aid for hearing and language difficulties (TIDE project)
MUSE	MUltimedia distributed Services Environment (ISIS multimedia project) http://www.ispo.cec.be/isis/96muse.htm

MUSE	S/W quality and reliability metrics: safety management and clerical systems (ESPRIT project)
MUSIK	Project to give distributors, publishers and the public access to an electronic classical music catalogue (TEDIS project)
MUSIP	MUltiSensor Image Processor (ESPRIT project)
MUST	Next generation database management system (ESPRIT project)
MUSYC	MUlti-media SYstems for Customs (a Telematics for Administrations project within the TELEMATICS APPLICATIONS programme)
MUTATE	MUltimedia Tools for Advanced GIS Training in Europe (EMTF project)
MUWIC	MUltimedia for Women In the Cultural industries (NOW project) http://www.miid.net/now/muwic.html
MWW	Mastering the Wired World (a Telematics Information Engineering project within the TELEMATICS APPLICATIONS programme)
*NA	National Accounts statistical domain on the NEW CRONOS databank. *See* NA_FINA; NA_MNAG; NA_SEC1; NA_SEC2; NA_SECT
NA	*See* NI
NABS	*Nomenclature for the Analysis and Comparison of Scientific programmes and Budgets.* Published by EUR-OP for EUROSTAT 1993.1994. See also SIMONE

NACE Rev 1	*General industrial classification of economic activities within the EU.* Published by EUR-OP for EUROSTAT 1996. See also PRODCOM; SIMONE http://europa.eu.int/eurostat.html
NADC	Non-Associated Developing Countries
NA_FINA	National Accounts-Financial accounts statistical domain on the NEW CRONOS databank
NA_MNAG	Candidate countries non-financial accounts statistical domain on the NEW CRONOS databank
NANA	Novel Algorithms for New real-time VLSI Architectures (ESPRIT project)
NANOFET	Performance and physical limits of HFET transistors (ESPRIT project)
NANSDEV	NANostructures for Semiconductor DEVices (ESPRIT project)
NAOPIA	New Architectures for Optical Processing in Industrial Applications (ESPRIT project)
NAP	National Awareness Partners. A network to raise awareness of the existence and availability of electronic information services. Created under the IMPACT programme UK contact: Aslib, Staple Hall, Stone House Court, London EC3A 7PB
NAPPIES	*See* NAP
NARCISSE	Network of Art Research Computer Image SyStems in Europe (IMPACT project)
NARIC	National Academic Recognition Information Centres. Established in 1982 and coordinated by the Education and Culture DG of the European Commission with national centres. Currently within the SOCRATES programme http://europa.eu.int/en/comm/dg12/socrates/agenar.html

NA_SEC1	National Accounts aggregates statistical domain on the NEW CRONOS databank
NA_SEC2	National Accounts branches of production statistical domain on the NEW CRONOS databank
NA_SECT	National Accounts by sector statistical domain on the NEW CRONOS databank
NATALI PRIZE	An annual award to a journalist for articles in newspapers or magazines published anywhere in the world in one of the EU official languages on the topic of development cooperation
NATASHA	Network And Tools for the Assessment of Speech/language and Hearing Ability (a Telematics for Disabled and Elderly People project within the TELEMATICS APPLICATIONS programme)
NAT-LAB	Natural Learner Acquisition (DELTA project)
NATURA 2000	A Community ecological network of protected sites designated by Member States under the BIRDS and HABITATS Directives Contact: European Commission Environment DG
NCAP	New Cars Assessment Programme (1996-1997) to ensure safety testing of passenger cars
NCB	EU National Central Banks http://www.ecb.int/
NCC	National Coordinating Committee (of RELAYS in the UK) c/o Relay Europe, Charlemagne House, 2 Enys Rd, Eastbourne BN21 2DE, United Kingdom
NCE	Non-Compulsory Expenditure

*NCI	New Community Instrument. A financial mechanism (1979-1990). *NCI I* published in OJ L125/79; *NCI II* published in OJ L116/82); *NCI III* published in OJ L112/83; *NCI IV* published in OJ L71/87
NCP	National Contact Points in EU Member States, which form part of the CRAFT initiative
NCPI	New Commercial Policy Instrument
NCU	National Coordination Units
NDA	Non-Differentiated Appropriations
NDSNET	Harmonisation of Nephrology Data Systems within regional NETworks (a Telematics for Healthcare project within the TELEMATICS APPLICATIONS programme)
NEAPOL	Negotiated Environmental Agreements
NEC	Network of Employment Coordinators (OJ C328/89)
NECTAR	Networked Electronic storage and Communication of Telematics Applications programme Results (a Telematics Engineering project within the TELEMATICS APPLICATIONS programme)
NEGATIVE ASSENT	Process by which the EP can veto legislation by absolute majority in 14 policy areas. Introduced in the TREATY ON EUROPEAN UNION
NEMESYS	Traffic and quality-of-service management for IBCN (RACE project)
*NEPTUNE	New European Programme for Technology Utilisation iN Education (OJ C187/87). Never formally adopted by the Commission

NER	Network of UK European RELAYS
NERVES	Innovative architectures for neurocomputing machines and VLSI neuram networks (ESPRIT project)
NESC	Network for the Evaluation of Steel Components. Established by the JRC with the IAM as the Operating Agent and the Reference Laboratory
NESSIE	A CSCW project in the field of computers as a social medium (partially funded by the Commission under the TELEMATICS APPLICATIONS programme) http://orgwis.gmd.de/projects/nessie/
NESSTAR	Networked Social Science Tools and Resources (a Telematics Information Engineering project within the TELEMATICS APPLICATIONS programme)
NET	Next European Torus
NET	Norme Européenne de Télécommunication. An approved technical specification of the CEPT
Netd@ys Europe	Commission initiative to promote the effective use of on-line technology in education http://europa.eu.int/en/comm/dg22/netdays.index.html
NETLINK	Validation and coordination of implementation of interoperable data card systems and intranet solutions before nation wide implementation (a Telematics for Healthcare project within the TELEMATICS APPLICATIONS programme) http://www.ehto.org/vds/projects/netlink.html
NETLOGO	The European educational interactive site (EMTF project) http://www.netlogo.org/

NETMAN	Functional specification for IBC management (RACE project)
NETS	Net for NETS (a Telematics for Administration project within the TELEMATICS APPLICATIONS programme)
NETS	*See* TN-NETS
NETT	Network for Environmental Technology Transfer ave Louise 207, Boîte 10, B-1050 Brussels, Belgium
NEUTRABAS	NEUTRA1 product definition dataBASe for large multi-functional systems (ESPRIT project)
NEVIS	NEural Vehicle Information System (VALUE project)
NEW APPROACH Directives	Council Resolution on a new approach to technical harmonisation and standards (OJ C136/85) http://www.newapproach.org
NEW CRONOS	EUROSTAT databank of macroeconomic statistics. *Previously* CRONOS Available from EUROSTAT Data Shop and licence holders. Extracts available on request on paper, diskette, CD-ROM or via e-mail
NFP	National Focal Points for the Telematics for libraries programme UK National Focal Point for the Telematics Programme at the Library and Information Commission, 2 Sheraton Street, London W1V 4BH
NFS	Council Decision 1999/175/Euratom adopting a specific RTD programme in the field of nuclear energy (Nuclear Fission Safety) (1998-2002) (OJ L64/1999) http://europa.eu.int/comm/dg12/fission/fission3.html
NGAA	National Grant Awarding Authority (within the ERASMUS and SOCRATES programmes)

NGDO	Non-Governmental Development Organisation
NGL	*See* EUL/NGL
NGO	Non-Governmental Organisation
NGO VOICE	Voluntary Organisations In Cooperation in Emergencies within the Liaison Committee of NGDOs to the EU sq Ambiorix 10, B-1000 Brussels, Belgium
*NI	*See* IND
NIC	*See* NCI
NICE	NItrogen Cycling in Estuaries (ELOISE project)
*NICE	Nomenclature of the Industries in the European Communities. *See* NACE Rev 1
NIGHTINGALE	Nursing Informatics: Generic High-level Training in Informatics for Nurses; General Applications for Learning and Education (a Telematics for Healthcare project within the TELEMATICS APPLICATIONS programme)
NIGHT OF THE LONG KNIVES	Discussions to allocate portfolios to the incoming Commissioners
*NIMEXE	Nomenclature of goods for the external trade statistics of the Community and statistics of trade between Member States. *Replaced by the CN*
NINETEEN NINETY TWO	*See* SEM (Single European Market)
NIP	National Indicative Programme which is negotiated by each ACP country
NIPRO	*Common Nomenclature of Industrial Products.* Published by OOPEC in 1975
NIS	New Independent States (of the former Soviet Union)

NITRATES Directive	Dir 91/676/EEC on the protection of waters against pollution caused by nitrates from agricultural sources (OJ L375/91)
NITREX	Nitrogen Saturation Experiments (STEP project)
NIVEMES	A network of integrated vertical medical services targeting ships and other vessels and remote populations (a Telematics for Healthcare project within the TELEMATICS APPLICATIONS programme)
NJORD-TIDE	Methods for user sensitive evaluations of domotic environments (a Telematics for Disabled and Elderly People project within the TELEMATICS APPLICATIONS programme)
NL	Dutch
NL	Netherlands
NLPAD	Natural Language Processing of Patient Discharge (AIM project)
NMP	New Mediterranean Policy
NOHA	Network On Humanitarian Assistance diploma
NOISE	Electrical fluctuations and noise in advanced microelectronics… (ESPRIT project)
NONS	NOtification of New Substances. *See also* SENSE
NORCAR-TRAMET	Development of a special off-road machine for soil preparation in reforestation (EUREKA project)
NOROS	Quantum NOise Reduction schemes in Optical Systems (ESPRIT project)

*NORSPA	North Sea Special Action Programme to clean up coastal zones and coastal waters (OJ L370/91). *Replaced by* LIFE
NOSE	NOmenclature for Sources of Emissions. Developed by EUROSTAT to facilitate the description of emission sources. Manual published by EUROSTAT
*NOW	New Opportunities for Women. Part of EMPLOYMENT, the COMMUNITY INITIATIVE (1994-1999) (Guidelines in OJ C200/96). *See also* HORIZON; INTEGRA; IRIS; YOUTHSTART
NPAA	National Programme for the Adoption of the Acquis which is drawn up by each country applying for membership of the EU. *See also* ACQUIS COMMUNAUTAIRE
*NPCI	National Programme of Community Interest designated by the ERDF (1979-1999). *Replaced by* CI
NQ	Non-Quota programme
NSI	National Statistical Institute. Title of the organisation responsible for statistics within a Member State
NSIGHT	Vision systems for natural human environment (ESPRIT project)
NST/R	Revised Uniform Nomenclature of Goods for Transport Statistics http://europa.eu.int/en/comm/dg07/tif/nomenclatures_nst.htm
NT	New Technologies
NTB	Non-Tariff Barrier
NTO	National TEMPUS Office
NUTOX	Testing the impact of human activities on the development of toxic algae blooms (MAST III project)

NUTS	*Regions: Nomenclature of Territorial Units for Statistics* 1999. Published by EUR-OP for EUROSTAT
NVA	Net Value Added
OAR	Specification of an Open Architecture for Reasoning (AIM project)
OASIS	Open and Secure Information Systems (EUREKA project)
OBJECTIVES	Priority Objectives within the STRUCTURAL FUNDS currently 1. To promote regions lagging behind in development 2. To convert regions in structural crisis 3. Regions needing support for education, training and jobs
OBNOVA	Reg 1628/96 for the rehabilitation and reconstruction of Bosnia and Herzegovina, Croatia, the Federal Republic of Yugoslavia and the Former Yugoslav Republic of Macedonia (OJ L204/96 with latest amendment in OJ L122/98). *See also* EAFR http://europa.eu.int/comm/dg1a/obnova/index.htm
OBSERVATORY	A team of experts, brought together from each Member State by the European Commission, to advise on the situation regarding a particular topic. *See* EIRO; IMO; OEST; OETH; SME OBSERVATORY; SMO
OCDS	Open Control Display System for industrial automation (EUREKA project)
OCT	Council Decision 91/482/EEC on the association of Overseas Countries and Territories within the EEC (France, Netherlands, UK) (OJ L263/91 with latest amendment in OJ L329/97)
ODAS	Ocean Data Acquisition System (COST action project)

ODIN	Origin-Destination INformation versus traffic control (DRIVE project)
ODL	Open and Distance Learning (within the SOCRATES programme)
ODYSSEUS	Joint Action 98/244/JHA adopted by the Council introducing a programme of training, exchanges and cooperation in the field of asylum, immigration and the crossing of external borders (1998-2002) (OJ L99/98). *Previously* SHERLOCK http://europa.eu.int/comm/sg/tfjai/project/odysseus/index_en.htm
OECD	Organisation for Economic Cooperation and Development rue André Pascal 2, F-75775 Paris Cédex 16, France http://www.oecd.org/
OEDT	*See* EMCDDA
OEIL	An EP database which shows the status of EU legislative proposals http:wwwdb.europarl.eu.int/dors/oeil/en/search.shtm
OEITFL	Association of European Fruit and Vegetable Processing Industries ave de Cortenberg 172, Boîte 6, B-1000 Brussels, Belgium
OEST	OBSERVATORY for Science and Technology to be set up under the IPTS
OETH	European OBSERVATORY for Textiles and Clothing
OFCA	Organisation of Manufacturers of Cellulose Products for Foodstuffs c/o Hercules BV, PO Box 5822, NL-2280 AR Rijswijk, Netherlands
OFELIA	Optical Fibres for ELectrical Industry Applications (BRITE project)
OFL	Office for Legislation. Body responsible for checking conformity with the Acquis. *See* ACQUIS COMMUNAUTAIRE

OHIM	Office for Harmonisation in the Internal Market to register Trade Marks. Set up under Reg 40/94 (OJ L11/94 with latest amendments in Reg 2868/95 in OJ L303/95) ave de Aguilera 20, E-03080 Alicante, Spain http://oami.eu.int/
OII	Open Information Interchange service. Part of INFO 2000
OIL	A database of prices of petroleum products Access on-line via EUROSTAT official gateways
OISIN	Joint Action 97/12/JHA for the exchange and training of, and cooperation between, law enforcement authorities (1997-2000) (OJ L7/97) http://europa.eu.int/comm/sg/tfjai/project/oisin_en.htm
OJ	*Official Journal of the European Communities* which is published by EUR-OP Electronic access via the Internet: CELEX; EUDOR; EUR-Lex and via CD-ROM: CONTEXT (OJ 'C'); ELLIS; EUR-Lex
OJ ANNEX	*Official Journal of the European Communities: Annex* of Parliamentary Debates in the EP
OJ 'C'	*Official Journal of the European Communities: C series*: Information and notices. *See also* OJ 'C E' Electronic access *See* OJ
OJ 'C E'	*Official Journal of the European Communities: CE series*. An electronic version of OJ 'C' which became available in 1999. It does not duplicate the contents of OJ 'C' and currently contains the text of COM DOCS (which ceased publication in OJ 'C' in July 1999) and EP written questions (from 29 January 2000). Further additions are expected Access: It appears firstly on the EUR-Lex site but is also available on the OJ 'L' and 'C' monthly CD-ROMs and the CELEX and EUDOR databases
OJEC	*See* OJ

OJ 'L'	*Official Journal of the European Communities: L series*: Legislation Electronic access *See* OJ
OJ 'S'	*Official Journal of the European Communities: S series*: public works, public supplies, public services, EEA and research tenders. No longer available in paper format. *See also* TED CD-ROM available from CONTEXT; EUR-OP and TSO
OLAF	Commission Decision 99/352/EC establishing a European Anti-Fraud Office (OJ L136/99). Operational since 1 June 1999. *Successor to* UCLAF
OLDI	On-Line Data Interchange. One of two EUROCONTROL standards adopted by Dir 97/15/EC which covers the specifications for the procurement of air management equipment and systems (OJ L95/97). *See also* ADEXP
OLE	Organisational Learning in Enterprises (DELTA project)
OLEW	Open Learning Experimental Workshop (DELTA project)
OLIVES	OpticaL Interconnections for VLSI and Electronic Systems (ESPRIT project)
OLMO	On-vehicle Laser Microsystem for Obstacle detection (INNOVATION project)
OMBUDSMAN	The person appointed by the EP to investigate complaints concerning maladministration in any EU Institution or activity. Introduced in the TREATY ON EUROPEAN UNION Mr M J Söderman, ave du Président Schuman 1, BP 403, F-67001 Strasbourg, France http://www.euro-ombudsman.eu.int/

OMEX	Ocean Margin EXchange. One of the four major regional RTD projects of MAST III. OMEX covers the Atlantic. *See also* BASYS; CANIGO; MATER
OMNI	Office wheelchair with high Manoeuverability and Navigational Intelligence for people with severe handicap (TIDE project)
ONE	OPAC Networking in Europe (TELEMATICS APPLICATIONS project)
ON LIVE	ON-Line Interactive Virtual Educator (EMTF project)
ONP	Dir 90/387/EEC on Open Network Provision in the telecommunications sector (OJ L192/90 with latest amendment in OJ L295/97)
OOPEC	Office for Official Publications of the European Communities. *See* EUR-OP
OP	Official Publications. *See* EUR-OP
OP	Operational Programme (under the STRUCTURAL FUNDS)
OPEN	Observatoire Permanent de l'Environnement rue Charles Meert 25, B-1030 Brussels, Belgium
OPEN	Orientation by Personal Electronic Navigation (TIDE project)
OPENLABS	An OPEN system architecture addressed to LABoratorieS (AIM project)
OPET	Organisation for the Promotion of Energy Technology. A network set up under the THERMIE programme ave R Vandendriesche 18, B-1150 Brussels, Belgium http://www.cordis.lu/opet/home.html
OPHTEL	Telematics in Ophthalmology (a Telematics for Healthcare project within the TELEMATICS APPLICATIONS programme)

OPMODD	Operational Modelling of regional seas and coastal waters (EUREKA project)
OPOCE	Publications Office of the European Commission. *See* EUR-OP
ORA	Opportunities for Rural Areas (project within Area 7 of the TELEMATIC SYSTEMS and TELEMATICS APPLICATIONS programmes)
ORDIT	Development of a methodology for specifying non-functional requirements (ESPRIT project)
OREXPRESS	Logistical information and scheduling system for the transportation of bulk materials on Europe's inland waterways (EUREKA project)
ORGANIGRAMME	*See* IDEA (Inter-institutional Directory of the EU
ORNET	Origin Network on customs and indirect taxation. Set up under the IDA programme
ORQUEST	A telematics system for oral health quality enhancement (a Telematics for Healthcare project within the TELEMATICS APPLICATIONS programme)
ORTELIUS	Database on higher education in Europe set up in 1994 http://ORTELIUS.unifi.it
*ORTOLI INSTRUMENT	*See* NCI
OSA-TESMA	Open System Architecture for Telematics Services in Municipal Application (a Telematics for Urban and Rural Areas project within the TELEMATICS APPLICATIONS programme)
OSCAR	Optical Switching Systems, Components and Applications (RACE project)

OSCE	EUROSTAT Press releases Access via RAPID
OSHA	*See* EU-OSHA
OSIRIS	Open Systems Integrated Roadfreight Information Services (IMPACT project)
OSIRIS	Optimal standards for successful integration of multi-media on-line services (DELTA project)
OSIS	One Stop Internet Shop for business http://europa.eu.int/business
OSIS	Open Shops for Information Systems (COST action project)
OSLO DECLARATION	Declaration by the Heads of Government of the EFTA countries on the strengthening of the association and relations with the EC. Signed March 1989 but not published in official sources. An unofficial translation is to be found in *Agence Europe* 4982 of 24 March 1989 Documents Section 1549, dated 22 March 1989
OSSAD	Office Support Systems Analysis and Design (ESPRIT project)
OT	Overseas Territories
OT	*See* IOT
OUSR	Operating Unit Status Report which forms part of ERDS
'outs'	*See* 'pre-ins'
*OUVERTURE	Cooperation between EU regions and regions in Central and Eastern Europe. *Now within* INTERREG
*OVIDE/Epistel	Organisation du Videotex pour le Député Européen. The EP's videotex service which has been replaced by EUROPARL

OVPIC	Office for Veterinary and Plant health Inspection. *See* FVA
OWN-INITIATIVE OPINION	Opinions submitted by the EP and ESC on subjects which they consider merit specific comment even if an opinion has not been requested by the European Commission
OWN RESOURCES	EU budget comprising Member State's contributions for customs duties, agricultural levies, a fraction of VAT and a fraction of each Member State's GNP
OXODIPINE	Development of Oxodipine pharmacological and clinical development of oxodipine (EUREKA project)
P	Portugal
P	Series of Information memos issued by the Spokesman's group of the European Commission Access via RAPID
PA	Payment Appropriations
*PABLI	ECHO database of progress made by the EC's development projects
PACA	Absorption heat pump (EUREKA project)
*PACE	Community Action Programme for the Efficient Use of Electricity (1989-1992) (OJ L157/89). *Incorporated into* SAVE II
PACE	Perspectives for Advanced Communications in Europe (RACE project)
PACE	Prediction of Aggregated-scale Coastal Evaluation (MAST III project)
PACE	Programme of Advanced Continuing Education (COMETT project)

PACIFLOR	Development of a heat-resistant probiotic useful for animal productions (EUREKA project)
PACOMA	Performance Assessment of COnfinements for Medium-level and Alpha waste (part of the EURATOM research programme on the Management and Storage of Radioactive Waste)
PACT	PCTE - Added Common Tools (ESPRIT project)
PACT II	Reg 2196/98 concerning the granting of Community financial assistance for Pilot Actions for Combined Transport (1997-2001) (OJ L277/98) http://europa.eu.int/en/comm/dg07/pact/index.htm
*PACTE	Exchanges of experience between local and regional authorities in the EU (under Article 10 of the ERDF)
PADMAVATI	Parallel Associative Development Machine for Artificial Intelligence (ESPRIT project)
PAG	Projects Advisory Group
Pagis	Performance Assessment of Geological Isolation System (Radioactive waste research programme)
PAIR	Process oriented Agent based Information Retrieval (a Telematics Information Engineering project within the TELEMATICS APPLICATIONS programme)
PALABRE	Integration of artificial intelligence, vocal input-output and natural language dialogue - application to directory services (ESPRIT project)
PALAVDA	Parallel Architectures and Languages for AIP - a VLSI Directed Approach (ESPRIT project)

PALIO	European standard qualification in the design, delivery, marketing and evaluation of multimedia open learning (COMETT project)
PALMA DOCUMENT	A report by the Coordinators' Group to the European Council on the lifting of controls at intra-EC borders. Published by HMSO as House of Lords Papers 1988-89 (90)
PAM-AID	Personal Adaptive Mobility AID for the frail and elderly visually impaired (a Telematics for Disabled and Elderly People project within the TELEMATICS APPLICATIONS programme)
PAMELA	Pricing And Monitoring ELectronically of Automobiles (DRIVE project)
PAMINA	German-French border regions in Northern Alsace, Southern Palatinate and the Middle Upper Rhine (INTERREG project)
PANCAKE MOTORS	Axial low cost brushed axial flux DC Motors with high energy pressed rare earth permanent magnets (EUREKA project)
PANDORA	Prototyping A Navigation Database Of Road network Attributes (DRIVE project)
PANGLOSS	Parallel Architecture for Networking Gateways Linking OSI Systems (ESPRIT project)
PAN(N5)	Manufacturer of pilot equipment to produce then prove the feasibility of manufacturing flow-line style, high pressure sub-sea pipes (EUREKA project)
PANNENBORG REPORT	Report of the ERB to assess the progress of the ESPRIT programme (COM(85) 616)
PANORAMA	Perception and Navigation System for Autonomous Mobile Applications (ESPRIT project)

PAP	Policy Advice Programme
PAP	Prices of Agricultural Products (CADDIA project)
PAP	Priority Action Plan
PAQO	Plant Availability and Quality Optimisation (ESPRIT project)
PARADI	Automatic production management system using AI developments (EUREKA project)
PARALLEL CONVENTION	*See* LUGANO CONVENTION
PARASOL	ATM specific measurement equipment (RACE project)
PARCMAN	Parking Management control and information systems (DRIVE project)
*PARDOC	EP Documents. An EP internal database which *replaced* DOSE and has been *replaced by* EPOQUE
PARENTAL LEAVE Directive	Dir 96/34/EC on the framework agreement on parental leave (OJ L145/96 with an extension for the UK in OJ L10/98)
PARIS	Project for the economic assessment of road transport and traffic information (DRIVE project)
PARIS TREATY	European Coal and Steel Community Treaty. Signed by Belgium, France, Germany, Italy, Luxembourg and the Netherlands on 18th April 1951. Came into force 23rd July 1952
ParlEuNet	EMTF project which permits secondary school students to use networks and multimedia resources to learn about and to take part in collaborative projects on the EP http://parleunet.jrc.it/

PARNUTS	Dir 89/398/EEC on foodstuffs intended for particular nutritional uses (OJ L186/89 with latest amendment in OJ L172/99)
*PARQ	An internal EP database of parliamentary questions which has been *replaced by* EPOQUE
PARTS	Performing Arts Research and Training Studios. An international contemporary dance school founded in 1994 (KALEIDOSCOPE project) ave Van Volxem 164, B-1190 Brussels, Belgium
PASSERELLE	A metaphor to describe the transfer of a policy area from one PILLAR to another. For example under the AMSTERDAM TREATY, the subject of immigration, asylum and visas was moved from the third PILLAR to the first PILLAR
PASSYS	PAssive Solar components and SYStems testing (JOULE I project)
PATENT	Patent applications statistical domain on the NEW CRONOS databank
PATINNOVA	A conference to promote the value of patents and patent information, organised jointly by the EU and the EPO http://www.cordis.lu/patinnova99/home.html
PATLIB	A network of patent information centres throughout Europe http://www.european-patentoffice.org/epidos/conf/patlibal.htm
PATMAN	PATient workflow MANagement systems (a Telematics for Healthcare project within the TELEMATICS APPLICATIONS programme) http://www.ehto.org/vds/projects/patman.html
PATMOS	Power and Timing Modelling Optimisation and Specification (ESPRIT project)
PATRICIA	Proving and Testability for Reliability Improvement of Complex Integrated Architectures (ESPRIT project)

PAUL FINET FOUNDATION	To provide support for schooling and training the children of coal miners and steel workers killed by occupational disease or industrial accident Jean Monnet Building, Plateau du Kirchberg, L-2920 Luxembourg
PAVE	PCTE and VMS environment (ESPRIT project)
PBKAL	Paris, Brussels, Köln, Amsterdam, London High Speed Rail Link (TEN-TRANSPORT project)
*PBS	Passbook Scheme. An export subsidy scheme, abolished and replaced on 1 April 1997 by the DEPB
PC	Programme Committee
PCA	Partnership and Cooperation Agreement
PCAD	Portable Communication Assistant for people with acquired Dysphasia (a Telematics for Disabled and Elderly People project within the TELEMATICS APPLICATIONS programme)
PCTE	A basis for a Portable Common Tool Environment (ESPRIT project)
PDB	Preliminary Draft Budget
PDCS	Predictably Dependable Computing Systems (ESPRIT project)
PDO	Reg 2081/92 on the Protected Designation of Origin (in connection with the origin of foodstuffs) (OJ L208/92 with latest amendment in OJ L83/97)
PDWEB	The Public Data WEB (a Telematics for Urban and Rural Areas project within the TELEMATICS APPLICATIONS programme)
PE	*See* EP

PEA	Proposal Expansion Award (TELEMATICS APPLICATIONS project)
PEACE	Previously a COMMUNITY INITIATIVE for Peace and reconciliation in Northern Ireland and the border counties of Ireland, now incorporated within OBJECTIVE 1 of the STRUCTURAL FUNDS (2000-2004)
PEACOCK	Software development using concurrently executable modules (ESPRIT project)
PEARL	Pan European competency Assessment in Rural and Landbased industries (EMTF project)
PECH	Committee on Fisheries (of the EP)
PECO	*See* CEEC (Central and Eastern European Countries)
PECOS	Reg 636/82 on outward processing arrangements applicable to certain clothing and textile products re-imported into the EU after working or processing in certain THIRD COUNTRIES (OJ L271/82 with latest proposal for amendment in COM(94) 328)
PEDACTICE	Educational multimedia in compulsory school: from PEDagogical Assessment to product Assessment (EMTF project)
PEDAP	Reg 3828/85 for a programme for the Development of Portuguese Agriculture (1986-) (OJ L372/85)
*PEDIP	Programme for the Development of Portuguese Industry (1988-1992) (OJ L185/88)
PEDRAA	Development Programme for the Azores Region
PEGASE	An EP internal library management database containing the catalogue of the EP

PEGASUS FOUNDATION	European Association for Culture. An EP initiative which was created in 1991 and is operational under CULT
PENELOPE	Pan-European Network of Environmental Legislation Observatories for Planning, Education and research (a Telematics for Education and Training project within the TELEMATICS APPLICATIONS programme)
PEOPLE'S EUROPE	Reports prepared by a working party and chaired by Pietro Adonnino to encourage EC citizens to see themselves as Europeans (1st and 2nd reports published in *Bulletin of the EC Supplement 7/85*; further report published in *Bulletin of the EC Supplement 2/88*)
PEPMA	Parallel Execution of Prolog on Multiprocessor Architectures (ESPRIT project)
PEPPER I & II REPORTS	on the Promotion of Employee Participation in Profits and Enterprise Results. *PEPPER I* published by EUR-OP as *Social Europe Supplement 3/91*. *PEPPER II* published as COM(96) 697
PERICLES	Protocol for the Evaluation of Residues in Industrial Contaminated Liquid EffluentS (an Environmental Health and Safety Research project within the ENVIRONMENT AND CLIMATE programme)
*PERIFRA	An EP initiative for special action in peripheral regions (1991-1992). *Continued as* KONVER
PERINORM Europe	A bibliographic database of European Standards (including CEN/CENELEC) Available as a CD-ROM from CSS INFO

*PERIODIC REPORT	on the social and economic situation of the regions of the Community (COM(80) 816; COM(84) 40; COM(87) 230; COM(90) 609; COM(94) 322. *Replaced by* the triennial COHESION REPORT. *See also* SYNTHETIC INDEX. The text of the Sixth (and final) report can be accessed on the Internet at: http://inforegio.cec.eu.int/6rp
PERIPHERA	Telematics applications and strategies combating social and economic exclusion (a Telematics for Urban and Rural Areas project within the TELEMATICS APPLICATIONS programme)
Perla	Performance Calibration and Training Laboratory (JRC - fissile materials safeguards and management programme)
PERSONAL PROTECTIVE EQUIPMENT Directive	*See* PPE
*PERU	*See* RUEM
PES	Party of European Socialists (of the EP) http://www.eurosocialists.org/congress/english/3b.htm
PES	Public Employment Services. The Commission's Communication on modernising PESs is published as COM(98) 641
PESC	Statements on the subject of the CFSP Access via RAPID
*PESCA	COMMUNITY INITIATIVE to restructure the EU fishing industry (1994-1999) (Guidelines in OJ C180/94)
PETE	Portable Educational Tool Environment (DELTA project)
PETI	Committee on Petitions (of the EP)
PETrA	Pan European Transport Area developed in the Black Sea

PETRA

Project of Equipment for the Treatment of Radioactive Waste in ADECO (JRC - safety of nuclear materials programme)

*PETRA II

Community action programme for the vocational training of young people and their preparation for adult and working life (1992-1994) (OJ L214/91). *Continued as* part of the LEONARDO DA VINCI programme

PETTEN

JRC establishment
Westerduinweg 3, Postbus Nr 2, NL-1755 ZG-Petten, Netherlands

PGI

Reg 2081/92 on the Protected Geographical Indication (in connection with the origin of foodstuffs) (OJ L208/92 with latest amendment in OJ L156/97)

PHARE

Reg 3906/89 for Poland/Hungary Aid for the Reconstruction of the Economy (OJ L375/89). Extended to other CEEC (OJ L257/90 with latest amendment in OJ L161/99)

PHARE ACE

A programme to support academic and professional economists in CEE. *See also* ACE

PHARE LIEN

PHARE Link Inter European NGOs for PHARE projects involving NGOs (OJ C29/98)

PHASE

PHysical forcing and biogeochemical fluxes in Shallow coastal Ecosystems (ELOISE project)
http://europa.eu.int/comm/dg1a/PHARE/index.htm

PHILOXENIA

Proposal for a multiannual programme on tourism (1999-2002) (OJ C13/97)

PHOEBUS

30mw solar demonstration plant (EUREKA project)

PHOENIX

Hierarchical integration of logic and functional paradigms (ESPRIT project)

PHOS	PHARE Operational Service
PHOTON	PHOTONic communications (an ACTS project)
PHOTOTRONICS	Industrial development of amorphous silicon-based components for photoelectronic applications (EUREKA project)
PHOX	Extra interface processing of 3-D holographics images for analysis and control (ESPRIT project)
PHYSAN	Electronic system for national governments on PHYTOSANITARY CONTROLS. Set up under the IDA programme
PHYTOSANITARY CONTROLS	A series of proposals contained in the SEM initiative relating to plant health and the free movement of plants. *See also* PHYSAN
PIDEA	Packaging and Interconnection Development for European Applications relating to the interconnection and assembly of electronic components (1998-2003) (EUREKA project)
PILLARS	A metaphor commonly used to describe the structure of the EU. The first pillar comprises the EC and is supranational in character. The second pillar deals with the CFSP. The third pillar was originally referred to as dealing with justice and home affairs, but since the AMSTERDAM TREATY has been retitled police and judicial cooperation in criminal matters. The second and third pillars are intergovernmental. Subject matter may be moved from one pillar to another across a 'footbridge' or PASSERELLE
PIMS	Project Integrated Management Systems (ESPRIT project)

PINC	Illustrative Nuclear Programmes for the Community published by the Commission in 1966, 1972, 1984 (with an update in 1990) and 1997
PIP	Plant INDUSTRY PLATFORM http://europa.eu.int/comm/dg12/biotech/ip2.html#PIP http://www.noord.bart.nl/~biotech/pipfront.html
*PIP	Productivity Initiative Programme. A TACIS small-scale project to provide senior managers from the NIS with on-the-job training in companies in the EU. *Continued as* MTP
PIPA	Project for the Improvement of Public Administration (part of PHARE's 1997 programme in the Czech Republic)
PIPE	EDI project under the TEDIS programme
PIPER	Project Information Prepared for Exploitation and Reference (a Telematics for Administrations project within the TELEMATICS APPLICATIONS programme)
*PIR	Public Information RELAYS in Public Libraries in the UK. *Continued as* EPIC
PISC	Project for the Inspection of Steel Components (JRC project)
PISG	Permanent Inter Service Group on refugees. A Commission inter-departmental coordination body chaired by ECHO
PIU	Programme Implementation Unit
PJAECH	Preserving Jewish Archives as part of the European Cultural Heritage (RAPHAEL project)
PLAIL	Public Libraries and Independent Learners (project within Area 5 of the TELEMATIC SYSTEMS programme)

PLAIN LANGUAGE Directive	Dir 93/13/EEC on unfair terms in consumer contracts (OJ L95/93)
PLANEC	PLANning of the care of the elderly in the European Community (a Telematics for Healthcare project within the TELEMATICS APPLICATIONS programme)
PLANET	European Network for Multimedia Environmental Education (EMTF project)
PLASIC	Performance and reliability of plastic encapsulated CMOS (ESPRIT project)
*PLATFORM EUROPE	An award scheme for cultural events with a European profile. *Replaced by* KALEIDOSCOPE
PLATING Directive	Dir 76/114/EEC relating to statutory plates and inscriptions for motor vehicles and their trailers (OJ L24/76 with the latest amendment in OJ L155/78)
PLAY	Storage of various music input, conversion of different Braille syntax into sounds, graphics, Braille output and Telematic access (a Telematics for Disabled and Elderly People project within the TELEMATICS APPLICATIONS programme)
PLEASE	Permanent Liaison Committee of the European Associations in Education rue de la Concorde 60, B-1000 Brussels, Belgium
PLUMBER REGULATIONS	Regs 3/84; 1292/89 and 718/91 introducing arrangements for movement within the EC of goods sent from one Member State for temporary use in one or more other Member States (OJ L2/84; OJ L130/89 and OJ L78/91)
p.m.	Pour Mémoire. A token entry in the EU Budget - no money has been allocated but it is expected in due course

PMC	*See* ACPM
PME	*See* SME (Small and Medium-sized Enterprise)
PMG	Project Management Group
PMS	Project Management Services
PMU	Programme Management Unit
PNIC	*See* NPCI
POCKET	EC economic data Pocketbook statistical domain on the NEW CRONOS databank
PODA	Piloting of the Office Document Architecture (ESPRIT project)
POLINAT-2	POLlution from aircraft emissions IN the North ATlantic flight corridor (THESEO project)
POLIS	A network of cooperation of the European cities in advanced transport telematics (DRIVE project)
POLIS	UK Parliamentary On-Line Indexing Service which includes EU legislation Access on-line and on CD-ROM via CONTEXT http://www.polis.net.html
POLITeam	A tele cooperation system to support the cooperation of German ministries distributed between Bonn and Berlin (CSCW project) http://orgwis.gmd.de/projects/POLITeam/
POLLEN	Publishers on Information Highways (a Telematics for Education and Training project within the TELEMATICS APPLICATIONS programme)
POLYGLOT	Multi-language speech-to-text and text-to-speech system (ESPRIT project)
POMPIDOU GROUP	Established in 1971 (within the Council of Europe) to combat drug abuse

PONTIFEX	Planning Of Non-specific Transportations by an Intelligent Fleet EXpert (ESPRIT project)
*POP	The French acronym for Reg 4028/86 on Community measures to improve and adapt structures in the fisheries and aquaculture sector (1987-1993) (OJ L376/86)
POPCYCLE	Environmental CYCLing of selected Persistent Organic Pollutants in the Baltic region (ELOISE project)
POPRAM	Multifund Operational Programme for the Autonomous region of Madeira
PORTICO	Portuguese Road Traffic Innovations... (DRIVE project)
*POSEICAN	A regional programme for the ultraperipheral region of the Canary Islands (1994-1999). *Now covered* by REGIS II
*POSEIDOM	Programme of Options Specific to the Remote and Insular Nature of the French Overseas Departments (1994-1999). *Now covered* by REGIS II
*POSEIMA	Programmes of options specific to the remote and insular nature of Madeira and the Azores (1994-1999). *Now covered* by REGIS II
POST-DOC	POST graduate training for DOCtors in Europe (EMTF project)
POSTED WORKERS Directive	Dir 96/71/EC concerning the posting of workers in the framework of the provision of services (OJ L18/97)
*POVERTY 4	Proposal for a medium-term action programme to combat exclusion and promote solidarity (1994-1999) (COM(93) 435). Not agreed. *See* INTEGRA

POVES	Portable Opto-electronic Vision Enhancement System for visually impaired persons (TIDE project)
POWERMAG	Low cost brushless axial flux motor with a high energy rubber bonded rare earth permanent rotating magnet (EUREKA project)
PPE	Dir 89/686/EEC on Personal Protective Equipment (OJ L399/89 with latest amendment in OJ L236/96)
PPE-DE	*See* EPP/ED
PPF	Project Preparation Facility. Part of PHARE's investment strategy for Central Europe
PPG	Public Procurement Group
PPS	Purchasing Power Standard
PRACTITIONER	Support system for pragmatic re-use of software concepts (ESPRIT project)
PRAG	Agriculture prices and price indices statistical domain on the NEW CRONOS databank
PRECISE	Promoting and Realising ELTA through Communication and Information Strategies for Europe (DELTA project)
PRECISE	PRospects for Extra-mural and Clinical Information Systems Environment (AIM project)
PREDICT	Pollution Reduction by Information and Control Techniques (DRIVE project)
PREDICT	PREDICTion and assessment of the acquatic toxicity of mixtures of chemicals (an Environmental Health and Chemical Safety Research project within the ENVIRONMENT AND CLIMATE programme)

'pre-ins'	Non-participating Member States in the EMU. *See also* 'ins'
PREJEEMI	Bootstrap project for a multiple device file server (ESPRIT project)
Pre-JEP	Preparatory JEP. A compulsory first step before a proposal for a JEP can be submitted
PreLex	Commission database on inter-Institutional procedures, which provides details of current proposals and communications. *Replaces* the APC database http://europa.eu.int/prelex/apcnet.cfm?CL=en
PRES	Council of the European Union Press releases Access via RAPID
PRESS	Press and Communications DG of the European Commission
*PREST	Working Party on Scientific and Technical Research Policy. *See* CREST
PRESTIGE	Patient REcords Supporting Telematics and Guidelines (a Telematics for Healthcare project within the TELEMATICS APPLICATIONS programme) http://www.rbh.nthames.nhs.uk/prestige/prestige.htm
PREXCO	Precursor Exportation Control . Database on precursors created in 1994. Now maintained in the CIS
PRIAMOS	Validation and demonstration of GPRS Protocol Specifications for the Mobile Offices of the Future (ISIS Teleworking project) http://www.ispo.cec.be/isis/98priamo.htm
PRICE	Prices and purchasing power parities statistical domain on the NEW CRONOS databank
PRICE LABELLING	*See* UNIT PRICING Directive

PRIMAVERA	Priority Management for Vehicle Efficiency, Environment and Road safety on Arterials (DRIVE project)
PRINCE	Programme to Inform Citizens about Europe (1996-). It comprises 3 campaigns: CITIZEN'S FIRST; the EURO: one currency for all; BUILDING EUROPE TOGETHER
PRINT	Non-impact PRINTer and plotter for Braille/Moon characters and tactile graphics (a Telematics for Disabled and Elderly People project within the TELEMATICS APPLICATIONS programme)
*PRISMA	Preparing Regional Industry for the Single Market. A STRUCTURAL FUNDS Initiative (1991-1993) (Guidelines in OJ C33/91). *Continued in* the SME COMMUNITY INITIATIVE
PROCAT-GEN	PROduct CATalogues in the Global Engineering Network (a Telematics Information Engineering project within the TELEMATICS APPLICATIONS programme)
PROCOS	Provably Correct Systems (ESPRIT project)
PRODCOM	Reg 3924/91 for Products of the European Community. A classification of industrial production in mining, quarrying, manufacturing, electricity, gas and water supply which is related to NACE Rev 1 (OJ L374/91). 1998 ed published by EUR-OP for EUROSTAT Also available on EUROPROMS and on the Internet at: http://europa.eu.int/eurostat.html
PRODEC	EDI project under the TEDIS programme
PRO-DELTA	Portuguese Research on DELTA (DELTA project)

*PRODEP	Integrated Operational Programme in Portugal for the Development of Education (1990-1993)
PRODIS	PROduct Development and Innovation in Shipbuilding (TRANSPORT project)
PROFIL	Flexible fabrication of fresh fermented dairy products (EUREKA project)
PROGRESS	*See* POVERTY 4
PROGUIDE	Promoting the development, dissemination and evaluation of Guidelines of clinical practice (a Telematics for Healthcare project within the TELEMATICS APPLICATIONS programme)
PROINNO	PROmoting European INNOvation culture (INNOVATION project) http://www.rrz.uni-hamburg.de/kooperationsstelle-hh/proinno/prowelcome.html
PROMETEUS	PROmoting Multimedia access to Education and Training in the European Society (within the IST programme) http://www.prometeus.org
PROMETHEUS	Programme for a European Traffic system with Highest Efficiency and Unprecedented Safety (EUREKA project)
PROMIMPS	Process Module Integration in a Multichamber Production System (ESPRIT project)
PROMINAND	Extended office process migration with interactive panel displays (ESPRIT project)
PROMIS	Portable Reception Of Multimedia Information network (a Telematics Information Engineering project within the TELEMATICS APPLICATIONS programme)

PROMISE	Council Decision 98/253/EC Promoting the Information Society in Europe (1998-2002) (OJ L107/98)
PROMISE	Mobile and Portable Information System in Europe (DRIVE project)
PROMISE	Personal mobile traveller and traffic information (TELEMATICS APPLICATIONS project)
PROMISE	PRe-Operational Modelling In the Seas of Europe (MAST III project)
PROMISE	Process Operator's Multi-Media Intelligent Support Environment (ESPRIT project)
PROMPT	Programme for MOS Processing Technology (ESPRIT project)
PROMPT	Protocols for Medical Procedures and Therapies (a Telematics for Healthcare project within the TELEMATICS APPLICATIONS programme)
PROMPT	*See* IPTS
PRONET	Multimedia computer based on-line training and support service for professionals (a Telematics for Education and Training project within the TELEMATICS APPLICATIONS programme)
PROOF	Primary Rate ISDN OSI Office Facilities (ESPRIT project)
PROREC	PROmotion strategy for European electronic healthcare RECords (a Telematics for Healthcare project within the TELEMATICS APPLICATIONS programme)
PROSIM	Process Simulator development project (EUREKA project)

PROSIM	PROpagation Channel SIMulator (MAST III project)
PROSIT	PROmotion of Short sea shipping and Inland waterways Transport by use of modern Telematics (TRANSPORT project)
PROSOMA	Service launched by the EU to help businesses benefit from the successes achieved in the ACTS, ESPRIT and TELEMATICS APPLICATIONS programmes by facilitating access to and uptake of research results http://www.prosoma.lu
PROSPECTRA	PROgramme development by SPECification and TRAnsformation (ESPRIT project)
PROSPECTRA DEMO	Demonstration of PROSPECTRA methodology and system (ESPRIT project)
*PROTEAS	ECHO database to assist organisations to promote and commercialise the results of their R&D. *Now available* on CORDIS as RTD-RESULTS
PROTOS	PROduction and Transport of Organic Solutes: effects of natural climatic variation (TERI project)
PROTOS	Prolog tools for building expert systems development of software tools in the programming language prolog, aimed at expert systems (EUREKA project)
PROTOWET	PROcedures for The Operationalisation of techniques for the functional analysis of European WETland ecosystems (a Water, Wetland and Acquatic Ecosystem Research project within the ENVIRONMENT AND CLIMATE programme)
PROVE	Provision of Verification (RACE project)
PROVERBS	PRObabilistic design tools for VERtical BreakwaterS (MAST III project)

PRT	Social Protocol procedure regarding the passage of a COM DOC
PSCI	Proposed SCI
PSE	*See* PES (Party of European Socialists)
p.s.r.	Quality sparkling wines Produced in Specific Regions
PSU	Programme Support Unit
PT	Portuguese
*PTF	Preliminary Task Force of the European Commission
Ptiers	ACP/ALA/MED/ THIRD COUNTRY statistical domain on the NEW CRONOS databank
PTL	PHARE Topic Link. The extension of the EIONET to CEEC
PTL/AQ	PTL on Air Quality. Extends the EEA work on air quality to the PHARE countries
PTL/IW	PTL on Inland Waters
PubliCA	Concerted Action for Public Libraries in Europe http://www.croydon.gov.uk/publica/
PUBLIC INFORMATION RELAYS	*See* PIR
PUBLISHERS' FORUM	*See* FORUM (EU Publisher's Forum)
PULSAR	Parking Urban Loading unloading Standards And Rules (DRIVE project)
PUSHED	EDI project under the TEDIS programme
PUSSYCATS	Improvement of pedestrian safety and comfort at traffic lights (DRIVE project)
PWG	Permanent Working Group

QMIS	Quality Management Information System (EUREKA project)
QMV	Qualified Majority Voting. A device whereby draft Directives under the SEM initiative may be approved on a majority weighted vote. The weighting being 10 for France, Germany, Italy and the UK; 8 for Spain; 5 for Belgium, Greece, the Netherlands and Portugal; 4 for Austria and Sweden; 3 for Denmark, Finland and Ireland; 2 for Luxembourg (Total 87)
QOSMIC	QOS verification Methodology and tools for Integrated Communications (RACE project)
QUAD PARTNERS	Canada; the EU; Japan and the United States of America
QUALIFIED MAJORITY VOTING	*See* QMV
QUALITY	Council Decision 1999/167/EC adopting a specific programme for research, technological development and demonstration on the Quality of life and management of living resources (1998-2002) (OJ L64/99). One of the THEMATIC PROGRAMMES which form part of FP5
QUANTUM	QUAlity Network Technology for User-oriented Multi-media (a Telematics for Research project within the TELEMATICS APPLICATIONS programme)
QUAMS	QUality Assurance of Medical Standards (AIM project)
QUAMT	QUAlitätssicherung MedizinTechnik (COMETT project)
QUATTRO	QUality Approach in Tendering/contracting urban public TRansport Operations (TRANSPORT project) http://www.cordis.lu/transport/src/quattro.htm

QUEST	Database of questions and answers on the EURO and EMU http://europa.eu.int/euro/quest/normal/frame.htm?language_nb=5
QUEST	QUarterly European Simulation Tool. A modelling project of the Economic and Financial Affairs DG of the European Commission to link quarterly econometric models for the individual Member States and Japan
QUID	Dir 97/4/EC on Quantitative Ingredients and Declarations relating to foodstuffs (OJ L43/97)
QUIRT	Real-time imaging and Quality control in Radiation Therapy (AIM project)
QUOTA	Electronic control system involving national governments for the importation of goods from non-EU countries which are subject to quantity restrictions. Set up under the IDA programme
*RACE II	R&D programme in Advanced Communications Technologies for Europe (1990-1994) (OJ L192/91). *Continued as* ACTS
RA-D	Rig Automation Drilling (EUREKA project)
RADATT	RApid Damage Assessment Telematic Tool (a Telematics for Environment project within the TELEMATICS APPLICATIONS programme) http://www.trentel.org/environment/research/projects/radatt.html
RAID	Robot for Assisting the Integration of the Disabled (TIDE project)
RAIL	Railway transport statistical domain on the NEW CRONOS databank

RAINBOW	An object network for statisticians and administrations (a Telematics for Administrations project within the TELEMATICS APPLICATIONS programme)
*RAINBOW GROUP	*See* ARC
RA-IQSE	An Integrated Quality Support Environment (ESPRIT project)
RAISE	Rigorous Approach to Industrial Software Engineering (ESPRIT project)
RAMÓN y CAJAL SCHOLARSHIPS	Post-graduate scholarships to familiarise students with the activities of the EP. *Formerly* STOA Scholarships. *See also* ROBERT SCHUMAN SCHOLARSHIPS
RAP	Research Action Programme
RAPHAEL	Council Decision 2228/97/EC establishing a Community action programme in the field of cultural heritage (1997-2000) (OJ L305/97). *To be continued as* CULTURE 2000 http://europa.eu.int/comm/dg10/culture/raphael/index_en.html
RAPID	Full-text Press releases and other communications from the EU Institutions. *See also* BIO; CC; CES; CJE; DCP; DOC; IP; MEMO; OSCE; P; PESC; PRES; SPEECH http://europa.eu.int/en/comm/spp/rapid.html Username: guest; Password: guest
RAPIDUS	RAPId Delivery of Updates on Search-profiles. A CORDIS e-mail service http://www.cordis.lu/src/i_014_en.htm
RAPPORTEUR	A member of a committee or body appointed to act as author and spokesperson on a report
*RARE	*See* TERENA
RARP	Regional Agricultural Reform Project (1995-1998) (TACIS project)

Raxen	European information network on Racism and Xenophobia. Set up and coordinated by the Monitoring Centre on Racism and Xenophobia Rahlgasse 3, A-1060 Vienna, Austria
*RBW	*See* ARC
r.cade	Resource Centre at the University of Durham for Access to statistical Data on Europe http://www-rcade.dur.ac.uk
RD	Regional R&D statistical domain on the REGIO database
*RDE	European Democratic Alliance (of the EP)
RDF	*See* ERDF
*RDP	RACE Definition Phase
RDP	Regional Development Programme
RDTD	Research, Demonstration and Technological Development
REACT	REAl-time Communication Termina (a Telematics for Disabled and Elderly People project within the TELEMATICS APPLICATIONS programme)
READAPTATION GRANTS	for redundant workers in the coal and steel industries under Article 56 of the PARIS TREATY. Suspension of funding for certain ECSC social aid in OJ C178/94
REBUILD	Reusable Energy in Historic City Centres (RECITE project)
REC	Regional Environment Centres. A TACIS initiative to help environmental interest groups and NGOs to provide public access to environmental information
RECAP	RECycling of Automobile Plastics (EUREKA project)

RECEP	Russian-European Centre for Economic Policy (TACIS project)
*RECHAR II	Reconversion des bassins Charbonnière (Conversion of coal mining areas). A COMMUNITY INITIATIVE (1994-1999) (Guidelines in OJ C180/94)
*RECITE	Regions and Cities for Europe (set up under Article 10 of the ERDF). *Now within* INTERREG
RECOVER	REd-Cross OVerall Emergency Resource management system (a Telematics for Healthcare project within the TELEMATICS APPLICATIONS programme)
REDEVELOPMENT GRANTS	*See* READAPTATION GRANTS
REDIS	R&D and Innovation Statistics (EUROSTAT project)
REDO	Maintenance reliability, reusability and documentation of software systems (ESPRIT project)
REDS	Registered Excise Dealers and Shippers for VAT purposes
RED WASTES	*See* WASTES
REFERENCE PRICE	A minimum price fixed according to EU producer prices for certain fruits and vegetables, wines and some fisheries products imported from a non-Member State
REFLECT	REFLECTive expertise in knowledge-based systems (ESPRIT project)
REFLECT	A thematic network for teacher training in Europe (TSER project)

REFLECTION GROUP	A group consisiting mainly of Foreign Ministers appointed to meet June-December 1995 to prepare for the 1996-1997 IGC
Reg	EU Regulation which automatically becomes law in all the Member States
*REGEN	Regional Network Policy for energy transmission and distribution networks in the peripheral areas of the EU. A STRUCTURAL FUNDS Initiative (1990-1993) (Guidelines in OJ C326/90). *Continued within* INTERREG II
*REGI	Committee on Regional Policy (of the EP)
REGIE	A project to set up a databank to provide detailed information for firms who wish to expand activities in cooperation with partners in other Member States, thus benefitting from the practical experience of EEIGs Contact: European Commission Enterprise DG
REGIO	Regional policy DG of the European Commission
REGIO	A regional statistical domain on the NEW CRONOS databank
REGIOMAP	Statistical and topographical information on the EU regions up to level III of NUTS CD-ROM available from EUR-OP
REGIONAL FUND	*See* ERDF
REGIONET	Integrated multimedia services via a regional telematics information system – a cross-sectoral application pilot project (a Telematics for Urban and Rural Areas project within the TELEMATICS APPLICATIONS programme)
*REGIOSTAT	A database of selected regional statistics from the REGIO database loaded on EUROCRON

*REGIS II	Rég(ions) Is(olées). A COMMUNITY INITIATIVE for the isolated regions of the Azores, Canaries, Madeira and the French Overseas Departments (1994-1999) (Guidelines in OJ C180/94). *Previously* IRIS
REITOX	A European information network on drugs and drug addiction at the EMCDDA. Set up under the IDA programme by Reg 302/93 (OJ L36/93 with latest amendment in OJ L341/94))
*RELA	Committee on external economic relations (of the EP)
RELAY CENTRE	*See* IRC
RELAY EUROPE	A European affairs consultancy company which sells merchandise and provides services for the London Representation of the European Commission Charlemagne House, 2 Enys Rd, Eastbourne BN21 2DE, United Kingdom
RELAYS	Network of EU information providers with priority access to the EU Institutions and publications. For those set up by IRNU *See* CARREFOUR; DEP; EDC; EIP; LUIC. For those set up by the Enterprise DG *See* EIC. For those set up by the Health and Consumer Protection DG *See* EUROGUICHET. For those set up by the Research DG *See* IRC. For those set up by the UK Commission Representation *See* EPIC; ERC; EURO UNITS; SECTORAL RELAYS and *See also* NCC; NER; STOKE ROCHFORD CONFERENCES
RELEX	External Relations DG of the European Commission
REM	Radioactivity Environmental Monitoring. A database of radioactivity measurements made in EU countries http://java.ei.jrc.it

REM	Reseau d'Enseignement Multimedia. Collaborative Multimedia Learning Environments (a Telematics for Education and Training project within the TELEMATICS APPLICATIONS programme)
REMAIN	Modular system for REliability and MAINtainability management in European rail transport (TRANSPORT project)
REMIE	Specification and development of an isolating electrical mineral coating on metal support (EUREKA project)
REMOT	Remote Experiment MOniToring and control (a Telematics for Research project within the TELEMATICS APPLICATIONS programme)
REMSSBOT	Regional Environmental Management Support Based On Telematics (a Telematics for Environment project within the TELEMATICS APPLICATIONS programme) http://www.trentel.org/environment/research/projects /remssbot.html
REMUS	REference Models for Useability Specifications (RACE project)
*RENAVAL	Reconversion des zones de chantiers navals. A COMMUNITY INITIATIVE to assist the conversion of shipbuilding areas (1988-1993) (OJ L225/88)
REPA	Regional Economic Partnership Agreements
REPLAY	Replay and evaluation of software development plans using higher-order metasystems (ESPRIT project)
REPRESENTATIVE RATE	*See* GREEN RATE
REQUEST	Reliability and Quality of European Software (ESPRIT project)

RES	Integrated development of Renewable natural resources (FAST programme)
RES	Renewable Energy Sources
RESAM	Remote Expert Support for Aircraft Maintenance (RACE project)
RESEARCH AND TECHNICAL DEVELOPMENT programme	*See* FP5
RESEAU	European environmental, agricultural and urban development monitoring network. A database of environmental statistics within the CADDIA programme
*RESIDER II	Reconversion des zones sidérurgiques. A COMMUNITY INITIATIVE to assist the conversion of steel areas (1994-1997) (Guidelines in OJ C180/94)
RESIGMUR	Development of geographic information systems (RECITE project)
RESMA	RESeau des MArques. An electronic processing system, part of the OHIM. Pilot phase of installation completed in 1998
RESORT	REmote Service Of Rehabilitation Technology (a Telematics for Disabled and Elderly People project within the TELEMATICS APPLICATIONS programme)
RESPECT	Requirements Engineering and SPECification in Telematics (a Telematics Engineering project within the TELEMATICS APPLICATIONS programme)
RET	Renewable Energy Technologies (within the ALTENER programme)

*RETEX	Régions fortement dépandantes du secteur Textile - habillement. A COMMUNITY INITIATIVE to support areas where there is a declining textile industry (1992-1997) (Guidelines in OJ C142/92 and OJ C180/94)
RETI	Association of European Regions of Industrial Technology rue Archimède 50, B-1000 Brussels, Belgium
RETRANSPLANT	REgional and international integrated telemedicine network for medical assistance in end stage disease and organ TRANSPLANT project (a Telematics for Healthcare project within the TELEMATICS APPLICATIONS programme) http://www.ehto.org/vds/projects/retransplant.html
RETT	Committee on Regional policy, transport and tourism (of the EP)
REVOLVE	Regional Evolution Planning for IBC (RACE project)
*REWARD	Recycling of Waste R&D (Subprogramme of the Raw Materials and Recycling programme) (1990-1992) (OJ L359/89). *Continued as* BRITE/EURAM II
*REX	External Economic Relations Committee (of the EP)
REX	Reconfigurable and extensible parallel and distributed systems (ESPRIT project)
RFLP	Genetic improvement of corn by Restriction Fragment Length Polymorphisms (EUREKA project)
RGMG	Representatives of the Governments of the Member States
RICA	A system to transfer data under the FADN (CADDIA project)

RICE	Regional Information Centre. Developed out of ESATT and INDIS http://jukebox.isf.kiev.ua/rice/index.html
RICHE	European information and communication networks for hospitals (ESPRIT project)
RIDDLE	Rapid Information Display and Dissemination in a Library Environment (project within Area 5 of the TELEMATIC SYSTEMS programme)
RIGHT OF INITIATIVE	Under the TREATY ON EUROPEAN UNION the EP has powers to request the European Commission to propose legislation in areas of relevance to the EU
RIMES	Road Information and Management Euro-System (DRIVE project)
RIPARIUS	Risk of Inundation – Planning and Response Interactive User System (a Telematics for Environment project within the TELEMATICS APPLICATIONS programme) http://www.trentel.org/environment/research/projects/riparius.html
RIPE	RACE Integrity Primitives Evaluation (RACE project)
RIS	Regional Innovation Strategies (part of the INNOVATION/SMEs programme). *See also* RITTS; RITTS/RIS NETWORK http://www.innovating-regions.org/index.html
RISC	Chemical Sector Information Network. An initiative of the Enterprise DG of the European Commission. *See also* ChimEre; ChimStat; ComLégi; Légichim Access via Internet (password required): http://europa.eu.int/comm/dg03/directs/dg3c/risc/index.htm
RISE	Caring for the elderly in the Information Society era (a Telematics for Disabled and Elderly People project within the TELEMATICS APPLICATIONS programme)

RISI	Regional Information Society Initiatives (under Article 10 of the ERDF and Article 6 of the ESF) http://www.niaa.org.uk
RISK ASSESSMENT	Reg 1488/94 on risk assessment procedures for new and existing substances (OJ L161/94 and *Guidance* published in 4 vols in 1996 by EUR-OP)
*RITTER LIST	Commission list of pending proposals published in June and October annually as a COM DOC
RITTS	Regional Innovation and Technology Transfer infrastructures and Strategies (part of the INNOVATION/SMEs programme). *See also* RIS; RITTS/RIS NETWORK http://www.innovating-regions.org/index.html
RITTS/RIS NETWORK	A network to support all RIS and RITTS projects in order to facilitate the exchange of experience and to disseminate relevant information http://www.innovating-regions.org/index.html
*RMC	RACE Management Committee
*RMP	RACE Main Phase
ROAD	Road transport statistical domain on the NEW CRONOS databank
ROADACOM	En route applied data communications development of an integrated system for on-based electronic data collection and processing... (EUREKA project)
ROBERT SCHUMAN PROJECT	Council Decision 1496/98/EC establishing an action programme to improve awareness of EU law for the legal profession (1998-2001) (OJ L196/98)

ROBERT SCHUMAN SCHOLARSHIPS	Post-graduate scholarships in economics, law and political science for work experience in the EP DG for Research. *Formerly* STOA SCHOLARSHIPS. *See also* RAMÓN y CAJAL SCHOLARSHIPS; SCHUMAN, Robert European Parliament, Bâtiment Robert Schuman, L-2929 Luxembourg
ROBOSCOPE	Ultrasound-image-guided manipulator-assisted system for minimally invasive endo-neurosurgery (a Telematics for Healthcare project within the TELEMATICS APPLICATIONS programme) http://www.ehto.org/vds/projects/roboscope.html
ROBOTRAC	Development of a new vehicle drive gear technology for use in inaccessible terrain... (EUREKA project)
ROCK STADIUM	Public Halls in Rock (PHIR) (EUREKA project)
ROC NORD	Transfer of economic planning/environmental technology from Nordjylland to Crete (RECITE project)
ROCOCO	Real-time monitoring and Control of Construction site manufacturing (ESPRIT project)
ROME CONVENTION	Council Convention on contractual obligations (OJ L266/80). Signed by the UK on 1st April 1991
ROME TREATY	signed by France, Germany, Italy, the Netherlands, Belgium and Luxembourg on 25th March 1957. Came into force 1st January 1958
ROPS	Roll-Over Protective Structures relating to wheeled agricultural or forestry tractors

ROS	*Research in Official Statistics.* An international journal published twice a year by EUROSTAT
ROSA	New conception of a very high stability miniature frequency source for applications in navigation, telecommunications and metrology (EUREKA project)
ROSA	RACE Open Services Architecture (RACE project)
ROSAL	Robot for rose plants handling and grafting (EUREKA project)
ROSAMES	Road Safety Management Expert System (DRIVE project)
ROSE	Research Open Systems for Europe (ESPRIT project)
ROSES	Road Safety Enhancement System which takes into account road and weather conditions (DRIVE project)
Route map for reform	Timetable from Commissioner Kinnock in October 1999, for the reform of the Commission http://europa.eu.int/comm/reform/index_en.htm
RPPF	Romanian Post-Privatisation Fund set up by the European Commission (under the PHARE programme) and the EBRD to finance investments in the private sector in Romania
RSVP	RACE Strategy for Verification (RACE project)
RTD	Research DG of the European Commission
RTD-ACRONYMS	A CORDIS database relating to EU RTD activities
RTD-COMDOCUMENTS	A CORDIS database providing details of RTD COM and SEC DOCs

RTD-CONTACTS	A CORDIS database of contact points for RTD information and advice both at national and European level
*RTDE	Committee on Research, Technological Development and Energy (of the EP)
RTD FRAMEWORK programme	*See* FP5
RTD-NEWS	A CORDIS database giving news on all aspects of EU RTD activities
RTD-PARTNERS	A CORDIS database which enables researchers to identify partners for collaboration
RTD-PROGRAMMES	A CORDIS database containing information on all EU research and research-related programmes
RTD-PROJECTS	A CORDIS database covering individual contracts and studies within the EU-funded programmes
RTD-PUBLICATIONS	A CORDIS database of bibliographical information and abstracts of publications, reports and papers arising from EU research activities. *Previously* EABS
RTD-RESULTS	A CORDIS database of information on results from EU RTD research which are awaiting commercial exploitation
RTGS	Real-Time Gross Settlement (linked to TARGET)
RTI	Road Transport Informatics (DRIVE project)
RTIS	Regional Traffic Information Service (EURET project)
RTTS	Proposal on frequency bands to be designated for the introduction of Road Transport Telematic Systems (OJ C221/92)

RUBRIC	A Rule-Based Approach to information systems development (ESPRIT project)
RUDING REPORT	*of the Committee of Independent Experts on company taxation*. Published for the European Commission by EUR-OP in 1992
RUE	Rational Use of Energy
RUEM	Regional and Urban Energy Management action. *Incorporated into* SAVE II
*RULE	Committee on the Rules of Procedure, the verification of credentials and immunities (of the EP)
*RURALNET	On-line version of a directory which contained information on local (and primarily) rural development projects. Ceased 1989
S	*See* PES
SAAs	Stabilisation and Association Agreements http://europa.eu.int/comm/dg1a/see/sap/index.
SAARC	South Asia Association for Regional Cooperation
SABE	Strategy Advisory Body on Environment. Set up by CEN
*SABINE	Système d'Accès à la Banque Informatique des Nomenclatures Européennes. *See* SIMONE
SAC	Special Areas of Conservation. Part of the HABITATS Directive
SACODY	A high-performance FMS robot with dynamic compensation (ESPRIT project)

SAD	Single Administrative Document (in international trade). Applicable from January 1988. Sample in OJ L79/85. Since January 1993 it has been mainly used in trade with EFTA countries
SAELN	Students Across Europe Language Network (a Telematics for Education and Training project within the TELEMATICS APPLICATIONS programme)
SAFE	Safety Actions for Europe (1996-2000). Proposed programme of non-legislative measures to improve health and safety at work (Amended proposal in OJ C92/97)
SAFE	Standard Authority Facility Environment (DELTA project)
SAFE 21	Social Alarms For Europe in the 21st Century (a Telematics for Disabled and Elderly People project within the TELEMATICS APPLICATIONS programme)
SAFETY-NET	SAFETY critical industries workplace learning Telematic NETwork (a Telematics for Education and Training project within the TELEMATICS APPLICATIONS programme)
SAI	Space Applications Institute. Part of the JRC at ISPRA
SAM	Multi-lingual Speech Input/Output Assessment: Methodology and Standardisation (ESPRIT project)
SAMOVAR	Safety Assessment Monitoring On-Vehicle with Automatic Recording (DRIVE project)
SANCO	Health and Consumer Protection DG of the European Commission

SAPARD	Special Accession Programme for Agriculture and Rural Development. Pre-accession aid for countries in CEE http://europa.eu.int/comm/dg06/publi/fact/sapard/index_en.htm
SAPPHIRE	PCTE portability (ESPRIT project)
SARA	Simulation of Reactor Accident
SARA	Structural Adjustment and Reform Assistance (part of the PHARE 1997 programme)
*SAST	Strategic Analysis in Science and Technology programme (part of the MONITOR programme)
SATDOC	Satellite Mediated Controlled Experiment for Continuing Education and Monitoring Doctors (DELTA project)
SATURN	Smart Card and Terminal Usability Requirements and Needs (TIDE project)
SAVE II	Council Decision 96/737/EC for Specific Actions for Vigorous Energy Efficiency (1996-2000) (OJ L335/96). *See also* PACE; RUEM
SAVIE	Support Action to facilitate the use of VIdeoconferencing in Education (a Telematics for Education and Training project within the TELEMATICS APPLICATIONS programme)
SBIP	Structural Biology INDUSTRIAL PLATFORM http://europa.eu.int/comm/dg12/biotech/ip2.html# SBIP http://www.biodigm.com/science/ip.htm
SBS	Structural Business Statistical domain on the NEW CRONOS databank
SC	Scientific Committee
SC	Standing Committee

SCA	Shared-Cost Action
SCA	Special Committee on Agriculture
SCAD	Automated Central Documentation Service of the European Commission
SCAD	Community system for accessing documentation. A print and web-based bibliographical database of EU legislation, official publications and periodical articles developed by SCAD. *See also* SCADPlus http://europa.eu.int/scad CD-ROM access via CONTEXT; ELLIS; ILI
SCADPlus	SCAD database plus further EU information. Incorporates the former INFO 92 database http://europa.eu.int/scadplus
SCAHAW	Scientific Committee on Animal Health and Animal Welfare. *See also* SSC
SCALE	Small Countries improve their Audiovisual Level in Europe (MEDIA project) Contact: rua Dom João V, 8-R/C Dto, P-1200 Lisbon, Portugal
SCAN	Scientific Committee on Animal Nutrition. *See also* SSC
SCAN	Subcontracting Assistance Network. A pilot project to improve the communication of information on subcontracting exchanges and databases in Europe. Launched July 1994 Contact: Enterprise DG of the European Commission
SCAR	Standing Committee on Agricultural Research
SCCNFP	Scientific Committee on Cosmetic Products and Non-Food Products. *See also* SSC
SCE	Proposal for a European Cooperative Society (OJ C99/92 and amended in OJ C236/93)

SCE	Standing Committee on Employment
SCENT	System Customs Enforcement Network (CADDIA project)
SCENT-CIS/FISCAL	Management of tariff application for imports and exports of goods from and to THIRD COUNTRIES
SCF	Scientific Committee for Food. *See also* SSC
SCG	Space Coordination Group. Set up by the European Commission in 1996 http://europa.eu.int/comm/jrc/space/index_en.html
SCHEMA	Social Cohesion through Higher Education in Marginal Areas (EMTF project)
SCHENGEN ACQUIS	A body of rules relating to the relaxation of border controls between a number of EU states originating in the SCHENGEN AGREEMENT of 1985. The Schengen rules were incorporated into the framework of the EU as a Protocol to the AMSTERDAM TREATY
SCHENGEN AGREEMENT	Signed 14 June 1985 by Belgium, Luxembourg, the Netherlands, Germany and France to set up a border-free zone. Spain, Portugal, Italy, Greece, Austria, Sweden, Finland and Denmark have since signed the Agreement which has not been published in official sources. Iceland and Norway also became parties to the Agreement in 1999. The Agreement made the abolition of internal border controls possible as from 26 March 1995. *See also* SCHENGEN ACQUIS; SCHENGENLAND; SIS
Schengenland	An area of free circulation within the EU created by the signatories to the SCHENGEN AGREEMENT

SCHUMAN, Robert	*See* ROBERT SCHUMAN PROJECT; ROBERT SCHUMAN SCHOLARSHIPS; SCHUMAN DECLARATION
SCHUMAN DECLARATION	A Declaration of 9 May 1950 by the French Foreign Minister Robert Schuman on the formation of the ECSC. Reprinted in *European Documentation 3/1990. See also* 30th MAY MANDATE; SCHUMAN, Robert
SCI	Site of Community Interest. Part of the HABITATS Directive. *See also* PSCI
SCIC	Joint Interpreting and Conference Service of the European Commission
*SCIENCE	Programme to stimulate the international cooperation and interchange needed by European research scientists (1988-1992) (OJ L206/88). *Previously* SCIENCE STIMULATION programme. *Continued as* the HCM programme
*SCIENCE STIMULATION programme	Action to stimulate the efficacy of the EECs Scientific and Technical potential (1985-88) (OJ L83/85). *Continued as* SCIENCE. *See also* BRAIN
SCIMITAR	Support and Coordination for Integrated Multimedia Telematics Applications for Researchers (a Telematics for Research project within the TELEMATICS APPLICATIONS programme)
SCIT	Standing Committee on Information Technology
SCMPMD	Scientific Committee on Medicinal Products and Medicinal Devices. *See also* SSC
*SCOOP	Common Services Unit of the European Commission which was set up to improve the coordination of sections of DG 1 and DG VIII

SCOPE	Software Certification on Programs in Europe (ESPRIT project)
SCOPE	Support of Commission Objectives and the Environment for administrations and urban and rural areas (a Telematics for Administrations project within the TELEMATICS APPLICATIONS programme) http://scope.cscdc.bc/scope.htm
SCP	Scientific Committee on Plants. *See also* SSC
SCP	Single Cell Protein (COST action project)
SCP-ECG	Standard Communication Protocol for Computerised Electrocardiography (AIM project)
SCR	Common Service for External Relations DG of the European Commission
SCREEN	Internal (confidential) Information Society DG of the European Commission database on RTD programmes and results
SCREWDRIVER PLANTS	*See* LOCAL CONTENT
SCRIBO	Secure Card Reader In Bank cOmmunication (EUREKA project)
SCRIPT	Support for Creative Independent Production Talent (MEDIA project) UK contact: 39C Highbury Place, London N5 1QP
SCTEE	Scientific Committee on Toxicity, Ecotoxicity and the Environment. *See also* SSC
SCVPH	Scientific Committee on Veterinary Measures relating to Public Health. *See also* SSC
SD	Special Directive

SDR	Special Drawing Rights
SDT	Translation Service of the European Commission http://europa.eu.int/comm/sdt/en/index.html
SE	Societas Europea (European Company) (OJ C138/91). This was blocked in 1995
SEA	Single European Act signed by the 12 Member States in February 1986. Came into force in July 1987
SEA	Strategic Environmental Assessment
SEAHORSE	Support, Empowerment and Awareness for HIV/AIDS; the On-line Research and Self-Help Exchange (a Telematics for Healthcare project within the TELEMATICS APPLICATIONS programme). *See also* SEAHORSE II
SEAHORSE II	Follow up project to SEAHORSE http:www.ehto.org/vds/projects/seahorse2.html
SEALINK	Improved maritime transport connections (RECITE project)
SEALOOK	R&D for new real-time underwater acoustic optic systems (EUREKA project)
SEAMOS	Sea Environmental Monitoring System (EUREKA project)
SEC DOC(UMENT)	Document of the Secretariat-General of the European Commission. Not normally available to the general public
SECFO	Systems Engineering and Consensus Formation Office (DRIVE project)
SECTORAL RELAYS	EU information providers in the UK from various organisations which have national sectoral coverage. *See also* RELAYS
SED	SETL Experimentation and Demonstrator (ESPRIT project)

SEDESES	Selective Deposition of Silicides and Epitaxail Silicon (ESPRIT project)
*SEDOC	Reg 1612/68 for a European System for the International Clearing of Vacancies and Applications for Employment (OJ L257/68 with latest amendment in OJ L245/92). *Replaced by* EURES
SEDODEL	Secure Document Delivery for blind and partially sighted people (a Telematics for Disabled and Elderly People project within the TELEMATICS APPLICATIONS programme)
SEDOS	Software Environment for the Design of Open Distributed Systems (ESPRIT project)
SEDOS DEMO	SEDOS Estelle Demonstrator (ESPRIT project)
SEER	Social, Economic and Environmental Research (Area D III of the ENVIRONMENT AND CLIMATE programme)
SEISCAN	A project to rescue early seismic reflection profiles that exist only as paper records, by computer scanning and archiving to a CD-ROM (MAST III project) http://www.soc.soton.ac.uk/CHD/seisweb/SEISCAN.html
SEISMED	Security questions in Medical information systems (AIM project)
SELECT	Feasibilty and definition of integrated measurement, databases and computer-aided design for orthopaedic footwear (EUREKA project)
SELECT	Rating and filtering of scientific, technical and other network documents (a Telematics for Research project within the TELEMATICS APPLICATIONS programme)

SEM	Single European Market. An EC initiative to achieve a single internal market without trade or fiscal barriers and to enable the FREE MOVEMENT of persons throughout the 12 Member States by the end of 1992. *See also* COCKFIELD WHITE PAPER; INFO 92
SEM	South and Eastern Mediterranean Countries
SEM 2000	Sound and Efficient Management 2000. Set up in 1995 to improve the European Commission's administration and financial management
SEMAGRAPH	Semantics and pragmatics of generalised Graph rewiring (ESPRIT project)
SEMANTIQUE	Semantics-based program manipulation techniques (ESPRIT project)
SEMPER	Socio-economic analysis (ACTS project)
SEMRIC	Secure Medical Record Information Communication (ISIS healthcare network project) http://www.ramit.be/semric/
SENIOR ONLINE	Use of networks for reducing the isolation of elderly people and people with mobility impairments (a Telematics for Disabled and Elderly People project within the TELEMATICS APPLICATIONS programme)
SENSE	Solid ENforcement of Substances in Europe. A second enforcement project started in October 1996 as part of the implementation of Directive 67/548/EEC on the classification, packaging and labelling of dangerous substances (OJ No 196/67 as amended by Directive 92/32/EEC in OJ L154/92). *See also* NONS
SEPLIS	European Secretariat for the Liberal Professions Coudenberg 70, B-1000 Brussels, Belgium

SERG	European System of Geographical References (COST action project)
SERI	Dir 92/59/EEC for a Système d'Echange Rapide d'Information (Rapid information exchange system on dangerous consumer products) (OJ L228/92)
SERIS	State of the Environment Reporting Information System. A gateway to information about the state of the environment in European countries and regions. Part of the EEA http://service.eea.eu.int/seris/files/main.html
SERT	Business Statistics and Telematics Networks for the collection and dissemination of data
SERV	Service activities and technological change (FAST project)
SERVICE 2000	Project based on the concept of the one-stop-shop framework for integrated services on a community level (a Telematics for Disabled and Elderly People project within the TELEMATICS APPLICATIONS programme)
SERVIVE	SERvice for integrated VIrtual Environments (a Telematics for Education and Training project within the TELEMATICS APPLICATIONS programme)
SES	Structure of Earnings statistical domain on the NEW CRONOS databank
SESAME	Derivation of the relationship between land use, behaviour patterns and travel demand for political and investment decisions (TRANSPORT project)
*SESAME	On-line database of innovative energy technology projects supported by the EU. Closed December 1999

SESAME	Standardisation in Europe on Semantical Aspects in Medicine (AIM project)
SESEFA	Self-Service Facilities Architecture (ESPRIT project)
SESPROS	Social Protection statistical domain on the NEW CRONOS databank
SET ASIDE	A voluntary scheme set up in 1985 to encourage the setting aside of arable land. Article 7 of Reg 1765/92 covers the establishment of a support system for producers of certain arable crops (OJ L181/92 with latest amendment in OJ L160/99)
SEVESO I Directive	Dir 82/501/EEC on the major-accident hazards of certain industrial activities (OJ L230/82 with latest amendment in OJ L85/87)
SEVESO II Directive	Dir 96/82/EC on the control of major-accident hazards involving dangerous substances (OJ L10/97)
SEVILLE	JRC establishment World Trade Centre, Isla de la Cartuja s/n, E-41092 Seville, Spain
SFAC	Social Fund Advisory Committee
SFINX	Software Factory Integration and Experimentation (ESPRIT project)
SG	Secretariat-General of the European Commission
SGM	Standard Gross Margin
*SHERLOCK	Joint Action 96/637/JHA for a programme of training, exchanges and cooperation in the field of identity documents (1996-2000) (OJ L287/96). *Replaced by* ODYSSEUS

SHIFT	System for animal Health Inspections at Frontier posts. Set up under the IDA programme
SHOW	Standards for Home Working (ISIS teleworking project) http://show.iitb.fhg.de/
SIC	Standards Implementation Committee
SICAMOR-ED	Information System and Coordinated Action in favour of the rural community (CADDIA project)
SIERRA	Support for the Implementation of the Europe Agreement. A Polish programme set up under PHARE
SIG	Special Interest Group
SIGLE	An electronic system involving national governments for licence administration. Set up under the IDA programme
SIGLE	On-line System for Information on Grey Literature in Europe. A product of EAGLE UK contact: Mr A Smith, British Library Document Supply Centre, Boston Spa, Wetherby, Yorkshire LS23 7BQ Blaise line: http://www.bl.uk/ STN international: http://www.fiz-karlsruhe.de Internet: http: stneasy.fiz-karlsruhe.de CD-ROM available from SILVERPLATTER
SIGMA	An EU and OECD joint programme to support reforms in public administrations in CEEC http:www.oecd.org/puma/sigmaweb/
SIGMA	Integrated and global support system for environmental management and monitoring (a Telematics for Environment project within the TELEMATICS APPLICATIONS programme) http://www.trentel.org/environment/research/projects/sigma.html
SIGMA	A quarterly bulletin of European statistics published by EUR-OP for EUROSTAT

SIGNBASE	Development of Multimedia Signed Language Database (TIDE project)
SIGNING BOOKS	Signing Books for the deaf (a Telematics for Disabled and Elderly People project within the TELEMATICS APPLICATIONS programme)
*SII	Integrated Information Systems (Commission DG IX responsible for databases). *Previously* CIRCE
SILMAG	Thin film magnetic heads on silicon (EUREKA project)
SIMAP	Système d'Information pour les Marchés Publics, to promote, coordinate and manage change in public procurement. Set up under the IDA programme to access international procurement databases http:simap.eu.int
SIMBIOSE	Scientific Improvement of Biofilters and Sensors (EUREKA project)
SIMET	Smart Inter-Modal Transfer (EURET project)
SIMONE	A EUROSTAT database containing nomenclatures and the relationships between them, for example HS; NABS; NACE. *Previously* SABINE Access via floppy diskette or paper from EUROSTAT. Available on the Internet by early 2000
SIMPR	Structured Information Management Processing and Effective Retrieval (ESPRIT project)
SIMULAB	On-line SIMULAtions on the WeB (a Telematics for Education and Training project within the TELEMATICS APPLICATIONS programme)
SINAPSE-EUROCIM	Flexibile automated factory for the production of electronic equipment (EUREKA project)

*SINDAVE	Support for Investors in the Region of Vale do Ave (Portugal) (1992-1993)
SINGLE ACT	*See* SEA
SINGLE CURRENCY	*See* ECU; EURO
SINGLE DOCUMENT	*See* SAD
SINGLE EUROPEAN ACT	*See* SEA
SINGLE EUROPEAN MARKET	*See* SEM
SINGLE MARKET	*See* SEM
SIP	Advanced algorithms and architectures for Speech and Image Processing (ESPRIT project)
SIP	Sectoral Impact Programme and technical assistance for SMEs in Poland (PHARE programme)
SIR	*See* CRS
SIRCH	Societal and Institutional Responses to Climate change and climatic Hazards (ENVIRONMENT AND CLIMATE project)
SIREN	Security In REgional Networks (a Telematics for Healthcare project within the TELEMATICS APPLICATIONS programme)
SIRENE	Energy statistical domain on the NEW CRONOS databank
SIRENE MANUAL	*See* SYRENE MANUAL
SIRIUS	Sociopolitical Implications on Road transport Informatics implementation and Use Strategies (DRIVE project)

SIS	Schengen Information System. A computerised network to collect information from police forces and justice systems within the SCHENGEN AGREEMENT. *See also* SYRENE MANUAL
SITC	Standard International Trade Classification. A United Nations classification. A *Guide to the classification of overseas trade statistics* is published annually by TSO which contains the SITC Rev3 codes
SITE	Computerised System for VAT Exchanges set up under the VAT Directives introduced by the SEM
SITYA	Sharing Information on Troubled Young Adults (a Telematics for Integrated Applications for Digital Sites project within the TELEMATICS APPLICATIONS programme)
SJ	Legal Service DG of the European Commission
SKIDS	Signal and Knowledge Integration with Decisional control for multi-sensory Systems (ESPRIT project)
SLAPS	Spatial variability of Land Surface Processes (EPOCH project)
SLIM	Simpler Legislation for the Internal Market (COM(96) 559)
SLOM	Supplementary Levy on Milk
SLOM farmers	Dairy farmers who were not attributed a milk quota when the quota system was launched in 1984 because they had previously stopped producing milk on a voluntary basis
SMART	Electronic cards for travel and transport (DRIVE project)

SMART	System Measurement and Architectures Techniques (ESPRIT project)
SMARTS	Socio-economic analysis (ACTS project)
*SMCU	Single Market Compliance Unit to assist UK companies which are experiencing trade barriers in the SEM. Now part of the Action Single Market Team (DTI Europe) Contact: Kingsgate House, 66-74 Victoria St, London SW1E 6SW
*SME	A COMMUNITY INITIATIVE which continued the assistance previously given to SMEs under PRISMA; STRIDE and TELEMATIQUE in order to adjust to the SEM (1994-1999) (Guidelines in OJ C180/94)
SME	Small and Medium-sized Enterprise. A definition appears in Recommendation 96/280/EC (OJ L107/96). *See also* SMEAP
SME	Small and Medium-sized Enterprise statistical domain on the NEW CRONOS databank
SMEAP	Council Decision 97/15/EC for a 3rd SME Action Programme (1997-2000) (OJ L6/97). *See also* INTERPRISE
SME-NARIO	Revitalisation of SMEs: Enabling Management to Formulate New Telematics Needs (a Telematics Engineering project within the TELEMATICS APPLICATIONS programme)
SME OBSERVATORY	An OBSERVATORY for SMEs
*SME TF	Small and Medium-sized Enterprise Task Force of the EC. *Now* the Enterprise DG of the European Commission
SME-WEB	Services and Assistance for SMEs on the Information Highway (a Telematics Engineering project within the TELEMATICS APPLICATIONS programme)

SMILE	A Sign language and Multimedia-based Interactive Language course for deaf for the training of European written languages (EMTF project)
SMILE	Technical feasibility of high volt smart power ICs for lighting applications (ESPRIT project)
SMILER	Short-Wave Microwave Links (DRIVE project)
SMO	Single Market OBSERVATORY. Established in 1994 to look into the impact and effectiveness of the SEM and to propose changes http://www.ces.eu.int/en/smo/fr_s_market_forum.htm
SMP	Single Market Programme. *See* SEM
*SMT	Council Decision 94/803/EC for a Standardisation, Measurement and Testing programme (1994-1998) (OJ L334/94). *Previously* MEASUREMENTS AND TESTING. *Replaced by* GROWTH http://www.cordis.lu/smt/home.html http://europa.eu.int/comm/dg12/bcr1.html
SMU	*See* SME
SMUK	Supplementary Measure in favour of the UK
SNA	*System of National Accounts*. A publication containing macro-economic accounts, issued by EUR-OP for EUROSTAT in 1993 Also available as a CD-ROM from EUR-OP
SNMT	Strategic Niche Management as a tool for transition to an environmentally sustainable transportation system (ENVIRONMENT AND CLIMATE project)
SOAG	Senior Officials Advisory Group to assist the European Commission to define and implement measures for a common information market
SOC	*See* PES

*SOCI   Committee on Social Affairs and
                               employment (of the EP)

SOCIAL CHAPTER   A Protocol on Social Policy annexed to the
                               TREATY ON EUROPEAN UNION. The
                               UK opted out

SOCIAL CHARTER   A Community Charter of the fundamental
                               social rights of workers. Published by EUR-
                               OP in 1990. An action programme relating
                               to the SOCIAL CHARTER is published as
                               COM(89) 568. Both the Charter and the
                               Action programme appear in *Social Europe
                               1/90*. *See also* INFO 92

SOCIAL FUND   *See* ESF

SOCKER   Search and retrieval Origin Communication
                               KERnel (project within Area 5 of the
                               TELEMATIC SYSTEMS programme)

SOCOMAT   Development, production and investigation
                               of new soft coating materials into heavy
                               duty slide bearings for tribological
                               applications... (EUREKA project)

SOCPOL   Proposal for a Community Programme for
                               Older People (1995-1999) (OJ C115/95)

SOCRATES   EP and Council Decision 819/95/EC
                               establishing a Community action
                               programme for the development of quality
                               education and training and the creation of an
                               open European area for cooperation in
                               education (1995-1999) (OJ L87/95 amended
                               by Council Decision 576/98 in OJ L77/98).
                               A second phase (2000-2006) was
                               established by Council Decision
                               253/2000/EC (OJ L28/2000). *Combines
                               ARION; COMENIUS; ERASMUS;
                               EURYDICE; GRUNDTVIG; LINGUA;
                               MINERVA; NARIC; ODL*
                               SOCRATES Technical Assistance Office, rue
                               Montoyer 70, B-1040 Brussels, Belgium
                               UK contact: Central Bureau for Educational Visits and
                               Exchanges, 10 Spring Gdns, London SW1A 2BN

SOCRATES	System of Cellular Radio for Traffic Efficiency and Safety (DRIVE project)
SODA	Superoxide Dismutase Analogues - free radical scavengers (EUREKA project)
*SOEC	Statistical Office of the European Communities. *See* EUROSTAT
SOGITS	Senior Officials Group for Information Technology Standardisation. A committee composed of representatives of Member State administrations which assists the ISIS initiative http://www.ispo.cec.be/isis/
SOG-T	Senior Officials Group on Telecommunications
SOMIW	Secure Open Multimedia Integrated Work-station (ESPRIT project)
SOUR-CREAM	SOftware Use and Re-use: Computerised REquirements And Methodology (EUREKA project)
SOUTHERN CONE COMMON MARKET	*See* MERCOSUR countries
SPA	Special Protection Area. Part of the BIRDS Directive
SPACE	Signal Processing for Auditory Communication in noisy Environments (a Telematics for Disabled and Elderly People project within the TELEMATICS APPLICATIONS programme)
SPACE	Single Point of Access for Citizens of Europe (a Telematics for Administrations project within the TELEMATICS APPLICATIONS programme)

SPAN	Parallel computing systems for integrated symbolic numeric processing (ESPRIT project)
SPAN	Regional promotion of electronic commerce standards for SMEs (ISIS SME promotion project) http://www.ispo.cec.be/isis/95span.htm
SPAN	Safe Passage And Navigation. Project to design safer and more efficient ships, coordinated by NETS (BRITE/EURAM project)
SPARTACUS	System for Planning and Research in Towns and Cities for Urban Sustainabilty (ENVIRONMENT AND CLIMATE project)
SPC	Statistical Programme Committee
S-PCS	EP and Council Decision 710/97/EC on a coordinated authorisation approach in the field of Satellite-Personal Communication Services in the Community (OJ L105/97)
SPD	Single Programming Document (under the STRUCTURAL FUNDS). *See also* IDO
*SPEAR	Support Programme for a European Assessment of Research (1988-1992) (Part of the MONITOR programme)
SPEARHEAD	A database of information on the SEM legislation and other EU legislation relevant to the operation of businesses in the EU, compiled by the UK Department of Trade and Industry Access via DATASTAR; FT PROFILE; ILI Also available on CD-ROM (which includes EUROPEAN UPDATE and INFO 92) from CONTEXT
SPEC	Council Decision 93/464/EEC for a Statistical Programme of the EU (1993-1997) (OJ L219/93)

SPEC	Formal methods and tools for the development of distributed and real-time systems (ESPRIT project)
*SPEC	Support Programme for Employment Creation especially towards the completion of the SEM (1990-1994?). An EP initiative
SPECS	Specification Environment for Communication Software (RACE project)
SPECTRA	Sustainability, development and spatial planning (ENVIRONMENT AND CLIMATE project)
SPECTRE	Submicron CMOS technology (ESPRIT project)
SPECTRUM	Strategies for Preventing Road Traffic Congestion (DRIVE project)
SPEECH	Text of speeches by members of the European Commission Access via RAPID
SPEL/EU	Agricultural data relating to prices, quantities and values of agricultural output statistical domain on the NEW CRONOS databank Available on CD-ROM from EUROSTAT
SPEM	Software Production Evaluation Model (ESPRIT project)
*SPES	Stimulation Plan for Economic Science (1989-1992) (OJ L44/89). *Continued as* TMR
SPHERE	Small/medium sized Ports with Harmonised, Effective Re-engineered processes (TRANSPORT project)
SPIERENBURG REPORT	Proposals for the reform of the Commission 1979. Published by the Commission
SPIN	Speech Interface at office workstations (ESPRIT project)

| SPIRIT | High performance technical workstation (ESPRIT project) |

SPIRIT   High performance technical workstation
                         (ESPRIT project)

SPMMS   Software Production and Maintenance
                         Management Support (ESPRIT project)

SPNET   Science Parks Networks

SPOT   Signal Processing for Optical and cordless
                         Transmissions (RACE project)

SPP-ESF   Special Preparatory programme for
                         European STRUCTURAL FUNDS. It
                         prepares candidate countries for the future
                         administration of all EU STRUCTURAL
                         FUNDS (part of the PHARE programme)

SPRINT   Signal Processor using Innovative III/V
                         Technologies (ESPRIT project)

SPRINT   Software Programme for Research IN
                         Telecommunications (RACE project)

SPRINT   Speech Processing and Recognition using
                         Integrated Neuro-computing Techniques
                         (ESPRIT project)

*SPRINT   Strategic Programme for the promotion of
                         Innovation and Technology Transfer (1989-
                         1993-1994) (OJ L112/89 and OJ L6/94).
                         Continued as INNOVATION

SPRINTEL   Speedy Retrieval of Information on the
                         Telephone (project within Area 5 of the
                         TELEMATIC SYSTEMS programme)

SPRITE   Storage Processing and Retrieval of
                         Information in a Technical Environment
                         (ESPRIT project)

SPRITE-S2   Pilot action in the area of Support and
                         guidance in the Procurement of ICT systems
                         and services. Launched in July 1997.
                         Replaces EPHOS

SRV   Sustainability Reference Value

SSC	Scientific Steering Committee. Coordinates the work of the Scientific Committees run by the Health and Consumer Protection DG of the European Commission. *See also* CSTEE; SCAHAW; SCAN; SCCNFP; SCF; SCMPMD; SCP; SCTEE; SCVPH; STFC
SSE	*See* ESS
SSID	Specialised Service for Documentary data processing
SSS-CA	Concerted Action on Short Sea Shipping. To oversee the implementation of TRANSPORT RTD projects
*SSV	Short Study-Visits (1977-1987). *Incorporated into* the ERASMUS programme
STA	Science and Technology Agency which runs a Fellowship programme in Japan to enable young European scientists to carry out research in Japan's national laboratories and non-profit making institutions http://www.sta.go.jp
STABEX	(System of) Stabilisation of Export Earnings of agricultural products under the LOME CONVENTION
STABILITY PACT	on EMU. Proposals agreed by the Council of the European Union in Dublin, December 1995 (OJ C369/96). *See also* EURO
STABINE	Development of an advanced power generation system, compounding a diesel cycle to that of an industrial gas turbine (EUREKA project)
STACCIS	Support for Telematics Cooperation with the CIS (a Telematics for Education and Training project within the TELEMATICS APPLICATIONS programme)

STADIUM	Statistical Data Interchange Universal Monitor (CADDIA project)
STAGE 1 Directive	Dir 94/63/EC on VOC emissions resulting from the storage of petrol and its distribution (OJ L365/94). *See also* STAGE 2 Directive
STAGE 2 Directive	Dir 1999/13/EC on the limitation of emissions of VOCs due to the use of organic solvents in certain activities and installations (OJ L85/99). *See also* STAGE 1 Directive
STAGIAIRE	A graduate given training within the European Commission in order to gain experience of the workings of the EU - possibly before taking up a career in the European Commission
STAMMI	Definition of Standards for In-vehicle Man-machine interface (DRIVE project)
STANORM	Statistical Normalisation to study the standardisation of data exchange between various types of data processing environments (CADDIA project)
STAPLE	Development of an efficient functional programme system for the support of prototyping (ESPRIT project)
STAR	Comité des Structures Agricoles et du Développement Rural (Committee for agricultural structures and rural development)
STAR	Seamless Telematics Across Regions (a Telematics for Healthcare project within the TELEMATICS APPLICATIONS programme)
*STAR	Special Telecommunciations Action for Regional Development in certain less-favoured regions (1986-1991) (OJ L305/86). *Continued under* TELEMATIQUE

STAR	STAndardisation of interoperable Road tolling systems based on Dedicated Short Range Communications (DSRC) (ISIS Transport project) http://www.ispo.cec.be/isis/98star.htm
STAR	Sustainability Targets and References value database. An EEA database of current environmental policy targets and SRVs http://star.eea.eu.int
STARLAB	Self-Sustaining Tele-media Applications Research Laboratory (a Telematics Information Engineering project within the TELEMATICS APPLICATIONS programme)
*STARS	Database for business on legislation and advisory services relevant to the SEM. *Replaced by* INFORULES
START-UP	Suppliers for Technological Advanced Requirements Through Users Protocols (DELTA project)
STATEL	Statistics Telematics. Common interfaces for statistics applications (IDA project)
STATEL	Statistiques Télétransmission. Electronic data exchange between the SOEC and Institutions in the Member States (CADDIA project)
STATONIS	Insurance Services statistical domain on the NEW CRONOS databank
STC	Scientific and Technical Committee (EURATOM)
STC	Scientific and Technical Cooperation
*STD III	R&D programme in the field of Science and Technology for Developing countries (1990-1994) (OJ L196/91). *Continued as* INCO I
*STECLA	Standing Technological Conference of European Local Authorities

STEELCAL	Computer-Aided Learning in Structural STEELwork design (EMTF project)
STELCI	Short-term Earnings and Labour Costs Indices statistical domain on the NEW CRONOS databank
STEM	Sustainable Telematics for Environmental Management (a Telematics for Environment project within the TELEMATICS APPLICATIONS programme http://www.trentel.org/environment/research/projects/stem.html
STEMM	Strategic European Multi-modal Modelling (TRANSPORT project)
*STEP	Science and Technology for Environmental Protection (1989-1993) (OJ L359/89). *Continued in* the ENVIRONMENT AND CLIMATE programme
STEPS Handbook	*Solutions for Telematics between European Public Services*. Compiled by SCOPE. Latest handbook available at http://scope.cscdc.be/steps/index.htm#handbook
STFC	Scientific and Technical Fisheries Committee. *See also* SSC
STI	Safety Technology Institute. Part of the JRC at ISPRA
STID	Scientific and Technical Information and Documentation
*STIG	*See* TELEMATIC SYSTEMS programme
STILMED	Safety Technology in Laser Medicine (EUREKA project)
STIMULATION programme	*See* SCIENCE STIMULATION programme
STM	Supplementary Trade Mechanism

STMS	Short-Term Monetary Support under the EMS
STOA	Scientific and Technical Options Assessment. A unit in the EP DG for Research to provide expert scientific and technical advice to MEPs and EP Committees. *See also* EPTA; ETAN; STOA SCHOLARSHIPS
*STOA SCHOLARSHIPS	for first degree level young scientists and engineers to obtain work experience in the EP DG for Research. *Replaced by* RAMÓN y CAJAL SCHOLARSHIPS. *See also* ROBERT SCHUMAN SCHOLARSHIPS; STOA
STOKE ROCHFORD CONFERENCES	held at Stoke Rochford in January 1993 and January 1994 to establish the decentralisation of EU information provision in the UK. The concept of RELAYS and the NCC were set up as a result
STOP	Joint Action 96/700/JHA establishing an incentive and exchange programme for persons responsible for combating trade in human beings and the sexual exploitation of children (1996-2000) (OJ L322/96)
STORM	Process modelling and device optimisation for submicron technologies (ESPRIT project)
STORMS	A European agreement on the radio access system for third generation multi-media mobile communications (ACTS project)
STP	Scientific Training Programme in Japan. Set up in 1986 to create an exchange scheme for young scientists Contact: European Commission Research DG, rue de la Loi 200, B-1049 Brussels, Belgium
STRADA II	Standardisation of Traffic Data transmission and management (DRIVE project)

STRATEGIC PLANNING	Assistance to small and medium-sized cities in the area of strategic planning (RECITE project)
STRC	*See* CREST
STREAM III	Stratosphere - Troposphere Experiments by Aircraft Measurements III (THESEO project)
STRETCH	Extensible KBMS for large knowledge base applications (ESPRIT project)
*STRIDE	Science and Technology for Regional Innovation and Development in Europe (1990-1993). A STRUCTURAL FUNDS Initiative (Guidelines in OJ C196/90). *Continued in* the SME COMMUNITY INITIATIVE
STRIDE	Speech-analytical hearing aids for the profoundly deaf in Europe (TIDE project)
STRIKES	Industrial disputes statistical domain on the NEW CRONOS databank
STRINGS	Statistical Report Integrated Generation Service (CADDIA project)
STRUCTURAL FUNDS	Reg 1260/99 laying down general provisions on the Structural Funds to strengthen the economic and social cohesion of the EU (2000-2006) (OJ L161/99. *See also* COMMUNITY INITIATIVES; EAGGF; ERDF; ESF; FIFG; OBJECTIVES
STRUDER	STRUctural DEvelopment in selected Regions (in Poland) (under the PHARE programme)
STUTTGART DECLARATION	concerning the Institutions and policies of the EC. Issued by the European Council meeting in Stuttgart on 19 June 1983. Published in the *Bulletin of the European Communities 6/83* p24-29

SUAW	Stand Up And Walk (BIOMED project)
SUBCONTRACTORS Directive	*See* POSTED WORKERS Directive
Sub-GATE	Submarine Groundwater-fluxes and Transport-processes from methane rich coastal sedimentary Environments (ELOISE project)
SUBSIDIARITY	The principle of decision-making at the lowest possible level so that Brussels only becomes involved in issues which cannot be dealt with at national level
SUBSOITEC	High Performance Submicron SOI-CMOS Technologies (ESPRIT project)
SUITE	SUlfonates InTerrestrial Environments (TERI project)
SUMMIT	*See* EUROPEAN SUMMIT
SUM-PROJECT	Shoe Upper Material Project (EUREKA project)
SUNDIAL	Speech Understanding and Dialogue (ESPRIT project)
SUNSTAR	Integration and design of speech understanding interfaces (ESPRIT project)
SUPERDOC	Set of software tools for a document workstation (ESPRIT project)
SUPERNODE	Development and application of a low cost high performance multiprocessor (ESPRIT project)
SUPERNODE II	Operating systems and programming environments for parallel computers (ESPRIT project)

SUPER REGIONS	Listed as follows: I. Alpine regions II. ATLANTIC ARC III. Northern arc IV. Central capitals V. Diagonal Continental VI. Central Mediterranean VII. West Mediterranean VIII. New German Länder
SUPERSMOLT	Production system for salmonids at elevated temperatures using sterile supermolts (EUREKA project)
SUPER SUBSEA	To develop standardised modular subsea production systems (EUREKA project)
SUPRADYNAMICS	Lattice dynamics of high TC single crystal superconductors (ESPRIT project)
SURE	To promote safety in the nuclear sector especially within countries participating in the TACIS programme (1998-2002)
SUSCOM	SUStainable COMmunities in Europe (ENVIRONMENT AND CLIMATE project)
SUTHERLAND REPORT	on the operation of the Community's Internal Market after 1992 (SEC(92) 2277)
SVC	Standing Veterinary Committee
SWIFT	Specification for Working positions In Future air Traffic control (EURET project)
SWIFT	User oriented and workflow integrated federation of service providers for the elderly (a Telematics for Disabled and Elderly People project within the TELEMATICS APPLICATIONS programme)
SWPI	Standing Working Party on Investment

SYMBIOSIS	An information network of non-profit making organisations on the PEOPLE'S EUROPE to inform citizens of the advantages of the SEM (OJ C293/91)
SYMBOL	Multilingual and multiple lexical learning on CD-I environment (TIDE project)
SYN	*See* COOPERATION PROCEDURE
SYNAPSES	Federated healthcare record serve (a Telematics for Healthcare project within the TELEMATICS APPLICATIONS programme)
SYNERGY	Council Decision 99/23/EC adopting a multi-annual programme to promote international cooperation in the energy sector (1998-2002) (OJ L7/99) http://www.cordis.lu/synergy/home.html
SYNTHETIC INDEX	of regions, measuring the relative intensity of regional problems in the EC (COM(84) 40 Table 7.1.1.; COM(87) 230 p23; COM(90) 609 Statistical Annex p35; COM(94) 322 Table A.25; COM(96) 542 p133). *See also* COHESION REPORT; PERIODIC REPORT
SYRECOS	SYsteme REgional d'echange de COmpetences et des Services (a Telematics for Urban and Rural Areas project within the TELEMATICS APPLICATIONS programme)
SYRENE MANUAL	which defines procedures to exchange information under the SIS
SYSDEM	European System of Documentation on Employment Contact: European Commission Employment and Social Affairs DG
SYSMIN	SYstem of Stabilisation of export earnings from MINing products. A trade provision within the LOME CONVENTION

SYSTRAN	SYStems analysis TRANslator. An automated translating System (1970-) used by the European Commission
T3	Telematics for Teacher Training (a Telematics for Education and Training project within the TELEMATICS APPLICATIONS programme)
T3E	Drug Addiction-Europe-Exchange-Training. Part of the five-year Community programme for the prevention of drug dependence (1996-2000)
T4D	Telemployment for the disabled (a Telematics for Urban and Rural Areas project within the TELEMATICS APPLICATIONS programme)
TAC	Technical Advisory Committee
TAC	Total Allowable Catch (of fish). Latest published for 1999 (OJ L13/99 with amendement in OJ L187/99)
TACD	TransAtlantic Consumer Dialogue. A United States-EU consumer forum set up in 1998
TACIS	Tactile Acoustic Computer Interaction System (TIDE project)
TACIS II	Reg 1279/96 concerning Assistance to economic reform and recovery in the NIS and Mongolia (1996-1999) (OJ L165/96). Reg 99/2000 extends the programme from 2000-2006 (OJ L12/2000) TACIS Information Office: European Commission DG I, rue de Loi 200, B-1049 Brussels, Belgium
TACIS LIEN	TACIS Link Inter European NGOs for TACIS projects involving NGOs (OJ C29/98)
TAFI	Textile Antifraud Initiative

TAIE	Design and assessment of a vessel traffic management system (EURET project)
TAIEX	Technical Assistance and Information Exchange. Set up by the Commission in 1996 to help the EU applicant countries in CEEC ave de Cortenberg 80, B-1049 Brussels, Belgium
TAKEOVER Directive	13th company law Directive on Takeovers (Latest proposal OJ C378/97)
TALAT	Training for Aluminium Applications Technologies (COMETT project)
TALON	Testing and Analysis of Local area Optical Networks (ESPRIT project)
TAMCRA	Telematics Applications to Create Alternative Marketing Channels for SMEs (a Telematics for Urban and Rural Areas project within the TELEMATICS APPLICATIONS programme)
TANIT II	Telematics for ANaesthesia and Intensive Therapy II (a Telematics for Healthcare project within the TELEMATICS APPLICATIONS programme)
TANKER	Ecological economical European Tanker (EUREKA project)
TAO	Technical Assistance Office
TAP	*See* TELEMATICS APPLICATIONS programme
TAPPE	Telematics for Administrations: Public Procurement in Europe (a Telematics for Administrations project within the TELEMATICS APPLICATIONS programme)
TARDIS	Total traffic management environment (DRIVE project)

TARGET	Telematics Applications in Radiation and GEneral oncology (a Telematics for Healthcare project within the TELEMATICS APPLICATIONS programme)
TARGET	Trans-European Automated Real-time Gross settlement Express Transfers system of Inter-bank payments. Introduced on 1 January 1999 to regulate transactions between commercial banks and the ECB
*TARGET PRICE	The price which the Council of the European Union considered an agricultural producer should receive for the product on the open market
TARIC	Integrated Customs Tariff of the European Communities (now under the IDA programme) which is published annually in the OJ (Latest tables in OJ C212A/99 4 vols)
TASC	Telematics Applications Supporting Cognition (a Telematics for Disabled and Elderly People project within the TELEMATICS APPLICATIONS programme)
TASQUE	Tool for Assisting Software Quality Evaluation (EUREKA project)
TASTE	Technology ASsessment in TEle-neuro-medicine (a Telematics for Healthcare project within the TELEMATICS APPLICATIONS programme)
TAU	Technical Assistance Unit
TAXUD	Taxation and Customs DG of the European Commission
TAYLOR	Transputer based APD/INMOS language and operating system research (EUREKA project)
TC	Technical Committee

TCEU	Translation Centre for Bodies of the EU. Set up under Reg 2965/94 (OJ L314/94 with amendment in OJ L268/95) rue Joseph Junck 9, L-1839 Luxembourg http://europa.eu.int/en/agencies.html#tceu
TCI	Temporary Committee of Inquiry of the EP
TCT	COST Technical Committee on Transport
TDHS	Technological Developments in the Hydrocarbons Sector scheme
TDI	*See* TGI
TDSP	Training and Dissemination Schemes Projects (part of INNOVATION) http://www.cordis.lu/tdsp/home.html
TEAC HEALTH	Towards Evaluation And Certification of HEALTH care telematics services in Europe (a Telematics for Healthcare project within the TELEMATICS APPLICATIONS programme) http://www.ehto.org/vds/projects/teac-health.html
TEAM	Techno-Economic-Analysis network in the Mediterranean. Joint initiatives and strategies between the science and technology communities of Europe and the Mediterranean (an IPTS initiative)
*TEAM 92	*See* TEAM EUROPE
TEAM EUROPE	Team Europe Information Service. A team of speakers throughout the Member States who are available for conferences, training sessions and so on, covering all EU policies and activities. *Previously* TEAM 92 Berkenlaan 6, B-1831 Diegem, Belgium http://europa.en.int/comm/dg10/teameurope/index_en.html
TECAR	Training network for the European CAR Industry (a Telematics for Education and Training project within the TELEMATICS APPLICATIONS programme)

TECDOC	Portable information devices for Technical Documentation (IMPACT project)
TECHNOLOGY TRANSFER	Electronic communication and exchange of data in order to facilitate the search for target SMEs in partner regions (RECITE project)
TECLA	*Multilingual glossary of head-words used for the Court's case-law.* 4 vols 1994.1995. Published by EUR-OP
TED	Tenders Electronic Daily. A free database of EU Tenders. *See also* OJ 'S'; TED - Alert http://ted.eur-op.eu.int
TED - Alert	A service to alert subscribers to relevant tenders listed on TED Available on subscription via EUR-OP agents
*TEDIS II	Council Decision 91/385/EEC establishing the Trade Electronic Data Interchange Systems programme (1991-1994) (OJ L208/91)
TEISS	Telematics - European Industry Standards Support (a Programme Support Actions project within the TELEMATICS APPLICATIONS programme)
TELEFARMS	TELEmatics multimedia application for FARMers Support (a Telematics for Administrations project within the TELEMATICS APPLICATIONS programme)
TELEFLEUR	TELEmatics-assisted handling of FLood Emergencies in URban areas (a Telematics for Environment project within the TELEMATICS APPLICATIONS programme) http://www.trentel.org/environment/research/projects /telefleur.html
TELEFLOW	TELEmatics supported workFLOW analysis and business process enhancement (a Telematics Engineering project within the TELEMATICS APPLICATIONS programme)

TELE-INSULA	TELEmatic services for Islands (a Telematics for Urban and Rural Areas project within the TELEMATICS APPLICATIONS programme)
TELEINVIVO	3D ultrasound TELEmatics medical emergency workstation (a Telematics for Healthcare project within the TELEMATICS APPLICATIONS programme) http://www.ehto.org/vds/projects/teleinvivo.html
*TELEMAN	Research into remote-controlled handling in nuclear hazardous and disordered environments (1989-1993) (OJ L226/89)
TELEMAN	TELEteaching and training for MANagement of SMEs - studies (a Telematics for Education and Training project within the TELEMATICS APPLICATIONS programme)
TELEMART	TELEmatics MARketing of Teleworkers (a Telematics for Urban and Rural Areas project within the TELEMATICS APPLICATIONS programme)
TELEMATE	TELEmatic Multidisciplinary Assistive Technology Education (a Telematics for Disabled and Elderly People project within the TELEMATICS APPLICATIONS programme)
*TELEMATICS APPLICATIONS programme	Council Decision 94/801/EC on RTD in the field of telematics applications of common interest (1994-1998) (OJ L334/94). *Successor to* the TELEMATIC SYSTEMS programme. *See also* DELTA; ICT; ORA; TIDE. *Continued as* IST
*TELEMATIC SYSTEMS programme	Telematic Systems in areas of general interest (1990-1994) (OJ L192/91). *Incorporates* AIM; DELTA; DRIVE; LRE; ORA. *Continued as* TELEMATICS APPLICATIONS programme

*TELEMATIQUE	A STRUCTURAL FUNDS Initiative for regional development services and networks related to data communication (1991-1993) (Guidelines in OJ C33/91). *Continued as* the SME COMMUNITY INITIATIVE
TELENURSE	TELEmatic applications for NURSEs (a Telematics for Healthcare project within the TELEMATICS APPLICATIONS programme) http://www.ehto.org/vds/projects/telenurse.html
TELEPLANS	TELEmedicine for citizens (a Telematics for Healthcare project within the TELEMATICS APPLICATIONS programme) http://www.ehto.org/vds/projects/teleplans.html
TELEPROMISE	TELEmatics to PROvide for MISsing sErvices (a Telematics for Urban and Rural Areas project within the TELEMATICS APPLICATIONS programme)
TELER	TELmatics for Enterprise Reporting (a Telematics for Administrations project within the TELEMATICS APPLICATIONS programme)
TeleRegions SUN2	TELEapplications for European Regions (a Telematics for Integrated Applications for Digital Sites project within the TELEMATICS APPLICATIONS programme)
TELESCAN	The first European Internet service for cancer research, treatment and education (MARIA project) http://telescan.nki.nl
TELETEENS	Methods and services to provide European TEENagers with long-term illnesses usual access to TELEmatics (a Telematics for Urban and Rural Areas project within the TELEMATICS APPLICATIONS programme)

TELEVISION WITHOUT FRONTIERS	*See* TWF Directive
TELEXPER	Dissemination Action on TELEmatics EXPERiences (a Programme Support Actions project within the TELEMATICS APPLICATIONS programme)
TELI	European Language Initiative. Language learning materials in EU official languages for local government European Language Initiative, PO Box 1901, Wicken, Milton Keynes MK19 6DN, United Kingdom
TELOS	Telematics Enhanced Language learning and tutoring Systems (a Telematics for Education and Training project within the TELEMATICS APPLICATIONS programme)
TEMPLE	Telematic Employment engine (a Telematics for Urban and Rural Areas project within the TELEMATICS APPLICATIONS programme)
TEMPORA	Integrating database technology, rule-based systems and temporal reasoning for effective software (ESPRIT project)
TEMPUS II and III	Council Decision 93/246/EEC for a Trans-European Mobility Scheme for University Studies (in CEEC) (1994-1998) (OJ L112/93 and extended until 2006 by Council Decision 1999/311/EC in OJ L120/99) ave des Arts 19H, B-1040 Brussels, Belgium UK contact: British Council, Europe Unit, Education and Science Division, Medlock St, Manchester M15 4PR
TEMPUS PHARE	To extend TEMPUS awards to new applicant countries
TEMPUS LIEN	To extend TEMPUS awards to the NIS and Mongolia

TEMSIS	Transnational Environmental Management Support and Information System (a Telematics for Environment project within the TELEMATICS APPLICATIONS programme) http://www.trentel.org/environment/research/projects /temsis.html
TEN	Reg 2236/95 on Trans-European Networks: an EU action programme (OJ L228/95 with an extension to 2006 in OJ L197/99). *See also* TEN-ENERGY; TEN-TELECOMMUNICATIONS; TEN-TRANSPORT http://europa.eu.int/en/agenda/ten/ten.html
TEN	Trans-European tele-education Network (a Telematics for Education and Training project within the TELEMATICS APPLICATIONS programme)
TEN-34	Trans-European Network interconnect at 34 Mbps (a Telematics for Research project within the TELEMATICS APPLICATIONS programme)
TEN-ENERGY	EP and Council Decision 1254/96/EC for Trans-European Energy Networks (Guidelines in OJ L161/96 with latest amendment in OJ L207/99). *See also* TEN
TEN-IBC	*See* TEN-TELECOMMUNICATIONS
TEN-T	*See* TEN-TRANSPORT
TEN-TELECOMMUNICATIONS	EP and Council Decision 1336/97/EC on a series of guidelines for Trans-European Telecommunications Networks (OJ L183/97). *See also* TEN
TEN-TRANSPORT	EP and Council Decision 1692/96/EC for Trans-European Transport Networks (Guidelines in OJ L228/96). *See also* TEN
TEP	Territorial Employment Pact in favour of employment with funding from the EAGGF; ERDF; ESF http://inforegio.cec.eu.int/pacts/index.htm

TEPIT	EDI project under the TEDIS programme
TEPSA	Trans-European Policy Studies Association rue d'Egmont 11, B-1000 Brussels, Belgium
TERA	Development and manufacture of high performance, high capacity optical disc storage systems for data library applications (EUREKA project)
TERENA	Trans European Research and Educational Networking Association Singel 466-468, NL-1017 AW Amsterdam, Netherlands
TERES	*European Renewable Energy Study* which was published (together with 3 Annexes) for the European Commission DG XVII by EUR-OP in 1994
TERI	Terrestrial Ecosystems Research Initiative (part of the ENVIRONMENT AND CLIMATE programme) http://europa.eu.int/comm/dg12/teri/teri-pro.html
TERICA	Concerted action for coordination of TERI (TERI project)
*TERMINALS GUIDE	ECHO database giving descriptions of terminals with the addresses of suppliers and service operators in Europe
TERN	Trans-European Road Network
*TERRA	Networks of local/regional authorities to carry out innovative and/or demonstration pilot projects on spatial planning (under Article 10 of the ERDF)
TERRACE	TMN Evolution of Reference configurations for RACE (RACE project)
TES/IOT	Tableaux Entrées-Sorties. A database containing input-output tables of the national accounts of the Member States Access via CD-ROM from EUROSTAT

TESCO	TESt on COperative driving (DRIVE project)
TESEMED	TElematics in Community pharmacies for responsible SElf-MEDication (a Telematics for Healthcare project within the TELEMATICS APPLICATIONS programme)
TESS/SOSENET	Telematics for Social Security/Social Security Network to exchange information about insured persons. Set up under the IDA programme
TESTLAB	TEsting Systems using Telematics for Library Access for Blind and visually handicapped readers (a Telematics for Libraries project within the TELEMATICS APPLICATIONS programme)
TESUS	TEleSUrgical Staff (a Telematics for Healthcare project within the TELEMATICS APPLICATIONS programme)
TET	Technology, Employment and Labour (FAST project)
TET-ADAPT	Adaptation of Techno-Economic Evaluation Tools for RACE (RACE project)
TETJAPAN	Telematics for Education and Training in JAPAN (a Telematics for Education and Training project within the TELEMATICS APPLICATIONS programme)
TETRISS	Telematics for Education and TRaining - Intermediate Support Structure (a Telematics for Education and Training project within the TELEMATICS APPLICATIONS programme)
TEU	*See* TREATY ON EUROPEAN UNION

TEXATWORK	TEXtile Application of TeleWORKing (a Telematics for Urban and Rural Areas project within the TELEMATICS APPLICATIONS programme)
TF	European Commission Task Force. Launched in 1995, the initial six TFs covered Car of the future; Multimedia educational software; New generation of aircraft; Vaccines and viral illnesses; Train of the future; Transport intermodality. Two further TFs cover: Environment-water; Maritime systems
*TFAN	Task Force for Accession Negotiations. Set up by the Commission in 1998. Now merged with the services responsible for pre-accession in the Enlargement DG of the Commission
*TF-HR(ETY)	European Commission Task Force Human Resources, Education, Training and Youth. *Now* the Education and Culture DG of the European Commission
TFTS	Terrestrial Flight Telecommunications Service (EUREKA project)
TFTS	Terrestrial Flight Telecommunications System (OJ C222/92)
TGI	Technical Group of Independent Members (of the EP)
THEATRON	Theatre History in Europe: Architectural and Textual Resources ON-line (EMTF project)
THEMATIC NETWORK	*See* TN
THEMATIC PROGRAMMES	Focused programmes to implement KEY ACTIONS, RTD activities of a generic nature and activities in support of research infrastructures. A component of FP5. *See* EESD; GROWTH; IST; QUALITY. *See also* HORIZONTAL PROGRAMMES

*THERMIE II	The demonstration component of the Non-Nuclear RTD programme JOULE-THERMIE. *Continued as* ENERGIE within the EESD programme http://www.europa.eu.int/en/comm/dg17/thproj.htm
*THESAURI	An on-line analytical inventory of current structured vocabularies which have appeared in at least one of the official EU languages
THESEO	THird European Stratospheric Experiments on Ozone. A campaign to monitor and study the ozone loss over Europe (1998-99) (ENVIRONMENT AND CLIMATE project) http://europa.eu.int/comm/dg12/envsc/theseo.html
THETIS	A data management and data visualisation system for supporting coastal zone management for the Mediterranean sea (a Telematics for Research project partly funded by the TELEMATICS APPLICATIONS programme)
THIN	Travel Health Information Network (a Telematics for Healthcare project within the TELEMATICS APPLICATIONS programme)
THIRD COUNTRY	Any country outside the Member States
THIRTIETH MAY MANDATE	*See* 30th MAY MANDATE
THORN	The obviously required name server (ESPRIT project)
THREE PILLARS	*See* PILLARS
THREE WISE MEN REPORT	on air transport, chaired by De Croo and published in 1994 by EUR-OP for the European Commission DG VII as *Expanding horizons: Civil aviation in Europe, an action programme for the future*
THREE WISE MEN REPORT	on EC steel policy (OJ C9/88)

THREE WISE MEN REPORT	on the European Institutions. Published by the Council of Ministers in 1979
THREE WISE MEN REPORT	on the institutional implications of enlargement. October 1999 http://europa.eu.int/igc2000
*THRESHOLD PRICE	The minimum price at which agricultural produce from non-EU countries could enter the EU
THTPs	Transnational High-Technology Projects
TIAH project	Total Income for Agricultural Households. A EUROSTAT project to provide a measure of the aggregate disposable income of farmers (1992-)
TIBIA	Technology Initiative in BICMOS for Applications (JESSI/ESPRIT project)
T-IDDM	Telematic management of Insulin Dependent Diabetes Mellitus (a Telematics for Healthcare project within the TELEMATICS APPLICATIONS programme)
*TIDE	Technology Initiative for Disabled and Elderly People (1993-1994) (OJ L240/93). *Continued in* the TELEMATICS APPLICATIONS programme
TIERRAS	Trans-European research on telematics applications for Regional Administration development Strategies (a Telematics for Urban and Rural Areas project within the TELEMATICS APPLICATIONS programme)
TII	European Association for the Transfer of Technologies, Innovation and Industrial Information rue des Capucins 3, L-1313 Luxembourg

TINA	Transport Infrastructure Needs Assessment. A transport initiative to identify the infrastructure requirements of the candidate countries (part of the PHARE programme)
TINDEMAN's REPORT	on European union. Published in the *Bulletin of the EC Supplement 1/76*
TIP	Technology Integration Project (within the ESPRIT programme)
TIP	TEMPUS Information Point (in TEMPUS and TACIS partner countries)
TIPPS	Transnational Innovation Pilot Programme in SMEs (INNOVATION project)
TIRONET	Interconnected broadband islands between Northern Ireland and the Republic of Ireland: a fibre interconnection initiative to prepare for TEN-TELECOMMUNICATIONS
TITAN	Tactical Integration of Telematics Applications across intelligent Networks (a Telematics for Integrated Applications for Digital Sites project within the TELEMATICS APPLICATIONS programme) http://www.trentel.org/environment/research/projects/titan.html
TMIE	Tutoring and Monitoring Intelligent Environment (DELTA project)
*TMR	Council Decision 94/916/EC on the Training and Mobility of Researchers: Activity 4 of the 4th RTD Framework programme (1994-1998) (OJ L361/94). *Previously* HCM; SPES. *Continued as* IMPROVING http://europa.eu.int/comm/dg12/tmr1.html
TN	Thematic Network. A means of RTD coordination and cooperation, bringing together technologies around specific on-going and complementary fields throughout the EU. This ensures the exchange of information and resources between partners

TNG	Thematic Network Group. Established by EU-OSHA
TN-NETS	The BRITE/EURAM Thematic Network: NEw concepts and technologies for the next century maritime TranSport
TOBIAS	Tools for Object-Based Integrated Administration of Systems (ESPRIT project)
TODOS	Automatic TOols for Designing Office information Systems (ESPRIT project)
TOM	*See* FOD
ToMeLo	Towards a strategic alliance between developers of Medical terminology and health care record systems (a Telematics for Healthcare project within the TELEMATICS APPLICATIONS programme)
TOMPAW	A TOtally Modular Prosthetic Arm with high Workability (a Telematics for Disabled and Elderly People project within the TELEMATICS APPLICATIONS programme)
TOOL-USE	Advanced support environment for method driven development and evolution of packaged software (ESPRIT project)
TOOTSI	Telematic Object Oriented Tools for Services Interfaces (ESPRIT project)
TOPILOT	To Optimise the Individual Learning process of Occupational Travellers (a Telematics for Education and Training project within the TELEMATICS APPLICATIONS programme)
TOPMUSS	TOols for Processing of MUlti-Sensorial Signals for plant monitoring and control (ESPRIT project)

TOPOZ-2	TOwards the Prediction of stratospheric OZone (THESEO project)
TOPP	Transverse Optical Patterns (ESPRIT project)
TOROS	Tinto Odiel River Ocean Study (ELOISE project)
TOSAFES	Treatment of Obstructive Sleep Apnea with Functional Electrical Stimulation (a Telematics for Disabled and Elderly People project within the TELEMATICS APPLICATIONS programme)
*Tosca	A CSCW project to provide an organisational knowledge base http://orgwis.gmd.de/projects/TOSCA/
TOSKA	TOols and methods for a Sophisticated Knowledge-based content free Authoring facility (DELTA project)
TOUR	Tourism statistical domain on the NEW CRONOS databank
TOUR-R	Tourism statistical domain on the REGIO database
TOY SAFETY Directive	Dir 88/378/EEC concerning the safety of toys (OJ L187/88)
TPA	Third Party Access to national gas and power grids
TPC	Committee on the Adaptation of Directives to Technical Progress
*TPF	Technology Performance Financing set up under the SPRINT programme to strengthen the innovative capacity of SMEs in Europe
TPF	Third Party Financing
TQC	Total Quality Control in the production industry (COMETT project)

TRA	Targeted Research Action. Set up by the Commission at the end of the Third RTD Framework Programme in 1994 under the BRITE/EURAM programme. *See also* TRA NESS
TRACE	Employment access routes. Mentoring programme for young people in France under a CEDEFOP three year plan
TRACE	TRAde Cooperation and Economic policy reform in South-Asia. Part of the EU's cooperation with Asia
TRACIT	Transponders for R/T Activity Control of manufacturing links to CIM IT systems (ESPRIT project)
TRADE	EDI project under the TEDIS programme
TRADE	Trade DG of the European Commission
TRAINING	Vocational training in enterprises statistical domain on the NEW CRONOS databank
TRAIN-IT	TRAINing of IT Innovators (ESPRIT programme)
TRAINS	Carriage of goods statistical domain on the NEW CRONOS databank
*TRAN	Committee on Transport and Tourism (of the EP)
TRAN	Regional transport statistical domain on the REGIO database
TRA NESS	New ship concept in the framework of short sea shipping. A project to group together seven Community-funded RTD projects. Part of TRA
TRANS	Transport DG of the European Commission
TRANSFERS Directive	*See* ACQUIRED RIGHTS Directive

| TRANSIT | An electronic system for national governments on customs clearance for goods in transit between the EU and EFTA countries. Set up under the IDA programme |

TRANSIT — An electronic system for national governments on customs clearance for goods in transit between the EU and EFTA countries. Set up under the IDA programme

TRANSMETE — Seminars for TRAiNing SMEs in the use of TElematics (a Telematics for Education and Training project within the TELEMATICS APPLICATIONS programme)

TRANSPARENCY — A term used to mean opennness, especially with regard to public access to information

*TRANSPORT — Council Decision 94/914/EC on RTD in the field of transport: Activity 1.6 of the 4th RTD Framework programme (1994-1998) (OJ L361/94). *Previously* EURET
http://www.cordis.lu/transport/home.html

TRANSPOTEL — A worldwide reproduceable concept for physical distribution centres where central facilities are offered of which the major provision is an integral data and communications processing system (EUREKA project)

TRANSTEC — Internet-based multimedia knowledge TRANSfer for innovative Engineering TEChnologies (EMTF project)

TRANSWHEEL — TRANSportation WHEELchair with high impact safety and advanced sensor comfortability for people with mobility problems (a Telematics for Disabled and Elderly People project within the TELEMATICS APPLICATION programme)

TRAPCA — Risk assessment of exposure to traffic-related air pollution for the development of inhalent allergy, asthma and other chronic respiratory conditions in children (an Environmental Health and Chemical Safety Research project within the ENVIRONMENT AND CLIMATE programme)

TREATY OF ACCESSION	*See* ACCESSION TREATY
TREATY OF AMSTERDAM	*See* AMSTERDAM TREATY
TREATY OF PARIS	*See* PARIS TREATY
TREATY OF ROME	*See* ROME TREATY
TREATY ON EUROPEAN UNION	Signed by the 12 Member States at Maastricht on 7 February 1992. Came into force 1 November 1993
TREES	TRopical Ecosystem Environment observations by Satellites (Commission/ESA project)
TREMOR	Development and validation of new assistive devices for the treatment of disability caused by Tremor (a Telematics for Disabled and Elderly People project within the TELEMATICS APPLICATIONS programme)
*TREND	An ECHO database to monitor trends in the development of computer hardware and software
TRENDS	Training Educators through Networks and Distributed Systems (a Telematics for Education and Training project within the TELEMATICS APPLICATIONS programme)
TRESHIP	Technologies for Reduced Environmental impact from SHIPs. One of the TNs supported by the TRANSPORT programme relating to Short Sea Shipping
TREVI GROUP	Member States' Interior Ministers meeting to discuss Terrorism, Radicalism, Extremism and VIolence
TRIDISMA	Three-DImensional Sediment transport Measurements by Acoustics (MAST III project) http://www.uea.ac.uk/~e470/www_trid.htm

TRIM	Main aggregates of the national accounts statistical domain on the NEW CRONOS databank
TRIMS	Trade-Related Investment Measures within the GATT and subsequent negotiations
TRIPS	Trade-Related aspects of Intellectual Property Rights within the GATT and subsequent negotiations
TRITON	Training material and courses on the technology for environmental protection in water resources management (COMETT project)
TROÏKA	The current Presidency, the previous Presidency and the following Presidency of the Council of the European Union
TROPICS	Transparent Object-oriented Parallel Information Computing System (ESPRIT project)
TRUST	Testing and consequent reliability estimation for real-time embedded software (ESPRIT project)
TrustHealth	TRUSTworthy HEALTH telematics (a Telematics for Healthcare project within the TELEMATICS APPLICATIONS programme)
TrustHealth II	Project based on TRUST HEALTH http://www.ehto.org/vds/projects/trusthealth2.html
TS	Technology Stimulation actions
TSE IP	Transmissable Spongiform Encephalopathies INDUSTRIAL PLATFORM http://tse-ip.org/

*TSER	Council Decision 94/915/EC for a Targeted Socio-Economic Research programme: Activity 1.7 of the 4th RTD Framework programme (1994-1998) (OJ L361/94). *Previously* MONITOR. *Continued as* IMPROVING http://www.cordis.lu/tser/home.html http://europa.eu.int/comm/dg12/tser1.html
TSIs	Technical Specifications for Interoperability of the trans-European high-speed rail system. Drawn up by the AEIF
TSME	Technology Stimulation Measures for SMEs
TSUNAMI II	Technology in Smart antennas for the UNiversal Advanced Mobile Infrastructure Part II (ACTS project)
TTA	All terrain amphibious vehicle (EUREKA project)
TTA	Time-Triggered-Architecture. Development of a new concept in on-board automotive electronic systems (ESPRIT project)
TT-CNMA	Testing Technology for Communications Networks for Manufacturing Applications (ESPRIT project)
TTER	Two-Tier Exchange Rate
TTNet	Community Training of Trainers Network. Set up in 1998 by CEDEFOP
TTP+TVP	Technology Transfer and Technology Validation Projects (INNOVATION project) http://www.cordis.lu/tvp/home.html
TT-RT-SMEIRT	Business-opportunity creation for SMEs (TIDE project)
TUDOR	Usability issue for people with special needs (RACE project)
TUNICS	Tunnel Integrated Control System (DRIVE project)

TUPE	Transfer of Undertakings introducing the ACQUIRED RIGHTS Directive into the United Kingdom (SI 1981 No 1794; SI 1995 No 2587)
TUTB	European Trade Union Technical Bureau for Health and Safety bd du Roi Albert II 5, B-1210 Brussels, Belgium http://www.etuc.org/tutb/index_en.html
TVA	*See* VAT
TV-Anytime	Home storage multimedia systems based on standards (ISIS Multimedia systems project) http://www.ispo.cec.be/isis/98tvanyt.htm
TWE	The relationship between Technology, Work and Employment (FAST programme)
TWENTY-ONE	Multimedia information transaction and dissemination tool (a Telematics Information Engineering project within the TELEMATICS APPLICATIONS programme)
TWEUROPA	TeleWork EUROPA (a Telematics for Urban and Rural Areas project within the TELEMATICS APPLICATIONS programme)
TWF Directive	Dir 89/552/EEC for Television Without Frontiers to coordinate the provision of television broadcasting activities (OJ L298/89 with latest amendment in OJ L202/97)
TWG-DFO	Technical Working Group on Data exchange and Forecasting for Ozone episodes in Northwest Europe. Set up in 1996 and coordinated by the ETC/AQ
*u.a.	Unit of Account. *See* ECU
UAA	Usable (utilised) Agricultural Area

UAC	Users Advisory Council. Set up by the European Commission in 1994 to encourage the dissemination of information on EU affairs
UACES	University Association for Contemporary European Studies c/o King's College, Strand, London WC2R 2LS, United Kingdom http://www.uaces.org/u-info/
UAM	Union of the Arab MAGHREB countries
U-CARE	Unexplained Cardiac Arrest Registry of Europe (BIOMED project)
UCITS Directive	Dir 85/611/EEC on the coordination of laws…relating to Undertakings for Collective Investment in Transferable Securities (OJ L375/85 with latest amendment in OJ L168/95)
*UCLAF	EU Anti-Fraud Coordination Unit within the European Commission Secretariat-General. *Replaced by* OLAF
UCOL	Ultra wideband Coherent Optical LAN (ESPRIT project)
UEAPME	*See* EUROPMI
UEN	Union for a Europe of Nations group (of the EP). *Previously* EDN; UPE
UETP	University-Enterprise Training Partnership (Strand A in the COMETT programme and continued in the LEONARDO DA VINCI programme)
UFE	*See* UPE
UHP	Unit of Homogeneous Production
UITP	*See* UETP
UK	United Kingdom

UK CEE	United Kingdom Centre for European Education. Now merged with the Central Bureau for Educational Visits and Exchanges Central Bureau for Educational Visits and Exchanges, 10 Spring Gdns, London SW1A 2BN
UKOP	Catalogue of UK Official Publications which includes EU publications listed in TSO catalogues Access via a CD-ROM produced by CHADWYCK-HEALEY and via the Internet (subscription required) http://www.ukop.co.uk
UKREP	United Kingdom Permanent Representative at the EU rond-point R Schuman 6, B-1040 Brussels, Belgium http://www.fco.gov.uk/ukrep
UKRHEEO	UK Research and Higher Education European Office rue de la Loi 83, Boîte 10, B-1040 Brussels, Belgium
ULIC	*See* LUIC
ULISIS	Ultrasonic Images of System Interfaces (EUREKA project)
ULTRA	Exposure and risk assessment for fine and ultrafine particles in ambient air (Environmental Health and Chemical Safety research project within the ENVIRONMENT AND CLIMATE programme)
ULYSSES	Urban LifestYles, SuStainability and integrated Environment aSsessment (ENVIRONMENT AND CLIMATE project)
UNEMP	Unemployment statistical domain on the REGIO database
UNEMPLOY	Unemployment statistical domain on the NEW CRONOS databank

UNESDA	Union of the EC Soft Drinks Associations bd Louis Schmidt 35, Boîte 14, B-1040 Brussels, Belgium
UNICE	Union of Industrial and Employers' Confederations of Europe rue Joseph II 40, Boîte 4, B-1000 Brussels, Belgium
UNIPOS	A UNIX-LIKE Parallel Operating System (EUREKA project)
UNISTOCK	Union of Cereal Storage Firms in the EEC Michelangelolaan 68, B-1000 Brussels, Belgium
UNITED	High-T superconducting thin films and tunnel junction devices (ESPRIT project)
UNITEL	Unified architectural specification for the set-top box (ISIS multimedia project). *See also* UNITEL-2 http://192.33.150.101/unitel/
UNITEL-2	Set-top functionalities in the multimedia chain. Extends the UNITEL project (ISIS multimedia project) http://192.33.150.101/unitel/
UNIT PRICING Directive	Dir 98/6/EC on consumer protection in the indication of the prices of products offered to consumers (OJ L80/98)
UNIVERSE	Large sale demonstrator for global, open distributed library services (a Telematics for Libraries project within the TELEMATICS APPLICATIONS programme)
UNIXIM	CT and Planar image acquistion by means of solid state linear x-ray image detector for slit scan digital radiology (EUREKA project)
*UPE	Union for Europe Group (of the EP). *See* UEN
UPI	User validation best Practice manual for Information engineering (a Telematics Information Engineering project within the TELEMATICS APPLICATIONS programme)

*UPP	Urban Pilot Project under Article 10 of the ERDF (1979-1999)
URBAN	A COMMUNITY INITIATIVE for integrated programmes concerned with economic, social and environmental problems in depressed urban areas (1994-1999) (Guidelines in OJ C180/94 and extended to 2006 in COM(99) 477)
URBAN OBSERVATORY	Establishment of an Urban Observatory to compile comparative data (RECITE project)
URB-LA	A programme to develop cooperation between local authorities in Latin America and EU Member States (1996-1999). Based on ASIA URBS
UROP	Universal Roadside Processor (DRIVE project)
URUGUAY ROUND	Multilateral trade negotiations established in 1986 with GATT countries
UseDHE	User-group on the architecture of Healthcare information systems (a Telematics for Healthcare project within the TELEMATICS APPLICATIONS programme)
Use MARCON	User-controlled generic MARC Convertor (project within Area 5 of the TELEMATIC SYSTEMS programme)
USER	USability requirements Elaboration for Rehabilitation technology (TIDE project)
UTE	Union des Théâtres de l'Europe. Founded in 1990, it aims to develop cultural cooperation across national borders (KALEIDOSCOPE project) pl. Paul Claudel 1, F-75006 Paris, France

UTILITIES Directive	Dir 93/38/EEC on the procurement procedures of entities operating in the water, energy, transport and telecommunications sectors (OJ L199/93 with latest amendment in OJ L101/98)
UVECOS	Effects of UV-B radiation on sensitive European ECOSystems (Environmental Health and Chemical Safety Research project within the ENVIRONMENT AND CLIMATE programme)
*V	Green group (of the EP). *See* GREENS/EFA
VALASPI	Developing and eVAluating culture and LAnguage-learning multimedia telematics for primary School PupIls (EMTF project)
VAL DUCHESSE	Château near Brussels where a number of high-level discussions have taken place
VALID	VALIDation methods and tools for knowledge-based systems (ESPRIT project)
VALIDATA	VALIdated DATAbank and dissemination for prescribers (AIM project)
*VALOREN	Exploitation of indigenous energy potential in certain less-favoured regions (1987-1991) (OJ L305/86)
*VALUE II	Dissemination and exploitation of results from research Valorisation and Utilisation for Europe (1989-1992-1994) (OJ L200/89 and OJ L141/92). *Continued as* INNOVATION
VALUE RELAY CENTRES	*See* IRC
VAMAS	International Scientific and Technical Collaboration on Advanced Materials and Standards (COM(84) 642)
VAMOS	Requirements and system specification for dynamic traffic messages (DRIVE project)

VAN EYCK	Visual Arts Network for the Exchange of Cultural Knowledge (project within Area 5 of the TELEMATIC SYSTEMS programme)
VAP	Vision As Process (ESPRIT project)
VASARI	Visual Arts System for Archiving and Retrieval of Images (ESPRIT project)
VAT	Value Added Tax
VATAM	VAlidation of Telematics Applications in Medicine (a Telematics for Healthcare project within the TELEMATICS APPLICATIONS programme)
VEDILIS	VEhicle DIscharge LIght System (EUREKA project)
VEGETATION	An Earth observation system launched on March 24 1998 on the SPOT4 satellite. Co-financed by the Commission http://spot4.cnes.fr/waiting.htm
VEINS	Variability of Exchanges In the Northern Seas (MAST III project)
VENICE	Virtual Enterprises Nurtured using Intelligent Collaborative Environment (a Telematics for Urban and Rural Areas project within the TELEMATICS APPLICATIONS programme)
VERTS/ALE	*See* GREENS/EFA
VES	Virtual European School (EMTF project)
VIC	Vehicle Inter-Communication (DRIVE project)
VICO	Cultural Values in Information and COmmunication technology (a Telematics for Healthcare project within the TELEMATICS APPLICATIONS programme)

VIDIMUS	Generic vision system for industrial applications (ESPRIT project)
VIENNA CONVENTION	*See* MONTREAL PROTOCOL
VIES	VAT Information Exchange System. An electronic system for national governments. Set up under the IDA programme
VIEWS	Visual Inspection and Evaluation of Wide-area Scenes (ESPRIT project)
VILAR	Landscape Virtual gallery (RAPHAEL project)
VIMP	Vision based on-line Inspection of Manufactured Parts (ESPRIT project)
VIP	VDM Interface for PCTE (ESPRIT project)
VIPS	Scientific press service designed to disseminate the results of EU-funded research to the media http://www.cordis.lu/innovation-smes/vips/en/src/about_en.htm
VIRTUOSO	Virtual Simulation and treatment via Telematics Applications in clinical radio Oncology (a Telematics for Healthcare project within the TELEMATICS APPLICATIONS programme) http://www.ehto.org/vds/projects/virtuoso.html
VISA	Universal access to WIMP-software for partially sighted and blind users (TIDE project)
VISEGRAD AGREEMENTS	Poland (OJ L348/93); Hungary (OJ L347/93); Czech Republic (OJ L360/94); Slovak Republic (OJ L359/94)
VISILOG	Advanced data processing for management support (EUREKA project)
VISIMAR	VIsualisation and SImulation of MARine environmental processes (EUREKA project)

VISIOBOARD	Gaze control system to provide services and applications to severely handicapped citizens (a Telematics for Disabled and Elderly People project within the TELEMATICS APPLICATIONS programme)
VISTEL	Visual Impaired Screen based TELephony (a Telematics for Disabled and Elderly People project within the TELEMATICS APPLICATIONS programme)
VITAL-Home	VITAL signs monitoring from HOME with open systems (ISIS Bioinformatics project) http://www.ispo.cec.be/isis/98vitalh.htm
VITAMIN	VIsualisation sTAndard tools in Manufacturing INdustry (ESPRIT project)
VIVA	Validation Initiative for Vital Application (ISIS Bioinformatics project) http://www.ispo.cec.be/isis/98viva.htm
VOC	Volatile Organic Compounds. *See* STAGE 1 and STAGE II Directives
VOICE	Giving a Voice to the deaf, by developing awareness of voice to text recognition capabilities (a Telematics for Disabled and Elderly People project within the TELEMATICS APPLICATIONS programme)
VOICE	*See* NGO VOICE
VOILA	Variable Object Identification, Location and Acquisition (ESPRIT project)
VREDELING INITIATIVE	Proposal for a Directive on procedures for informing and consulting the employees of undertakings with complex structures (originally published in *Bulletin of the EC Supplement 3/1980* with a revision in *Bulletin of the EC Supplement 2/1983* and a Council Conclusion in OJ C203/86)

VREPAR	Virtual Reality Environments for Psycho-neuro-physiological Assessment and Rehabilitation (a Telematics for Healthcare project within the TELEMATICS APPLICATIONS programme)
VRLEARNERS	Virtual Reality Learning Environment for Network of advanced Educational multimedia Resource centres, museums and Schools (EMTF project)
VSB	Very Small Businesses
VSOP	Voice Supported Optical Publisher (EUREKA project)
VULCANUS III	Traineeships in European industrial companies for Japanese students Contact: European Commission Enterprise DG
VUSEC	Voluntary work and employment. A Commission study published in 1986 in the *Document series* by OOPEC within the Programme of Research and Actions on the Development of the Labour Market in the EC entitled *The extent and kind of voluntary work in the EEC...*
WAI	Web Accessibility Initiative (a Telematics for Disabled and Elderly People project within the TELEMATICS APPLICATIONS programme)
WALCYNG	How to enhance WALking and CYcliNG instead of shorter car trips and to make these modes safer (TRANSPORT project)
WAMM	WAter Management Model. The project involves the application of a new satellite-based technology to improve flood forecasting in the Venice lagoon (INNOVATION project)
WASP	WAdden Sea Project (MAST I project)

WASTEBASE	Database launched by ETC/W containing detailed data and information on all relevant waste management issues covered by the ETC/W http://www.hull.ac.uk/cwpr/html/body_database.html
WASTE CATALOGUE	*See* EWC
WASTES	Reg 259/93/EEC on the supervision and control of shipments of wastes within, into and out of the EU (OJ L30/93 with latest amendment in OJ L298/98). Categories of Green, Amber and Red wastes are listed
WATCH-CORDIS	Windows Access To Commission Host - CORDIS. A Windows application to provide easy access to CORDIS on-line (INNOVATION project)
WAtER	Wetland and Aquatic Ecosystem Research. A TN, launched formally in 1998, to assemble projects covering a wide spectrum of water and wetland related tasks
WATERNET	Distributed WATER quality monitoring using sensor NETworks (a Telematics for Environment project within the TELEMATICS APPLICATIONS programme) http://www.trentel.org/environment/research/projects/waternet.html
WATIS	Work and Training Information System (a Telematics Information Engineering project within the TELEMATICS APPLICATIONS programme)
WEB4GROUPS	Transfer of knowledge between research, education, business and public administration through World Wide Web extended for Group communication (a Telematics for Research project within the TELEMATICS APPLICATIONS programme)

W.E. PRO	Women Entrepreneurs Project. Launched in the framework of the medium-term Community action programme on equal opportunities for men and women, the project looks at access to credit for women entrepreneurs in SMEs Credit Italiano Bruxelles, AIDDA, sq de Meeûs 35, B-1006 Brussels, Belgium
WERNER REPORTS	on monetary union. Published in the *Bulletin of the EC Supplement 11/1970. See also* EMU
WESTENDORF GROUP	REFLECTION GROUP report on Institutional reform which was issued in December 1995 in preparation for the IGC. Published in *Bulletin of the EU 12/1995* p46-51
WETS	Worldwide Emergency Telemedicine Services (a Telematics for Healthcare project within the TELEMATICS APPLICATIONS programme) http://www.ehto.org/vds/projects/wets.html
WGCS	Working Group "Codes and Standards"
WHITE PAPER	A policy paper. *See also* GREEN PAPER
WIDE	Network Women in Development Europe rue du Commerce 70, B-1040 Brussels, Belgium http://www.eurosur.org/wide
WILD BIRDS Directive	*See* BIRDS Directive
WISE	Women's International Studies Europe University van Utrecht, Heidelberglaan 2, NL-3584 Utrecht, Netherlands http://women-www.uia.ac.be/women/wise
WISE	Working In Synergie for Europe (a Telematics for Healthcare project within the TELEMATICS APPLICATIONS programme) http://www.ehto.org/vds/projects/wise.html

WISECARE	Workflow Information Systems for European nursing CARE (a Telematics for Healthcare project within the TELEMATICS APPLICATIONS programme)
WITTY	WIreless Traffic and Transport information sYstem for urban areas (ISIS Transport project) http://www.ispo.cec.be/isis/98witty.htm
WOMAN	Intelligent telematics services for women care by a European network (a Telematics for Healthcare project within the TELEMATICS PPLICATIONS programme) http://www.ehto.org/vds/projects/woman.html
*WOME	Committee on Women's Rights (of the EP)
WORK EQUIPMENT Directive	Dir 89/655/EEC concerning minimum safety and health requirements for the use of work equipment by workers at work (OJ L393/89 with amendment in OJ L335/95)
WORKERS' CHARTER	*See* SOCIAL CHARTER
WORKING HOURS Directive	*See* WORKING TIME Directive
WORKING TIME Directive	Dir 93/104/EC on certain aspects of the organisation of working time (OJ L307/93)
WORKS COUNCIL Directive	*See* EWC
WOW	Women at Work project P.O. Box 94, Strada Commenda 5/A, I-50028 Tavarnelle di Pesa, Florence, Italy
WRC	Water Research Centre. The lead organisation of the ETC/IW under contract to the EEA pl Madou 1, B-1030 Brussels, Belgium http://www.wrcplc.co.uk
WSI	Wafer Scale Integration (ESPRIT project)

WTO	World Trade Organisation (1995-). *Previously* GATT
	Centre William Rappard, rue de Lausanne 154, CH-1211 Geneva 21, Switzerland
	http://www.wto.org/
X-by-wire	Project to develop a safety-related fault-tolerant system in vehicles (supported by the BRITE/EURAM programme)
XML/EDI	European XML (Extensible markup language)/EDI Pilot Project (ISIS Electronic Commerce project)
	http://www.ispo.cec.be/isis/98xmledi.htm
YB_1999	Regions Statistical yearbook 1999 statistical domain on the REGIO database
YEE	Youth and Environment Europe
	Oudergracht 42, NL-3511 AR Utrecht, Netherlands
	http://www.netg.se/oppen/org/y/yee/yee.htm
*YES FOR EUROPE	*See* YOUTH FOR EUROPE
YFE	*See* YOUTH FOR EUROPE
YIP	Yeast INDUSTRIAL PLATFORM
	http://europa.eu.int/comm/dg12/biotech/ip2.html#YIP
	http://www.tech-know.be/
*YIP	Youth Initiative Projects (within the PETRA programme)
*YOUNG WORKERS' EXCHANGE programme	*Incorporated into* the PETRA programme
YOUTH	Common Position 22/99/EC adopted by the Council with the view to the adoption of a Decision establishing the Youth Community action programme (OJ C210/99). This will incorporate the two programmes YOUTH FOR EUROPE and EVS

*YOUTH FOR EUROPE III	EP and Council Decision 818/95/EC for a programme for the promotion of youth exchanges (1995-1999) (OJ L87/95). *See* YOUTH
*YOUTHSTART	Part of EMPLOYMENT, the COMMUNITY INITIATIVE for the promotion of access to work and continuing education for the under twenties (1994-1999) (OJ C180/94 and new guidelines in OJ C200/96)
YWU	Year-Work-Unit
ZPA1	Agricultural products statistical domain on the NEW CRONOS databank
ZPA1_CC	Agricultural production in candidate countries statistical domain on the NEW CRONOS databank
ZRD1	Government R&D statistical domain on the NEW CRONOS databank
ZRD2	Regional data statistical domain relating to government R&D on the NEW CRONOS datatabank

APPENDIX ONE

POSTAL ADDRESSES OF PUBLISHERS AND ELECTRONIC HOSTS

Agra Europe Ltd
80 Calverley Road
Tunbridge Wells
Kent TN1 2UN
United Kingdom

Blaise-Line
British Library National Bibliographical Service
Boston Spa
Wetherby
Yorkshire LS23 7BQ
United Kingdom

British Standards Institution
389 Chiswick High Road
London W4 4AL
United Kingdom

Butterworths
Halsbury House
35 Chancery Lane
London WC2A 1EL
United Kingdom

CAB International
Wallingford
Oxford OX10 8DE
United Kingdom

Chadwyck-Healey Ltd
The Quorum
Barnwell Road
Cambridge CB5 8SW
United Kingdom

Context Electronic Publishers (Justis)
Grand Union House
20 Kentish Town Road
London NW1 9NR
United Kingdom

CSS Information
Perinorm Desk
Miller Avenue 310
Ann Arbor MI
48103 United States of America

Dialog/Datastar
The Communications Building
48 Leicester Square
London WC2H 7DB
United Kingdom

Dimdi
Weisshausstrasse 27
Postfach 420580
D-50939 Cologne
Germany

EINS (European Information Network)
c/o United Kingdom National Centre
Mr R Kitley, DIALTECH
British Library
St Pancras
96 Euston Road
London NW1 2DB
United Kingdom

Ellis Publications (also distributed by Chadwyck-Healey Ltd)
PO Box 1059
NL-6201 BB Maastricht
Netherlands

EPRC Ltd
Graham Hills Building
40 George Street
Glasgow G1 1QE
United Kingdom

ESA-IRS
via Galileo Galilei
I-00044 Frascati
Italy

Eurokom
Dale House
30 Dale Road
Stillorgan
Co Dublin
Eire

EUR-OP
rue Mercier 2
L-2985 Luxembourg

EUR-OP official gateways and sales agents
See full list in EUR-OP catalogues, *EUR-OP news* and on the Internet at:
http://europa.eu.int/general/en/s-ad.htm

EUROSTAT
Bâtiment Jean Monnet
L-2920 Luxembourg

EUROSTAT data shops and sales offices
See full list in *Eurostat publications and databases: practical mini-guide* and on
the Internet at:
http://europa.eu.int.eurostat.html

FT Profile
Financial Times Electronic Publishing
Fitzroy House
13-17 Epworth Street
London EC2A 4DL
United Kingdom

HMSO (now TSO)

ILI
Index House
Ascot
Berkshire SL5 7EU
United Kingdom

Justis
c/o Context Electronic Publishers

Lawtel
St Giles House
50 Poland Street
London W1V 4AX
United Kingdom

Lexis-Nexis Europe
International House
1 St Katherine's Way
London E1 9NU
United Kingdom

Raabe-Fachuerlag für Wissenschaftsinformation
Kaiser-Friedrich Strasse 90
D-10585 Berlin
Germany

SilverPlatter Information Ltd
Merlin House
20 Belmont Terrace
Chiswick
London W4 5UG
United Kingdom

Springer Verlag London Ltd
Sweetapple House
Catteshall Road
Godalming GU7 3DJ
Surrey
United Kingdom

STN International
Postfach 2465
D-76012 Karlsruhe 1
Germany

Technical Indexes
Willoughby Road
Bracknell
Berkshire RG12 8DW
United Kingdom

Thomson Financial Services
22 Pittsburgh Street
Boston MA
02210 United States of America

TSO (formerly HMSO)
51 Nine Elms Lane
London SW8 5DR
United Kingdom

Westlaw
PO Box 64833
St Paul MN
55164-0833 United States of America

BIBLIOGRAPHY

A to Z of European terms and acronyms. Joe Mitchell and Associates.
http://www.ecu-notes.org/atoz997/atozint.html

Bainbridge, Timothy and Teasdale, Anthony *The Penguin companion to European Union* (sic). 2nd ed 1998. Penguin Books. ISBN 0-14-026879-0

Crampton, Stephen *1992 Eurospeak explained.* [1990]. Rosters Ltd in association with Consumers in the European Community Group. ISBN 0948-03291-X

European Commission. Directorate General for Education and Culture *Glossary: Institutions, policies and enlargement of the European Union*. 2000. Office for Official Publications of the European Communities. ISBN 92-828-8282-9

The European Union encyclopaedia and directory 1999. 3rd ed 1999. Europa Publications Limited. ISBN 1-85743-056-5

Gondriand, François *Eurospeak a user's guide: the dictionary of the Single Market*, translated by Peter Bowen. 1992. Nicholas Brealey. (Originally published in France in 1991 by Les Editions d'Organisation). ISBN 1-85788-004-8

Yearbook of international organizations Vol 1 Organization descriptions and cross references. 35th ed 1998/99. K.G. Saur. ISBN 3-598-23362-0